Insurance Operations

by

Kathy Stokes
KSM Communications LLC
Arlington, Virginia

Publisher
The Goodheart-Willcox Company, Inc.
Tinley Park, Illinois
www.g-w.com

Copyright © 2013
by
The Goodheart-Willcox Company, Inc.

All rights reserved. No part of this work may be reproduced, stored, or transmitted in any form or by any electronic or mechanical means, including information storage and retrieval systems, without the prior written permission of
The Goodheart-Willcox Company, Inc.

Manufactured in the United States of America.

Library of Congress Catalog Card Number 2011045457

ISBN 978-1-60525-774-7

1 2 3 4 5 6 7 8 9 – 13 – 17 16 15 14 13 12

The Goodheart-Willcox Company, Inc. Brand Disclaimer: Brand names, company names, and illustrations for products and services included in this text are provided for educational purposes only and do not represent or imply endorsement or recommendation by the author or the publisher.

The Goodheart-Willcox Company, Inc. Safety Notice: The reader is expressly advised to carefully read, understand, and apply all safety precautions and warnings described in this book or that might also be indicated in undertaking the activities and exercises described herein to minimize risk of personal injury or injury to others. Common sense and good judgment should also be exercised and applied to help avoid all potential hazards. The reader should always refer to the appropriate manufacturer's technical information, directions, and recommendations; then proceed with care to follow specific equipment operating instructions. The reader should understand these notices and cautions are not exhaustive.

The publisher makes no warranty or representation whatsoever, either expressed or implied, including, but not limited to, equipment, procedures, and applications described or referred to herein, their quality, performance, merchantability, or fitness for a particular purpose. The publisher assumes no responsibility for any changes, errors, or omissions in this book. The publisher specifically disclaims any liability whatsoever, including any direct, indirect, incidental, consequential, special, or exemplary damages resulting, in whole or in part, from the reader's use or reliance upon the information, instructions, procedures, warnings, cautions, applications or other matter contained in this book. The publisher assumes no responsibility for the activities of the reader.

Library of Congress Cataloging-in-Publication Data

Stokes, Kathy E.
  Insurance operations / by Kathy E. Stokes. -- 1st ed.
    p. cm.
  Includes index.
  ISBN 978-1-60525-774-7
  1. Insurance--Juvenile literature. I. Title.
  HG8052.5.S76 2013
  368--dc23
                                2011045457

Attributions for unreferenced images:

Cover: Andrey Armyagov /Shutterstock
Real World Case: Alistair Cotton/Shutterstock
Consumer Laws: Sergey Mironov/Shutterstock
History of Insurance: Vladimir Radosa/Shutterstock
Math: Jackiso/Shutterstock
Go Green: Mashe/Shutterstock

Ethical Insurance Practices: Image Wizard/Shutterstock
Unit 1 image: Andrey Armyagov/Shutterstock
Unit 2 image: Tom Plesnik/Shutterstock
Unit 3 image: joyfull/Shutterstock
Unit 4 image: SVLuma/Shutterstock

Introduction

As a young adult, one of the most important keys to your success is preparation and preparedness for a career, which will allow you to be financially independent. This text is a step toward a career in finance within the insurance services industry. In addition to the insight you will gain into the insurance industry through this text, you will be learning to be financially capable as well. Being financially capable means you understand topics related to finance such as the importance of insurance and risk management. With our rapidly changing economy, it has become clear that as a young person, you will need to learn how to make wise financial decisions at an early age. Wise financial decisions will help you lead a productive life, as well as enable you to be a positive contributor to the economic stability of the nation.

As you progress through *Insurance Operations*, you will have many opportunities to learn about the insurance industry and how it has evolved in this century, new offerings to its clients, and avenues for a future potential career.

A new learning tool has been provided to help you as you study. QR codes are provided to use with your smartphone to go directly to selected text activities. In addition, the G-W Learning mobile site makes it easy for you to study on the go!

About the Author

Kathy Stokes is a communication consultant for businesses and nonprofits. She has a deep background in retirement income security and financial education. Kathy has worked on these and related issues with AARP, The American Savings Education Council, the Employee Benefit Research Institute, the MetLife Mature Market Institute, the US Chamber of Commerce, the Women's Institute for a Secure Retirement, and other organizations. She holds a bachelor's degree in Rhetoric and Communication from the University of Pittsburgh and a master's degree in American Government from the Johns Hopkins University.

Reviewers

The author and publisher would like to thank the following industry and teaching professionals, who provided valuable input to the development of this text.

Mark Andruss
Vice President of Corporate
 Development
Assurant Employee Benefits
Kansas City, MO

Stacey Armstrong
DECA Advisor, Business Teacher
Beaverton School District
Beaverton, OR

Summer Basgier
Business and Marketing Teacher
McAdory High School
McCalla, AL

Lora Cherry, MLS (ASCP)
Health Science Instructor
Bastrop High School
Bastrop, TX

Dana Farris
Marketing Teacher
Seabreeze High School
Daytona Beach, FL

Beth Felts
Business Educator
Elkin High School
Elkin, NC

Keith Fortmann
Assistant Director of Underwriting
 Group Non-Medical Benefits
Principal Financial Group
Overland Park, KS

Jennifer Gatlin, Ed. D.
Lead Teacher for the Academy of
 Marketing and Business
Hunters Lane High School/
 Metropolitan Nashville Public
 Schools
Nashville, TN

John Ghilardi
Regional Vice President,
 Underwriter and Marketing
RGA Reinsurance Company
Chesterfield, MO

Jennifer Hair
Business Education Instructor
Shawnee Mission East High School
Prairie Village, KS

Valerie McGuire
Vice President, Human Resources
Weil-McLain
Bennettsville, SC

Robert J. Mendelson
Vice President
Five Star Life Insurance Company
Alexandria, VA

Elizabeth Mosher
Marketing Teacher/ DECA Advisor
Farmington High School
Howell, MI

Stuart Powell
Vice President of Insurance Operations
 and Technical Affairs
Independent Insurance Agents of
 North Carolina
Cary, NC

Amber Reed
Business Teacher and DECA Advisor
Bremen High School
Bremen, IN

Cindy Storey
Business Teacher
Merrol Hyde Magnet School
Hendersonville, TN

Catherine Summers
High School Business Teacher
Community Schools of Frankfort
Frankfort, IN

Eric Swick
Business Education Teacher
Clark Public School District
Clark, NJ

Alan Watts B.S., B.A., M.S.
Business Teacher and DECA Advisor
Dayton High School
Dayton, NV

Brief Contents

Unit 1 The World of Insurance 18

Chapter 1 Basics of Insurance......................19

Chapter 2 Property and Casualty Insurance for Homes and Businesses 35

Chapter 3 Property and Casualty Insurance on Land, Sea, and Air............................49

Chapter 4 Health Insurance........................67

Chapter 5 Disability, Long-Term Care, and Life Insurance 85

Chapter 6 Additional Types of Insurance 107

Unit 2 Social Insurance 126

Chapter 7 Worker Protections 127

Chapter 8 Public Health Insurance Programs 143

Chapter 9 Social Security 159

Unit 3 Nature of the Industry 176

Chapter 10 Nature of the Insurance Industry..........177

Chapter 11 How Insurance Companies Make Money.....197

Chapter 12 State Regulation of Insurance 211

Chapter 13 Federal Insurance Industry Regulations 227

Chapter 14 Legal Principles........................243

Chapter 15 Ethics and Social Responsibility 257

Unit 4 Careers 272

Chapter 16 Roles and Responsibilities 273

Chapter 17 Benefits of a Career in the Insurance Industry................................293

Glossary.................... 304

Index.................... 315

Table of Contents

Unit 1 The World of Insurance

Chapter 1 Basics of Insurance ... 19
Section 1.1 Why Insurance? ... 20
  Concept of Risk ... 20
  Role of Insurance in Managing Risk ... 21

Section 1.2 What Risks Do You Face? ... 23
  Risks by Life Stage ... 23
  Risks of Life Choices ... 25

Section 1.3 Considerations When Buying Insurance ... 27
  Is the Company Financially Healthy? ... 27
  What Is the Company's Customer Service Record? ... 27

Special Features
  Reading Prep ... 19
  Go Green ... 19
  History of Insurance ... 21
  Real World Case ... 24
  Ethical Insurance Practices ... 26
  Careers in Finance: Insurance Sales Agent ... 30
  Event Prep: Student Organizations ... 33

Chapter Review and Assessment
  Chapter Summary ... 31
  Review Your Knowledge ... 31–32
  Apply Your Knowledge ... 32
  Working in Teams ... 32
  Common Core ... 33

Chapter 2 Property and Casualty Insurance for Homes and Businesses ... 35
Section 2.1 Homeowner's and Renter's Insurance ... 36
  Protecting Your Home and Yourself ... 36
  Policy Types ... 37
  Floods and Earthquakes ... 39
  Homeowner's Liability Protection ... 40
  How Much Coverage Is Enough? ... 40

Section 2.2 Commercial Insurance ... 42
  Commercial General Liability Insurance ... 42
  Commercial Property Insurance ... 42
  Commercial "Package" Policy Insurance ... 42
  Business Owner's Policy Insurance ... 43

Special Features
  Reading Prep ... 35
  Go Green ... 35
  Real World Cases ... 37, 40
  Ethical Insurance Practices ... 39, 42
  History of Insurance ... 40
  Careers in Finance: Claims Adjuster ... 44
  Event Prep: Insurance Ethics ... 48

Chapter Review and Assessment
  Chapter Summary ... 45
  Review Your Knowledge ... 46
  Apply Your Knowledge ... 47
  Working in Teams ... 47
  Common Core ... 48

Table of Contents

Chapter 3 Property and Casualty Insurance on Land, Sea, and Air ... 49

3.1 Automobile Insurance ... 50
What Is Automobile Insurance? ... 50
State Coverage Requirements ... 53
How Insurers Determine Premiums ... 54
Ways to Reduce the Premium ... 55
Claims Process ... 56

3.2 Marine and Aviation Insurance ... 58
Ocean Marine Insurance ... 58
Inland Marine Insurance ... 60
Aviation Insurance ... 61

Special Features
Reading Prep ... 49
Go Green ... 49
History of Insurance ... 52, 56, 62
Real World Cases ... 52, 55, 60
Ethical Insurance Practices ... 60
Careers in Finance: Insurance Appraiser ... 51
Event Prep: Public Speaking ... 65

Chapter Review and Assessment
Chapter Summary ... 63
Review Your Knowledge ... 63
Apply Your Knowledge ... 64
Working in Teams ... 65
Common Core ... 65

Chapter 4 Health Insurance ... 67

Section 4.1 The High Cost of Health Care ... 68
Health Insurance Costs ... 68
Patient Protection and Affordable Care Act ... 69

Section 4.2 Private Health Insurance ... 71
Group Health Plans ... 71
Individual Health Plans ... 72
Fee-for-Service Plans ... 73
Managed-Care Plans ... 74
Consumer-Driven Health Plans ... 75

Section 4.3 Protection When Group Coverage Is Lost ... 77
COBRA ... 77
HIPAA ... 78
Impact of the Uninsured ... 79

Special Features
Reading Prep ... 67
Go Green ... 67
Ethical Insurance Practices ... 69
History of Insurance ... 72
Real World Case ... 73
Consumer Laws ... 74
Careers in Finance: Health Insurance Claims Examiner ... 79
Event Prep: Insurance Concepts ... 84

Chapter Review and Assessment
Chapter Summary ... 81
Review Your Knowledge ... 82
Apply Your Knowledge ... 83
Working in Teams ... 83
Common Core ... 84

Chapter 5 Disability, Long-Term Care, and Life Insurance. .85

Section 5.1 Disability Insurance 86
Insuring Against Disability 86
Why Disability Insurance Is Important 87
Policy Definitions 87
Social Security Disability Income 88

Section 5.2 Long-Term Care Insurance 90
Benefit of Carrying Long-Term Care Insurance 90
Role of Medicare and Medicaid in Long-Term Care Coverage 92
Long-Term Care Policy Types 92

Section 5.3 Life Insurance. 96
How Life Insurance Works 96
Insuring Another Person 97
Types of Life Insurance 97
How Much Life Insurance Is Enough? 100
Role of Life Insurance as an Investment 101

Special Features
Reading Prep. 85
Go Green 85
Ethical Insurance Practices 87
History of Insurance. 97, 99
Real World Cases 99, 101
Careers in Finance: Life Insurance Claims Examiner 95
Event Prep: Community Service Project 106

Chapter Review and Assessment
Chapter Summary. 103
Review Your Knowledge 104
Apply Your Knowledge 105
Working in Teams 105
Common Core. 106

Chapter 6 Additional Types of Insurance 107

Section 6.1 Insurance That Plugs the Holes 108
Umbrella Liability Insurance. 108
Gap Insurance 109

Section 6.2 Other Insurance for Homeowners 111
Earthquake Insurance 111
Title Insurance 112

Section 6.3 Medical Malpractice Insurance 114
What Is Medical Malpractice? 114
How Medical Malpractice Insurance Works. 114

Section 6.4 Trends in Insurance Products. 117
Identity Theft Insurance 117
Hacker Insurance. 120

Special Features
Reading Prep. 107
Go Green 107
Real World Cases 109, 119
History of Insurance. 112
Ethical Insurance Practices 112, 120
Consumer Laws. 120
Careers in Finance: Insurance Investigator 118
Event Prep: Role Playing and Interviews 124

Chapter Review and Assessment
Chapter Summary. 121
Review Your Knowledge 122
Apply Your Knowledge 123
Working in Teams 123
Common Core. 124

Table of Contents

Unit 2 Social Insurance

Chapter 7 Worker Protections 127

Section 7.1 Workers' Compensation Insurance................. 128
Basics of Workers' Compensation........................128
State Rules..130
Making a Claim..132

Section 7.2 Unemployment Insurance 133
Unemployment Insurance 133
Unemployment Insurance During the Great Recession 134
Unemployment Insurance Funding 135
Program Administration 135
Applying for Benefits 136

Special Features
Reading Prep..127
Go Green...127
History of Insurance..............................130, 135
Ethical Insurance Practices..............................131
Real World Case..135
Careers in Finance: Insurance Underwriter...............129
Event Prep: Written Events..............................141

Chapter Review and Assessment
Chapter Summary.......................................138
Review Your Knowledge.................................139
Apply Your Knowledge............................139–140
Working in Teams.......................................140
Common Core...140

Chapter 8 Public Health Insurance Programs........ 143

Section 8.1 Medicare 144
Public Health Insurance..................................144
Overview of Medicare...................................145
Medigap..148
Choosing a Medicare Plan...............................149
Rising Costs of Medicare................................149

Section 8.2 Medicaid 151
Overview of Medicaid 151
Eligibility and Covered Services 152
Rising Costs of Medicaid................................152

Special Features
Reading Prep..143
Go Green...143
History of Insurance..............................145, 152
Ethical Insurance Practices..............................147
Consumer Laws..148
Real World Case..149
Careers in Finance: Customer Service Representative....154
Event Prep: Team Presentation..........................158

Chapter Review and Assessment
Chapter Summary.......................................155
Review Your Knowledge.................................156
Apply Your Knowledge............................156–157
Working in Teams.......................................157
Common Core...157

Chapter 9 Social Security 159

Section 9.1 Social Security Retirement Benefits................ 160
Social Security: Just One Source of Retirement Income ...160
How Social Security Works..............................163
Spousal Benefits..164
Social Security's Funding 164

Section 9.2 Other Social Security Benefits 167
    Social Security Disability Benefits 167
    Supplemental Security Income 169
    Social Security Survivors Benefit. 170
Special Features
    Reading Prep. 159
    Go Green 159
    Real World Cases 161, 164
    History of Insurance 163
    Ethical Insurance Practices 169
    Careers in Finance: Actuary 162
    Event Prep: Extemporaneous Speaking. 174
Chapter Review and Assessment
    Chapter Summary. 171
    Review Your Knowledge 172
    Apply Your Knowledge 173
    Working in Teams 173
    Common Core. 174

Unit 3
Nature of the Industry

Chapter 10 Nature of the Insurance Industry 177
Section 10.1 Insurance Contracts. 178
    Overview of Insurance Contracts. 178
    Basics of an Insurance Contract 179
Section 10.2 How Insurers Manage Risk 182
    Law of Large Numbers. 182
    Underwriting. 183
    Reinsurance. 187
Section 10.3 Insurance Claims 188
    Nature of Insurance Claims 188
    Claims-Filing Pitfalls. 189
Section 10.4 Consumer Resources 191
    Ratings Agencies. 191
    State Consumer Resources. 191–192
Special Features
    Reading Prep. 177
    Go Green 177
    Ethical Insurance Practices 183
    History of Insurance 184
    Real World Case 190
    Careers in Finance: Insurance Sales Manager 185
    Event Prep: Careers 196
Chapter Review and Assessment
    Chapter Summary. 193
    Review Your Knowledge 194
    Apply Your Knowledge 195
    Working in Teams 195
    Common Core. 196

Chapter 11 How Insurance Companies Make Money. . 197
Section 11.1 Premiums. 198
    Overview of Premiums. 198
    Underwriting. 199
    Ratemaking 201
    Accounting for Disasters 202
Section 11.2 Investments. 204
    Income from Investments. 204
    Float 204
    Short- and Long-Tail Policies 205
Special Features
    Reading Prep. 197
    Go Green 197

Table of Contents

　　History of Insurance. 199
　　Ethical Insurance Practices 201
　　Real World Case 203
　　Careers in Finance: Insurance Policy Processing Clerk 205
　　Event Prep: Job Interview 209

Chapter Review and Assessment
　　Chapter Summary. 207
　　Review Your Knowledge 207–208
　　Apply Your Knowledge 208
　　Working in Teams 208
　　Common Core. 209

Chapter 12 State Regulation of Insurance. 211

Section 12.1 Purpose of State Regulation 212
　　Why States Regulate the Insurance Industry 212
　　Roles of State Government Branches 213
　　State's Role in Consumer Protection 215

Section 12.2 What States Regulate 217
　　Solvency 217
　　Market Regulation 219
　　Rate Regulation 220

Section 12.3 State Risk Pools 222
　　Purpose of Risk Pools 222
　　Replacing Risk Pools. 222

Special Features
　　Reading Prep. 211
　　Go Green 211
　　History of Insurance. 213, 222
　　Ethical Insurance Practices 217
　　Careers in Finance: Insurance Claims Processing Clerk 214
　　Event Prep: Business Calculations. 226

Chapter Review and Assessment
　　Chapter Summary. 224
　　Review Your Knowledge 225
　　Apply Your Knowledge 225
　　Working in Teams 226
　　Common Core. 226

Chapter 13 Federal Insurance Industry Regulations . . . 227

Section 13.1 COBRA. 228
　　Overview of COBRA 228
　　Eligibility. 229
　　Regulation and Enforcement 230

Section 13.2 HIPAA 231
　　Overview 231
　　Preexisting Conditions Rule. 232
　　Special Enrollment Rule. 233
　　Individual Health Plan Rule 233

Section 13.3 PPACA 235
　　PPACA Overview. 235
　　Expanding Coverage 236
　　Health Plan Changes. 236
　　Medicare Changes. 237

Special Features
　　Reading Prep. 227
　　Go Green 227
　　Ethical Insurance Practices 229
　　Consumer Laws. 230
　　Real World Case 229
　　History of Insurance. 232
　　Careers in Finance: Insurance Loss Control Representative 237
　　Event Prep: Business Communication 242

Chapter Review and Assessment
    Chapter Summary... 239
    Review Your Knowledge... 240
    Apply Your Knowledge.. 241
    Working in Teams.. 241
    Common Core... 242

Chapter 14 Legal Principles 243

Section 14.1 Utmost Good Faith 244
    Principle of Utmost Good Faith 244
    Three Components of Utmost Good Faith............................... 244

Section 14.2 Insurable Interest............................. 247
    Insurable Interest in Property and Casualty Insurance 247
    Insurable Interest in Life Insurance 248

Section 14.3 Indemnity and Subrogation....................... 249
    Indemnity... 249
    Subrogation... 250

Special Features
    Reading Prep.. 243
    Go Green.. 243
    History of Insurance.. 248
    Real World Case 245
    Ethical Insurance Practices... 245
    Careers in Finance: Financial Planner............................... 251
    Event Prep: Business Law 256

Chapter Review and Assessment
    Chapter Summary... 253
    Review Your Knowledge... 254
    Apply Your Knowledge.. 255
    Working in Teams.. 255
    Common Core... 255

Chapter 15 Ethics and Social Responsibility 257

Section 15.1 Insurance Industry Ethics 258
    Ethical Codes in the Insurance Industry 258
    State Regulation of Ethics 259

Section 15.2 Insurance Fraud................................ 262
    Overview of Insurance Fraud... 262
    External Fraud.. 263
    Internal Fraud.. 263

Section 15.3 Insurance Industry's Role in Society 265
    Social and Economic Contributions................................... 265
    Responsibility to Society 266

Special Features
    Reading Prep.. 257
    Go Green.. 257
    Working in Teams... 263
    Ethical Insurance Practices................................... 259, 260
    Real World Cases 263, 264
    History of Insurance.. 263
    Careers in Finance: Insurance Marketing Manager..................... 266
    Event Prep: Proper Attire 270

Chapter Review and Assessment
    Chapter Summary... 267
    Review Your Knowledge... 268
    Apply Your Knowledge.. 269
    Working in Teams.. 269
    Common Core... 269

Table of Contents

Unit 4 Careers

Chapter 16 Roles and Responsibilities 273
Section 16.1 Licensing and Professional Designations 274
Licensing 274
Certification and Professional Designation 275
Section 16.2 Administrative Support Occupations. 277
Secretaries and Administrative Assistants. 277
Accounting and Auditing Clerks. 278
Policy and Claims Processing Clerks 278
Customer Service Representatives 278
Section 16.3 Management Occupations. 280
Top Executives. 280
Marketing Managers 280–281
Sales Managers 281
Section 16.4 Financial Occupations. 282
Claims Examiners 282
Investigators. 284
Loss Control Representatives 284–285
Underwriters. 285
Actuaries 285
Section 16.5 Sales Occupations 287
Overview 287
Sales Agents/Producers 287
Special Features
Reading Prep. 273
Go Green 273
Ethical Insurance Practices 275
History of Insurance. 281, 285
Event Prep: Leave Nothing to Chance 292
Chapter Review and Assessment
Chapter Summary. 289
Review Your Knowledge 290
Apply Your Knowledge 291
Working in Teams 291
Common Core. 292

Chapter 17 Benefits of a Career in the Insurance Industry . . 293
Section 17.1 Industry Outlook. 294
Compensation and Benefits. 294
Industry Outlook. 295
Section 17.2 Insights from the Inside 298
From the Source 298
Future. 298–299
Special Features
Reading Prep 293
Go Green. 293
Ethical Insurance Practices 295
History of Insurance. 296
Event Prep: Day of the Event 302
Chapter Review and Assessment
Chapter Summary. 299
Review Your Knowledge 300
Apply Your Knowledge 301
Working in Teams 301
Common Core. 302

Glossary 304
Index 315

Excellent Organization

Student Focused

Each chapter and section opener begins with a consistent plan of learning for success.

- **Reading Prep** sets the stage for reading by applying Common Core State Standards for reading.

- The **Check Your Insurance IQ** pretest opens each chapter with an opportunity to evaluate what the student knows about the insurance topic to be presented in the chapter.

- Sharing best practices for the environment, **Go Green** gives tips on ways businesses are wisely using resources.

- A **QR code** makes it convenient to use a smartphone to launch the pretest. Access the pretest without a smartphone on the G-W Learning companion website.

Workplace Spotlighted

Special features in this book bring content to life in a way that allows the reader to understand and apply what is learned. In each chapter, emphasis is given to selected insurance topics that are important to building knowledge of insurance operations.

- Chapters are divided into smaller learning sections for easier comprehension of content that is being presented.

- **Objectives** define the goals for learning the section content and are related to the main headings in the section.

- Through the presentation of important business and academic **terms**, a framework is created to build an insurance glossary.

Engaging Features

History of Insurance

Unemployment insurance has been around since the Great Depression. It was enacted in 1935 to help stabilize the economy when millions of people were out of work.

www.m.g-wlearning.com
www.g-wlearning.com

History of Insurance features provide information about the history of the insurance industry. An expanded article is provided on the G-W Learning mobile and companion websites. The QR code allows the expanded article to be accessed with a smartphone.

Careers in Finance
Insurance Services

What Does an Insurance Appraiser Do?

An **insurance appraiser** assesses the cost to repair damaged vehicles for insurance purposes. He wo... insurers. An appraiser:
- examines damaged vehicl...

Careers in Finance features highlight careers in the Insurance Services pathway of the Finance Cluster to provide awareness of potential opportunities.

Real World Case

Two years ago, Jacob got hurt at the skateboard park. Even though he wore a helmet, he landed a jump badly and was knocked unconscious. He awakened to find...

and received...

Meet Maria and Jacob, both 16 years old. They will help illustrate experiences people have with insurance at various points in their lives. These **Real World Cases** will help show you how your career in insurance will affect consumers.

Ethical Insurance Practices

It is important to be completely truthful when applying for insuranc... The carrier has no... of knowing if an ap... is really a non-smo... or does not engage... dangerous pastime... But, if the undisclo... information plays a... in a claim, the insurer will deny the claim and will likely cancel the policy.

By presenting topics related to **ethics in insurance**, real-life information is given to provide insight on issues that arise in the insurance industry.

Consumer Laws

Under Medicare Part C, beneficiaries have the right to information, to participate in treatment decisions, to emergency services, and to file complaints. Some states provide additional consumer protections for Part C beneficiaries.

Consumer Laws features highlight legal aspects of the insurance industry as they relate to the consumer.

G-W Learning Mobile Site

The G-W Learning mobile site is a study reference to use when you are on the go. The mobile site is easy to read, easy to use, and fine-tuned for quick access.

For *Insurance Operations*, the G-W Learning mobile site contains chapter pretests and post tests, expanded History of Insurance articles, and e-flash card vocabulary practices. If you do not have a smartphone, these same features can be accessed using an Internet browser to visit the G-W Learning companion website.

G-W Learning mobile site: www.m.g-wlearning.com
G-W Learning companion website: www.g-wlearning.com

Scan now!

Goodheart-Willcox QR Codes

This Goodheart-Willcox product contains QR codes, or quick response codes. These codes can be scanned with a smartphone bar code reader to access information or online features. If you do not have a smartphone, these same features can be accessed using an Internet browser to visit the G-W Learning companion website. For more information on using QR codes and a recommended QR reader, visit the G-W Learning companion website.

G-W Learning companion website: www.g-wlearning.com

An Internet connection is required to access the QR code destination. Data-transfer rates may apply. Check with your mobile Internet service provider for information on your data-transfer rates.

Scan now!

Ongoing Assessments

Oriented Outcomes

Multiple opportunities are provided for self-assessment within the chapter, as well as at the conclusion, to check learning as the content is explored. Each activity is unique to cover the concepts and critical thinking skills that are developed in each chapter. Additionally, each unit concludes with an assessment to measure student knowledge.

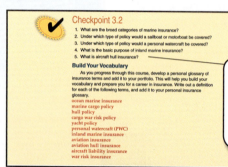

Through point-of-coverage assessment at the end of each chapter section, understanding of content is confirmed before progressing through the remaining content. Solutions to the **checkpoint** questions are located on the G-W Learning companion website at www.g-wlearning.com.

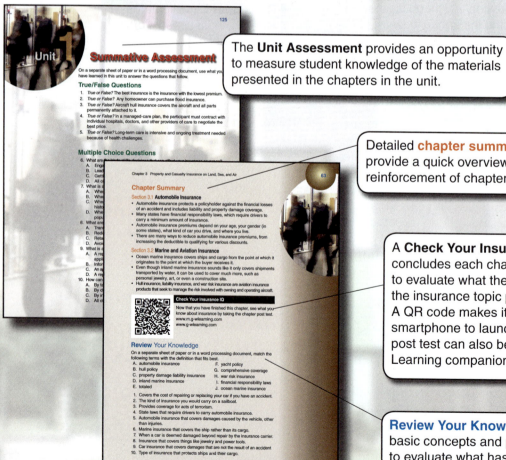

The **Unit Assessment** provides an opportunity to measure student knowledge of the materials presented in the chapters in the unit.

Detailed **chapter summaries** provide a quick overview and reinforcement of chapter content.

A **Check Your Insurance IQ** post test concludes each chapter with an opportunity to evaluate what the student learned about the insurance topic presented in the chapter. A QR code makes it convenient to use a smartphone to launch the post test. The post test can also be accessed on the G-W Learning companion website.

Review Your Knowledge questions review basic concepts and provide an opportunity to evaluate what has been learned.

Engaging Features

History of Insurance

Unemployment insur[ance] has been around sin[ce] the Great Depression[.] [It] was enacted in 1935 [to] help stabilize the eco[nomy] when millions of peo[ple] were out of work.

www.m.g-wlearning.com
www.g-wlearning.com

History of Insurance features provide information about the history of the insurance industry. An expanded article is provided on the G-W Learning mobile and companion websites. The QR code allows the expanded article to be accessed with a smartphone.

Careers in Finance
Insurance Services

What Does an Insurance Appraiser Do?

An **insurance appraiser** assesses the cost to repair damaged vehicles for insurance purposes. He wo[rks for] insurers. An appraiser:
- examines damaged vehic[les]

Careers in Finance features highlight careers in the Insurance Services pathway of the Finance Cluster to provide awareness of potential opportunities.

Real World Case

Two years ago, Jacob got hurt at the skateboard park. Even though he wore a helmet, he landed a jump badly and was knocked unconscious. He awakened to find...and received...

Meet Maria and Jacob, both 16 years old. They will help illustrate experiences people have with insurance at various points in their lives. These **Real World Cases** will help show you how your career in insurance will affect consumers.

Ethical Insurance Practices

It is important to be completely truthful when applying for insuran[ce.] The carrier has no [way] of knowing if an ap[plicant] is really a non-smo[ker] or does not engag[e in] dangerous pastime[s.] But, if the undisclo[sed] information plays a [part] in a claim, the insurer will deny the claim and will likely cancel the policy.

By presenting topics related to **ethics in insurance**, real-life information is given to provide insight on issues that arise in the insurance industry.

Consumer Laws

Under Medicare Part C, beneficiaries have the right to information, to participate in treatment decisions, to emergency services, and to file complaints. Some states provide additional consumer protections for Part C beneficiaries.

Consumer Laws features highlight legal aspects of the insurance industry as they relate to the consumer.

G-W Learning Mobile Site

The G-W Learning mobile site is a study reference to use when you are on the go. The mobile site is easy to read, easy to use, and fine-tuned for quick access.

For *Insurance Operations,* the G-W Learning mobile site contains chapter pretests and post tests, expanded History of Insurance articles, and e-flash card vocabulary practices. If you do not have a smartphone, these same features can be accessed using an Internet browser to visit the G-W Learning companion website.

G-W Learning mobile site: www.m.g-wlearning.com
G-W Learning companion website: www.g-wlearning.com

Scan now!

Goodheart-Willcox QR Codes

This Goodheart-Willcox product contains QR codes, or quick response codes. These codes can be scanned with a smartphone bar code reader to access information or online features. If you do not have a smartphone, these same features can be accessed using an Internet browser to visit the G-W Learning companion website. For more information on using QR codes and a recommended QR reader, visit the G-W Learning companion website.
G-W Learning companion website: www.g-wlearning.com

An Internet connection is required to access the QR code destination. Data-transfer rates may apply. Check with your mobile Internet service provider for information on your data-transfer rates.

Scan now!

Ongoing Assessments

Oriented Outcomes

Multiple opportunities are provided for self-assessment within the chapter, as well as at the conclusion, to check learning as the content is explored. Each activity is unique to cover the concepts and critical thinking skills that are developed in each chapter. Additionally, each unit concludes with an assessment to measure student knowledge.

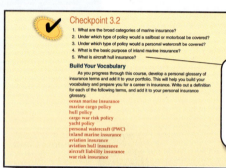

Through point-of-coverage assessment at the end of each chapter section, understanding of content is confirmed before progressing through the remaining content. Solutions to the **checkpoint** questions are located on the G-W Learning companion website at www.g-wlearning.com.

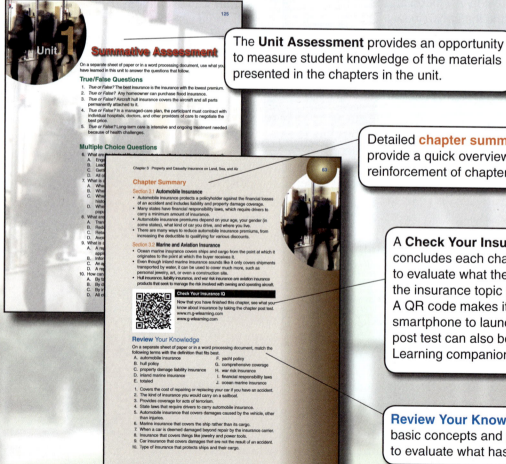

The **Unit Assessment** provides an opportunity to measure student knowledge of the materials presented in the chapters in the unit.

Detailed **chapter summaries** provide a quick overview and reinforcement of chapter content.

A **Check Your Insurance IQ** post test concludes each chapter with an opportunity to evaluate what the student learned about the insurance topic presented in the chapter. A QR code makes it convenient to use a smartphone to launch the post test. The post test can also be accessed on the G-W Learning companion website.

Review Your Knowledge questions review basic concepts and provide an opportunity to evaluate what has been learned.

Working in Teams features provide collaborative work experiences to encourage leadership and cooperation.

The **G-W Learning** mobile site contains e-flash cards to practice vocabulary, as well as the chapter pretest and post test and expanded History of Insurance articles. If students do not have access to a smartphone, these activities can be completed on the G-W Learning companion website.

College and Career Readiness activities give students an opportunity to apply the **Common Core** State Standards to improve reading and writing skills.

Apply Your Knowledge questions present critical-thinking activities that allow individual interpretation of content learned in the chapter.

Event Prep creates an opportunity to prepare for competitive activities for career and technical student organization (CTSO) competitions.

This product aligns with the National Standards in K–12 Personal Finance Education published by the Jump$tart Coalition for Personal Financial Literacy®.

Unit 1: The World of Insurance

Each of us faces uncertainty in life. While some uncertainties cannot be managed, others can be. In the following unit, you will learn about the basics of insurance and the types of insurance products that exist. One of the best ways to understand insurance is from the consumer perspective. Unit 1 takes this approach. When you begin to understand how insurance plays a role throughout your life, you will be better able to understand it as a business. There are some remarkable career opportunities in the field of insurance. You will learn about them as you move through this text.

Chapter 1
Basics of Insurance

Chapter 2
Property and Casualty Insurance for Homes and Businesses

Chapter 3
Property and Casualty Insurance on Land, Sea, and Air

Chapter 4
Health Insurance

Chapter 5
Disability, Long-Term Care, and Life Insurance

Chapter 6
Additional Types of Insurance

Chapter 1

Basics of Insurance

 **Reading Prep.** Before reading this chapter, review the objectives. Based on this information, analyze the author's purpose for this chapter.

College and Career Readiness

The way financial risk is managed in many aspects of life is through insurance. With it, we protect ourselves from financial loss from car accidents, house fires, and other risks. When someone buys insurance, he or she pays an insurance carrier to assume the financial risks. Insurance plays an important role in our lives and in our economy.

Section 1.1
Why Insurance?

Section 1.2
What Risks Do You Face?

Section 1.3
Considerations When Buying Insurance

 Paperless billing is one way that insurance companies are protecting the environment. By providing electronic billing rather than printing and mailing statements, tons of paper is saved from going to the landfill each year.

Check Your Insurance IQ

Before you begin this chapter, see what you already know about insurance by taking the chapter pretest.

www.m.g-wlearning.com
www.g-wlearning.com

Section 1.1
Why Insurance?

Terms
risk
risk management
risk reduction
risk avoidance
risk retention
risk transfer
insurance
claim
deductible
premium
policyholder

Objectives
After completing this section, you will be able to:
- Explain the concept of risk.
- Identify the role of insurance in managing risk.

Concept of Risk

When you head out for school in the morning, it might rain. Then again, it might not. You have two choices: take your umbrella or leave it at home. If you do not protect yourself by carrying an umbrella, you will get wet if it rains. Then again, you are stuck carrying the umbrella if it is a dry day.

This scenario is a small, but straightforward, example of assessing risk. **Risk** is simply the probability of an event occurring and the possible consequences of that event. Some risks are minor—like leaving the umbrella at home. In this example, the worst-case scenario is you get wet and are uncomfortable for the first hour of classes. Other risks have the potential to result in greater harm or loss.

When you are faced with a risk, you can make one of four choices: reduce it, avoid it, take it on, or transfer it. These strategies are known as risk management. **Risk management** is the process of evaluating risk and choosing how to minimize or manage the loss. A fifth choice

By buckling your seat belt, you are reducing the risk of being injured in a traffic accident.

Source: Shutterstock (mangostock)

could be to do nothing about the risk. Since this is a bad idea, it is not part of risk management.

Risk reduction is taking steps to minimize the amount of risk. Using a seat belt when you are in a car is an example of risk reduction. This simple act lessens the chance you will be injured or killed in a traffic accident.

Risk avoidance, on the other hand, is taking steps to eliminate risk. You could avoid the risk of injury or death from a car accident by never riding in one. This is an extreme example of risk avoidance.

The third choice in risk management is to take it on. **Risk retention** is the act of assuming the risk on your own. If you put money aside to pay for your health care instead of buying insurance, you retain the risk of paying for all of your health care costs.

Finally, you can choose to transfer risk. **Risk transfer** is when you shift the risk of financial loss to an insurance carrier. When you transfer risk to an insurer, you make a decision to pay the company to take on the risk for you. Sometimes, as with automobile insurance, the state makes the decision for you. Most states require drivers to carry insurance.

Role of Insurance in Managing Risk

Insurance is a financial product that offers protection against a specific type of loss. For example, automobile insurance protects you against the financial consequences of wrecking your car. Following an accident, you submit a **claim**—a request for payment—to your insurer. You have to pay a set portion (the **deductible**) of the cost to fix your car, but the insurance company, more properly called the insurance carrier, will cover costs beyond that amount.

Likewise, health insurance helps pay for the cost of medical care. You may be able to pay the cost of a visit to the doctor for a sore throat, but could you afford to pay for a tonsillectomy if it turns out you need one? The average cost for this procedure (not including surgeon or other physician's fees) is about $5,300. You carry health insurance, or in this stage of your life your parents carry it for you, to protect against having to pay for expensive, but necessary medical care.

Insurance cannot prevent a loss. Life insurance, for example, does not protect anyone from dying. Rather, it protects those who rely on the insured person for financial support. The basic intent of insurance is to make the policyholder whole. In other words, it should return the policyholder to the financial situation he or she was in before the loss.

An entire industry exists that helps people and businesses manage risk. Insurance carriers offer financial protection against things like high health care costs, fire damage to homes, car accidents, and the loss of income. Insurance can also protect businesses from risks such as reputational damage, fraud, operational failure—even terrorism. When we purchase insurance, we transfer risk from our businesses or ourselves to the insurance carrier.

History of Insurance

The insurance industry as we know it today began to emerge at the start of the Industrial Revolution. But, the concept of transferring risk dates back to ancient times. For example, Babylonian traders used a form of insurance to protect caravans in the second millennia BC.

www.m.g-wlearning.com
www.g-wlearning.com

Insurance carriers do not take on our risks out of the goodness of their hearts. They do it because it is how they make money. In return for accepting our risk, insurance carriers charge a fee called a **premium** for the coverage they provide. **Policyholders** are the people who buy the insurance policies. They typically pay premiums on a monthly or quarterly basis. The cost of premiums varies based on what risks the insurance carrier covers. We will cover specifics on how insurance companies make money in Chapter 11. We will go into detail about the types of insurance in the next chapter.

Checkpoint 1.1

1. What is risk?
2. What are four ways to manage risk?
3. Describe the concept of risk transfer.
4. What is the basic intent of insurance?
5. When an insurance carrier takes on a risk for you, what do you give the carrier in return?

Build Your Vocabulary

As you progress through this course, develop a personal glossary of insurance terms and add it to your portfolio. This will help you build your vocabulary and prepare you for a career in insurance. Write out a definition for each of the following terms, and add it to your personal insurance glossary.

risk
risk management
risk reduction
risk avoidance
risk retention
risk transfer
insurance
claim
deductible
premium
policyholder

Chapter 1 Basics of Insurance

Section 1.2
What Risks Do You Face?

Objectives

After completing this section, you will be able to:
- Describe how risks change through an individual's life stages.
- Identify how an individual's life choices can affect insurance coverage.

Terms

life stage
peril
hazard

Risks by Life Stage

Each of us runs the risk of experiencing events that can have a negative impact. The types of risk and the potential harm they may cause change throughout our lives. As you move through life, you will go through various stages.

A **life stage** is a distinct phase of a person's life. For example, after school you will be a young, probably single, adult. Then you might enter a new life stage when you get married, which brings a new set of financial risks. Adding children to the mix is another life stage, bringing yet more types of financial risk. Retirement, which is the final life stage, carries significant risk, such as running out of money.

As you progress through different life stages, such as getting married and starting a family, your insurance needs change.

Source: Shutterstock (ClickPop)

Children do not so much face risk as represent it. Parents come up with ways to protect against the financial risks they face by virtue of having children. The main financial risk children represent to their parents relates to health. A single illness or injury could cost tens of thousands of dollars. This is why most families purchase health insurance coverage. We will describe the various types of health insurance products in Chapter 3.

From the time you become a young adult, you will start to take on the responsibility of protecting yourself against risk. Risks you will face include the potential loss of earning power, unexpected health care costs, property loss, and premature death. As your life situation changes, so do your insurance needs, as shown in Figure 1-1.

Real World Case

When Maria's parents started their family, their insurance needs changed. First, they moved from a rental apartment to a house with a mortgage. Their mortgage lender required them to buy homeowner's insurance when they bought the house. They also signed up for health insurance through her father's employer. Knowing that the family would suffer financially if either of them died, her parents both bought life insurance, too. Even though these policies meant additional monthly bills, Maria's parents felt the cost was worth it for their peace of mind.

If you are...	You may need this type of insurance...
A young, single adult	Health insurance to protect against the financial impact of illness or injury
	Auto insurance to cover accidents and theft
	Renter's insurance to cover loss associated with incidents like fire or theft
	Disability insurance to replace some of your income if you become injured or ill and cannot work
Married	All of the above, plus:
	Life insurance to provide income for your spouse if you die, and vice versa
	Homeowner's or renter's insurance to protect against loss related to fire, theft, or other incidents and to protect you in the event someone is injured on your property
Married with kids	All of the above, plus:
	Life insurance that will provide income to the surviving spouse and children in the event one spouse dies
Retired	Health insurance
	Homeowner's or renter's insurance
	Life insurance
	Long-term care insurance to help pay for home-based or nursing home care

Figure 1-1. Insurance Needs

Chapter 1 Basics of Insurance

Risks of Life Choices

The types of risks represented in Figure 1-1 are those we face by virtue of being human. But, we can increase the risks we face by the choices we make on how and where we live our lives. These choices, in turn, may affect our ability to obtain affordable insurance. Figure 1-2 lists some examples of lifestyle choices that can affect what you pay for insurance.

Risky Behavior	Possible Consequences
Using Tobacco	Cancer Heart disease Respiratory difficulties Dental problems Shortened life expectancy
Being Overweight	Heart disease Diabetes Joint and bone problems Shortened life expectancy
Consuming Alcohol	Heart disease Liver disease Cancer Accidents/injuries Shortened life expectancy
Driving Dangerously	Accidents/injuries Death Property damage
Riding a Motorcycle	Accidents/injuries Death Property damage
Skydiving	Injuries Death
Climbing Mountains	Injuries Death
Having a Private Pilot's License	Accidents/injuries Death Property damage

Figure 1-2. Lifestyle Choices That May Affect Insurance Costs

Ethical Insurance Practices

It is important to be completely truthful when applying for insurance. The carrier has no way of knowing if an applicant is really a nonsmoker or does not engage in dangerous pastimes. If the undisclosed information plays a role in a claim, the insurer will deny the claim and will likely cancel the policy.

For example, smokers face greater health risks than nonsmokers. According to the Centers for Disease Control and Prevention, cigarette smoking is responsible for one in five deaths in the US every year. It can cause heart disease, emphysema, and other chronic diseases. Because of these health effects, insurers may charge smokers a higher premium for health insurance.

Choosing to engage in high-risk physical activity may also affect insurance coverage. A health insurance policy, for example, may state that it will not cover the costs of injuries resulting from high-risk behaviors. So, a person who breaks a leg skydiving may have to bear the full cost of medical care, despite having health insurance.

Another example of risk by life choice is deciding to live far away from a city. Homeowners in rural areas generally pay higher premiums for home insurance. This is because the biggest risk associated with a house is fire. Insurers see the potential for a house fire as a **peril;** that is, a potential cause of a loss. In this case, the distance from the fire department is a hazard. To insurance carriers, a **hazard** is a condition that increases the likelihood or extent of a loss. So, the farther the house is from the fire department, the greater the potential hazard, and the more the insurance may cost.

Checkpoint 1.2

1. What is a life stage?
2. How does an individual's life stage affect his or her need for insurance?
3. List three risks that a young person faces when entering the life stage of adulthood.
4. What are the kinds of life decisions that can affect your insurance coverage?
5. Describe the difference between a peril and a hazard.

Build Your Vocabulary

As you progress through this course, develop a personal glossary of insurance terms and add it to your portfolio. This will help you build your vocabulary and prepare you for a career in insurance. Write out a definition for each of the following terms, and add it to your personal insurance glossary.

life stage
peril
hazard

Chapter 1 Basics of Insurance

Section 1.3
Considerations When Buying Insurance

Objectives
After completing this section, you will be able to:
- Describe how to determine an insurer's financial health.
- Identify an insurer's customer service record.

Terms
independent ratings agencies
customer service
complaint ratio
NAIC

Is the Company Financially Healthy?

When looking to buy insurance coverage, you will find there are many insurance carriers. It is important to learn about the insurer before you purchase a product. The company that offers the lowest premium is not always the best choice.

Insurance carriers receive scores from **independent ratings agencies.** These agencies offer expert opinions on the financial strength of the companies they rate. The rating is an indication of the insurance carrier's ability to pay claims now and in the future. Since you want to be sure the company will be around when you need it to pay a claim, you will want to know the opinions of these agencies.

The major ratings agencies in the US are A.M. Best (www.ambest.com), Standard & Poor's (www.ratings.com), and Moody's (www.moodys.com). Each uses its own set of criteria to form an opinion, and each uses a slightly different rating system. Generally, letter grades are used along with pluses or minuses. For example, Standard & Poor's uses a rating scale with AAA as the highest and AA+ one level below. D is the lowest rating. It is worthwhile to compare ratings from two or more agencies before you make a purchase.

What Is the Company's Customer Service Record?

The independent ratings agencies only offer insight into an insurance carrier's financial health. The ratings do not tell you anything about a company's customer service record. **Customer service** is the manner in which a company engages with its customers. You know poor customer service when you experience it. The server who gives you cold food when it should be hot and does nothing to correct it has provided poor customer service.

As Figure 1-3 shows, customer service in the insurance industry relates to several points of contact between the insurance carrier and its policyholders. When a consumer has a complaint about an insurer, he or she can file it with state insurance regulators.

Figure 1-3. Aspects of Customer Service

Some of the states calculate a complaint ratio. A **complaint ratio** is a number that represents the rate of complaints an insurance carrier receives. States may post these ratios on the their websites.

The National Association of Insurance Commissioners (NAIC) collects complaint information from the states. The **NAIC** is a membership organization of state insurance regulators. The organization makes complaint information available online (www.naic.org). It offers a useful comparison chart to represent where a company's complaint ratio lies in relation to other companies, as shown in Figure 1-4. An educated consumer wants to know the customer service record of an insurance carrier before deciding to buy a product from it.

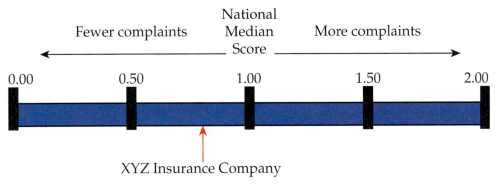

Figure 1-4. NAIC Complaint Ratio Chart

Checkpoint 1.3

1. How do you find out about the financial health of an insurance carrier?
2. Do independent ratings agencies score insurance carriers on customer service?
3. What is an example of customer service in the insurance industry?
4. Where can you find information about an insurer's record of customer service?
5. Explain why buying insurance based on the lowest premium may not be a good idea.

Build Your Vocabulary

As you progress through this course, develop a personal glossary of insurance terms and add it to your portfolio. This will help you build your vocabulary and prepare you for a career in insurance. Write out a definition for each of the following terms, and add it to your personal insurance glossary.

independent ratings agencies
customer service
complaint ratio
NAIC

Careers in Finance
Insurance Services

What Does an Insurance Sales Agent Do?

Insurance sales agents sell insurance to consumers and businesses. An **insurance sales agent** helps individuals and businesses complete the application process to obtain insurance policies. An agent:

- identifies potential clients;
- works with potential clients to determine the types and levels of insurance that fit their needs;
- submits the application to the company underwriter;
- notifies the applicant of the underwriter's decision;
- stays in touch with clients; and
- prepares reports and maintains records.

An agent is called a producer within the industry. An **insurance sales agent** may sell only one company's insurance. In this case, the agent is a captive agent and likely works for a salary and earns commissions. An independent agent, also known as an insurance broker, may sell products of many insurance carriers and most likely works on commission only.

What Is It Like to Work as an Insurance Sales Agent?

An **insurance sales agent** spends a lot of time working directly with people. Many agents work in small offices. Independent agents often spend much of their time traveling to meet with clients and close sales. They make their own work schedules, which often include evenings and weekends to accommodate their clients' availability.

An **insurance sales agent** must communicate with customers of many different social and ethnic backgrounds. In any kind of communication, the agent must follow accepted guidelines for use of e-mail, social networking, blogs, and texting. Knowledge of more than one language is not typically required to do the job, but it may open up more sales opportunities. However, in some locations, the ability to communicate in another language may be a requirement.

Insurance sales agents often dress in business-professional attire. In some cases, business-casual attire is acceptable.

What Education and Skills Are Needed to Be an Insurance Sales Agent?

- college degree is preferred
- excellent communication skills
- ability to work without direct supervision
- expertise in one or more financial products (this requires coursework and exams to obtain licensing)
- strong computer skills

Chapter 1 Basics of Insurance

Chapter Summary

Section 1.1 Why Insurance?
- Risk is the probability of an occurrence and its potential consequences.
- When you buy insurance, you are transferring the financial risk to the insurance carrier.

Section 1.2 What Risks Do You Face?
- The types of risks we face change as we progress through life stages.
- Sometimes we face risks created by the choices we make, such as engaging in dangerous activities or behavior.

Section 1.3 Considerations When Buying Insurance
- The financial health of an insurance carrier is important, because insurance is worthless if the company is not in business when you need to make a claim.
- An aspect to research when purchasing insurance is the insurer's history of consumer complaints.

Check Your Insurance IQ
Now that you have finished this chapter, see what you know about insurance by taking the chapter post test.
www.m.g-wlearning.com
www.g-wlearning.com

Review Your Knowledge

On a separate sheet of paper or in a word processing document, match the following terms with the definition that fits best.

- A. risk
- B. risk management
- C. insurance
- D. claim
- E. deductible
- F. premium
- G. policyholder
- H. peril
- I. hazard
- J. complaint ratio

1. A product that offers protection against a specific type of financial loss.
2. The out-of-pocket expense for a claim.
3. The probability of an event occurring and the possible consequences.
4. The fee paid for an insurance product.
5. A potential cause of a loss.
6. Represents complaints against the insurer compared to others in your state.
7. A condition that increases the likelihood or extent of a loss.
8. The person who purchases an insurance product.
9. A request by a policyholder for payment from an insurer based on a covered loss.
10. Process of evaluating risk and choosing how to minimize or manage the loss.

On a separate sheet of paper or in a word processing document, answer each of the following questions.

11. Describe the difference between risk reduction and risk avoidance.
12. How is insurance used to manage risk?
13. Explain life stages.
14. What is the purpose of the NAIC?
15. What do independent ratings agencies tell you about insurance carriers?

Apply Your Knowledge

16. If your yard has several 100-year-old trees, why might your homeowner's insurance premium be higher?
17. Do you think an insurer should be permitted to vary premiums by the risk represented? For example, is it fair to charge a rural homeowner more for homeowner's insurance than a city dweller? Why or why not?
18. Imagine your life 15 years from now. Describe what it would be like and what risks may come with your lifestyle. What insurance products might you buy?
19. Look up your state's insurance department on the Internet. List the types of information you can gather about insurers that do business in your state.
20. Go online and research three insurance carriers that offer car insurance in your state. Identify aspects you can compare, and write them down. Can you find the complaint ratios? If so, list them. Based on your research, which company would you choose and why?

Working in Teams

Working in a team, research the history of insurance. Where did the idea of insurance originate? Create a timeline of the evolution of insurance and present it to the class.

G-W Learning Mobile Site

Visit the G-W Learning mobile site to complete the chapter pretest and post test, to review the History of Insurance articles, and to practice vocabulary using e-flash cards. If you do not have a smartphone, visit the G-W Learning companion website to access these features.

G-W Learning mobile site: www.m.g-wlearning.com
G-W Learning companion website: www.g-wlearning.com

Common Core

Reading. Read a magazine, newspaper, or online article about the impact of technology on the operations of insurance carriers. Determine the central ideas of the article and review the conclusions made by the author. Provide an accurate summary of your reading, making sure to incorporate the *who, what, when,* and *how* of this situation.

Writing. Conduct research on how much money insurance carriers paid out in the last year due to natural disasters (flooding, tornados, etc.). Write an informative report based on your findings consisting of several paragraphs to describe the implications for the insurance industry.

Student Organizations

Career and technical student organizations are a valuable asset to any educational program. These organizations support student learning and the application of skills learned to real-world situations. There are a variety of organizations from which to select, depending on the goals of your educational programs. Competitive events may be written, oral, or a combination of both. To prepare for any competitive event, complete the following activities.

1. Contact the association a year before the next competition to have time to review and decide which competitive events are correct for you or your team.
2. Closely read all of the guidelines. These rules and regulations must be strictly adhered to or disqualification can occur.
3. Read about which skills are covered for the event you select. Research and preparation are important keys to successful competition.
4. Go to the organization's website to locate specific information for the events. Visit the site often, as information can change.
5. Pick one or two events that are of interest to you. Print the information for the events and discuss your interest with your instructor.

Property and casualty insurance is essential for homes as well as commercial property to protect against financial loss.

Source: Shutterstock (Alexander Chaikin)

Chapter 2
Property and Casualty Insurance for Homes and Businesses

 Reading Prep. Before reading this chapter, preview the illustrations. Translate the technical information in the illustrations into words. Assess the extent to which the illustrations support the content.

When you hear fire engines roar down the street, you might wonder what is on fire and if everyone is okay. But, have you ever thought about what happens *after* a fire? What happens to the business housed in the building that burned to the ground or to the family who just lost its home? What happens largely depends on whether or not the owners carried property and casualty insurance. In this chapter, you will learn about insurance for the places people live, whether they own or rent. Additionally, businesses large and small face many risks they can protect themselves against with insurance. A range of insurance products to meet specific business needs are covered in this chapter.

Section 2.1
Homeowner's and Renter's Insurance

Section 2.2
Commercial Insurance

 Corporate environmental reports are being created by many insurance companies. These reports create positive public relations to demonstrate the commitment of the company to protecting the environment. Some topics included in these reports may be the company's internal practices for preserving the environment, relationships with the community, and ongoing business partnerships that pursue sustainable business processes.

Check Your Insurance IQ

Before you begin this chapter, see what you already know about insurance by taking the chapter pretest.

www.m.g-wlearning.com
www.g-wlearning.com

Section 2.1
Homeowner's and Renter's Insurance

Terms

property and casualty insurance
mortgage
replacement cost
cash value
depreciation
endorsement
umbrella policy
scheduling

Objectives

After completing this section, you will be able to:
- Define the purposes of homeowner's and renter's insurance.
- Identify policy types.
- Describe flood and earthquake insurance.
- Identify what liability protection is provided by homeowner's insurance.
- Determine how much homeowner's insurance is enough.

Protecting Your Home and Yourself

Suppose the fire engines you heard roaring down the street were responding to a house fire. The firefighters were able to prevent the home's destruction, but the fire caused a lot of damage. Property and casualty insurance helps the family restore its home and possessions. **Property and casualty insurance** protects policyholders against financial loss associated with property damage or injury to others.

For most people, their home is their most valuable possession. This is why carrying the right amount of homeowner's insurance is so important. Homeowner's insurance is a form of property and casualty insurance. It protects the home, its structures (like a detached garage), and its contents against certain losses. This is "property" coverage. It also provides liability protection for the policyholder and his or her family. This is "casualty" coverage.

For most people, a house is the largest investment they will make. It is important to protect the house, but also to protect personal property and to provide liability protection.

Source: Shutterstock (Donald Joski)

Most people who own a home borrowed money to buy it. The loan is called a **mortgage.** The mortgage lender requires the borrower to carry homeowner's insurance to cover potential property damage.

Two important concepts in homeowner's insurance are replacement cost and cash value. **Replacement cost** pays the full cost of replacing a specific item with one just like it. **Cash value** (market value) pays for an item's current value—what you might get for it on eBay, for example. The difference between the two is depreciation.

Depreciation is the loss of an item's value over time. A sofa that cost $2,000 new, for example, may lose $500 in value each year based on the insurer's calculations. It would have no *cash value* after four years. But, its *replacement cost* would remain at $2,000 (minus a deductible) because that is what it would cost to buy a new one. It is important to be aware of these differences when considering a homeowner's insurance policy.

People who rent their house or apartment also need to carry insurance. While they are not responsible for the physical structure, they do need to cover their possessions. They also need to protect themselves from liability in the event someone gets injured at the house or apartment. An Insurance Research Council survey showed that 96% of homeowners have homeowner's insurance, but only 43% of renters have renter's insurance.

Real World Case

Maria's parents splurged on a beautiful Oriental rug for the living room. They spent $3,000 on it four years ago. Unfortunately, it was one of the items destroyed in a small house fire this past summer. Because they had replacement cost coverage, the insurance company reimbursed Maria's parents, and they were able to replace the rug with one just like it. If they had cash value coverage, the insurer may have valued the rug at a much lower price because it had been in use for four years.

Policy Types

Most homeowner's insurance products come in one of several standard types of policies (HO-2 through HO-8). The policy types vary in what they cover. Each contains a section on property protection and a section on liability protection. Liability protection is identical across all of the policies. With each policy type, the buyer can typically choose replacement cost or actual cash value coverage for the home.

Four of the policy types are for individuals who own their own homes, one is for renters, and another is for condominium owners. Yet another policy is for homes that have low value. Figure 2-1 explains each policy type. However, some states categorize insurance policies in a different way. Visit your state's insurance department website to find out how homeowner's insurance is categorized for its residents.

Form	Coverage	Perils Covered
HO-2	Covers home and personal property losses caused by 16 perils. Also covers personal and medical liability, damage to the property of others, living expenses if the home is damaged, legal defense in liability cases, and personal property when traveling. A version of HO-2 is available for mobile homes.	• Lightning or fire • Windstorm or hail • Explosion • Riot or civil commotion • Aircraft • Vehicles • Smoke • Vandalism • Theft • Damage by glass or safety glazing material that is part of a building • Volcanic eruptions • Falling objects • Weight of ice, snow, or sleet • Accidental discharge or overflow of water or stream • Sudden and accidental tearing apart, cracking, burning, or bulging of the structure • Freezing • Sudden and accidental damage from artificially generated electrical current
HO-3	Protects the home against all perils, with exceptions specifically listed.	Considered an "all perils" policy. Common exceptions are earthquakes, floods, and acts of war.
HO-4	Protects a renter's furniture, clothing, and other personal items from damages. Also provides the tenant with liability insurance in case someone is injured in the rented space.	All perils listed in HO-1 and HO-2.
HO-5	The most comprehensive coverage available. It is a "no perils" policy and it protects personal property without limitation to the perils listed for HO-2.	Considered a "no perils" policy.
HO-6	Covers personal property and alterations to a condominium unit. (A condominium is a unit in a multiunit building that is purchased instead of rented.)	Same as HO-2.
HO-8	Only protects the home against ten perils and typically offers cash value for losses. Often used to insure an older home that would cost more to replace than it is worth.	• Lightning or fire • Windstorm or hail • Explosion • Riot or civil commotion • Aircraft • Vehicles • Smoke • Vandalism • Theft (typically limited to $1,000) • Volcanic eruptions

Figure 2-1. Homeowner's Insurance Policy Types

Floods and Earthquakes

You may have noticed that none of the policies described in Figure 2-1 covers damage from floods or earthquakes. These perils are covered by separate policies. The next sections discuss earthquake insurance and flood insurance.

Earthquake Insurance

Earthquakes can be very destructive. The 2011 earthquake that struck northeast Japan was the strongest to ever hit that nation. More than 18,000 people lost their lives to the quake. The quake caused about $180 billion in damages, but only $35 million worth of damage was insured.

Each year in the US, about 5,000 earthquakes strike. The most costly US quake was the 1994 Northridge earthquake in southern California. It caused about $25 billion in property damage. Despite the somewhat common occurrence of earthquakes in California, only about 12% of the state's homeowners carry earthquake insurance.

Earthquake coverage is available as an add-on to a standard policy or as a separate policy. An add-on is called an **endorsement.** Comprehensive insurance on automobile policies covers earthquake damage, however. Earthquake insurance is covered in more detail in Chapter 3.

Flood Insurance

Flood insurance is a different story from other insurance. Congress created the National Flood Insurance Program (NFIP) to provide flood insurance. The goal of the NFIP is three-fold: to protect

Ethical Insurance Practices

Insurance professionals must abide by high ethical standards in the work they do. While laws and regulations require some forms of ethical behavior, more than laws motivate insurance professionals. Selling fair policies at reasonable prices and upholding promised coverage is not only the right thing to do, it makes good business sense.

Source: FEMA News Photo (Andrea Booher)

The Northridge earthquake hit California on January 17, 1994. It caused an estimated $25 billion in damages.

individuals from loss by providing flood insurance, reduce future floodplain damage by managing floodplains, and cut costs to the federal government for disaster assistance and flood control. The NFIP exists because private insurers are unable to provide affordable flood insurance. This is largely because floods cause such significant damage.

The Federal Emergency Management Administration (FEMA) runs the NFIP. The agency contracts with private insurers that offer the protection. Flood insurance is only available in communities that join NFIP and take measures to manage flood risks. Check out FEMA's Community Status Book on the web to find out if your area participates in NFIP.

History of Insurance

In the early 20th century, the US experienced severe river flooding. The federal government intervened with projects, such as building levees and dams, to control damages caused by flooding. Yet despite spending billions of dollars on these projects, flood loss continued to worsen. Eventually, the National Flood Insurance Act of 1968 created the NFIP.

www.m.g-wlearning.com
www.g-wlearning.com

Homeowner's Liability Protection

Homeowner's liability insurance protects the policyholder from claims or lawsuits. If someone gets hurt on the property, this policy will protect the homeowner from the financial consequences of a lawsuit. If a covered family member causes injury to someone not on the property, this insurance covers that incident, too. Homeowner's liability coverage also pays medical costs for someone who gets hurt on the property, regardless of who is at fault.

Most policies come with a standard $100,000 worth of liability protection. For homeowners who want protection beyond this amount, they can purchase an umbrella policy. An **umbrella policy** is like a safety net. Its protection kicks in when the homeowner's insurance reaches its coverage limits. Umbrella insurance is covered in more detail in Chapter 4.

Real World Case

Jacob's cousin Ellie was badly injured in a boating accident last year. After weeks in the hospital and months of rehabilitation, Ellie fully recovered. However, she had hundreds of thousands of dollars in medical bills. A family friend was driving the boat at the time of the accident, and his homeowner's insurance was responsible for covering the costs of Ellie's care.

How Much Coverage Is Enough?

It is important to know the value of the home and its structures, as well as the value of all personal items. If the house is worth $100,000 in today's market, is $100,000 worth of insurance enough? Probably not. This is because the cost to rebuild the house will likely rise over time. In addition, the amount does not account for personal property. Some experts recommend insuring a home for at least 125% of its value.

Most homeowner's policies cover personal possessions up to 50% of the total coverage. So, if the homeowner's policy provides $100,000 in coverage, it will cover electronics and other possessions up to $50,000. Individual items may be limited to $1,500 or $2,000. What if there are items that are more valuable than this limit? Those items can be added to the policy by scheduling them.

Scheduling simply means that an item and its value are stated on the policy. A small additional premium is paid for this. For example, a rare piece of art or expensive jewelry should be scheduled. In some cases, the receipt for the item may need to be supplied, or the item may need to be valued by an expert.

Checkpoint 2.1

1. What does homeowner's insurance cover?
2. What coverage protects you if somebody is hurt on your property?
3. How is earthquake coverage included in a homeowner's policy?
4. What determines if a homeowner can purchase flood insurance?
5. If a home is worth $100,000, what should the homeowner's minimum coverage amount be?

Build Your Vocabulary

As you progress through this course, develop a personal glossary of insurance terms and add it to your portfolio. This will help you build your vocabulary and prepare you for a career in insurance. Write out a definition for each of the following terms, and add it to your personal insurance glossary.

property and casualty insurance
mortgage
replacement cost
cash value
depreciation
endorsement
umbrella policy
scheduling

Section 2.2
Commercial Insurance

Terms

commercial general liability insurance
commercial property insurance
commercial package policy insurance
business owner's policy insurance

Objectives

After completing this section, you will be able to:
- Explain the purpose of commercial general liability insurance.
- Define commercial property insurance.
- Explain a commercial package policy.
- Identify what a business owner's policy covers.

Commercial General Liability Insurance

Commercial general liability insurance, known in the business as CGL, covers bodily injury and property damage. Let's say A-Plus Remodeling Company puts in a new staircase and fails to secure the railing. Grandma Kate goes for the railing and pulls it off the wall, causing her to fall down the stairs. A-Plus Remodeling Company's CGL policy pays for the damage to the wall and Grandma Kate's medical bills. If Grandma Kate sues the company, the CGL policy will cover legal expenses. CGL also covers the business premises, operations, products the business sells or distributes, medical payments, as well as personal and advertising injury (slander, libel, copyright infringement, and the like).

Commercial Property Insurance

Commercial property insurance pays for physical damage or loss of certain kinds of property. The coverage can include buildings, business personal property (like equipment, furniture, and merchandise), and the personal property of others. This insurance can either be for specific perils or no named perils. A business can buy coverage to pay either the cash value of lost property or its full replacement cost.

Commercial Package Policy Insurance

Commercial package policy insurance combines two or more insurance products into one policy. The benefit to buying a package policy typically comes in reduced premiums. The package would include only the insurance the particular business needs. These may be general liability insurance and property insurance, for example.

Ethical Insurance Practices

Everyone should behave in an honest and ethical manner. To manage the risk that an employee or contractor's action will potentially cause harm, companies and government entities can purchase surety insurance. This kind of insurance pays the policyholder should a bonded third party act dishonestly or fail to perform a contractual obligation.

Businesses must protect themselves against property damage, but there are other perils they need to be protected against as well.

Source: Shutterstock (Dennis Tokarzewski)

Business Owner's Policy Insurance

Business owner's policy insurance, known also as BOP, provides low-cost property and liability coverage to small businesses. It also covers loss of income if the business has to stop operating for a while. Let's say you open a small bookstore, and a bad storm tears off part of the roof. A business owner's policy would cover the damage to your shop, injury to the customer who happened to be browsing at the time, and payroll and taxes while your store is closed for repair. You can buy the coverage to pay either the cash value of your lost property or its full replacement cost.

Checkpoint 2.2

1. What is CGL?
2. What does CGL cover?
3. What does commercial property insurance cover?
4. What is the benefit to a business owner of purchasing a commercial package policy?
5. What does a business owner's policy protect against?

Build Your Vocabulary

As you progress through this course, develop a personal glossary of insurance terms and add it to your portfolio. This will help you build your vocabulary and prepare you for a career in insurance. Write out a definition for each of the following terms, and add it to your personal insurance glossary.

commercial general liability insurance
commercial property insurance
commercial package policy insurance
business owner's policy insurance

Careers in Finance
Insurance Services

What Does a Claims Adjuster Do?

A **claims adjuster** interviews the claimant (individual making the claim), witnesses, and others to determine whether a claim is covered by the customer's policy. A **claims adjuster** inspects property damage, estimates repair costs, and assesses the insurer's financial responsibility. An adjuster:
- plans and schedules the work required to process a claim;
- interviews witnesses and claimants;
- reviews police and hospital records;
- inspects property damage;
- develops a report that is used to evaluate the claim;
- negotiates with the claimant to settle the claim; and
- if a claim is denied, works with attorneys and witnesses to defend the insurer's position.

What Is It Like to Work as a Claims Adjuster?

Claims adjusters work in the property and liability insurance industry. An adjuster decides whether customers' policies cover their claims. Many adjusters work outside the office, inspecting damage claims. Others work in a centralized claims center, where they estimate payouts and issue checks.

When working in an office, a claims adjuster may be required to wear business-professional attire, but may be allowed to wear business-casual attire, depending on the office's dress policy. When working in the field inspecting damage, it may be acceptable to wear blue jeans. The adjuster is representing the company; so, it is important to be dressed in clothing appropriate to the situation. In addition, the claims adjuster must follow accepted guidelines for use of e-mail, social networking, blogs, and texting.

What Education and Skills Are Needed to Be a Claims Adjuster?

- a college degree is preferred, but not required
- solid communication skills
- good interview skills
- an assertive personality
- strong computer skills

Chapter 2 Property and Casualty Insurance for Homes and Businesses

Chapter Summary

Section 2.1 **Homeowner's and Renter's Insurance**

- Homeowner's insurance protects the home, its structures, and its contents against certain losses. It also provides liability protection for the policyholder and family.
- The standard homeowner's policies are HO-2 through HO-8, although some states have different categories.
- Flood insurance is only available through a federal program, the National Flood Insurance Program, while earthquake insurance can be added as an endorsement to a standard homeowner's policy.
- Homeowner's liability insurance protects the policyholder and family from claims or lawsuits related to injuries.
- A homeowner's policy typically should be for 125% of the home's value with especially valuable items placed on a schedule.

Section 2.2 **Commercial Insurance**

- Commercial general liability insurance covers a business against bodily injury and property damage.
- Commercial property insurance pays for the loss or damage of certain kinds of property associated with the business.
- To save on premiums, some companies purchase a commercial package policy, combining two or more policies into one.
- A common insurance policy for small businesses is the business owner's policy (BOP) insurance, which provides property and liability coverage. It also covers loss of income if the business has to stop operating.

Check Your Insurance IQ

Now that you have finished this chapter, see what you know about insurance by taking the chapter post test.
www.m.g-wlearning.com
www.g-wlearning.com

Review Your Knowledge

On a separate sheet of paper or in a word processing document, match the following terms with the definition that fits best.

A. commercial general liability insurance
B. cash value
C. property and casualty insurance
D. replacement cost
E. umbrella policy
F. business owner's policy insurance
G. depreciation
H. mortgage
I. endorsement
J. scheduling

1. Coverage that replaces an insured item's current market value.
2. A safety net that kicks in when the homeowner's insurance reaches the coverage limits.
3. General term for insurance that protects policyholders against financial loss associated with property damage or injury to others.
4. Policy that covers a business for bodily injury and property damage.
5. A loan to purchase a house.
6. Loss of an item's value over time.
7. Additional insurance coverage to increase the amount a policy would typically pay.
8. An insurance policy for small business owners to provide property and liability protection.
9. Coverage that replaces an insured item with one just like it.
10. An add-on to an insurance policy.

On a separate sheet of paper or in a word processing document, answer each of the following questions.

11. What is covered by the two basic components of "property" and "casualty" insurance?
12. How is earthquake coverage handled for a homeowner's insurance policy?
13. Which type of insurance protects a small business against loss of income due to the business closing for a period of time?
14. What does scheduling mean?
15. Why do renters need insurance?

Chapter 2 Property and Casualty Insurance for Homes and Businesses

Apply Your Knowledge

16. Browse a local newspaper for an article about an accident that involved property damage and an injury at a business. Explain how each part of the business insurance, "property" and "casualty," applies to the accident.
17. Explain why you think a mortgage lender requires homeowner's insurance on the home they helped finance.
18. If your grandfather leaves you an expensive watch, describe how you should insure it to be sure it is completely covered in case of a loss.
19. What type of homeowner's policy provides the best value, a named perils policy or a no named perils policy that lists specific exclusions? Why?
20. Suppose you start a small business printing T-shirts in a rented garage. What kinds of insurance should you purchase? Why?

Working in Teams

Working with a classmate, create a list of competitive advantages an insurance carrier could offer that would persuade a consumer to move his or her insurance business to that company. Focus on what is most significant to the consumer. After you finish your research, survey your class to see what services they perceive to be most important.

G-W Learning Mobile Site

Visit the G-W Learning mobile site to complete the chapter pretest and post test, to review the History of Insurance articles, and to practice vocabulary using e-flash cards. If you do not have a smartphone, visit the G-W Learning companion website to access these features.

G-W Learning mobile site: www.m.g-wlearning.com
G-W Learning companion website: www.g-wlearning.com

Common Core

College and Career Readiness

Reading. Research an entrepreneur that you know personally or one who is well known. List the person's name, business, and when the business was organized. Cite specific evidence that supports the person's entrepreneurial spirit.

Writing. Conduct a short research project to answer questions about the history of entrepreneurship. Use multiple authoritative print and digital sources. Where did the idea of entrepreneurship originate? Write several paragraphs about your findings to demonstrate your understanding of entrepreneurship.

Insurance Ethics

The insurance competitive event may include an objective test that covers multiple topics. Participants are usually allowed one hour to complete the event. One of the topics that may be included on the test is ethics. The ethics portion of the event may be an objective test. However, ethics may also be an event in the competition that has teams defending a position held on an ethical dilemma or topic. To prepare for the ethics portion of the event, complete the following activities.

1. On your own, review the special ethics features in this book.
2. Put together a team of others who are also interested in this event. Work collaboratively with your team to review and discuss each of the special ethics features in this book. How would you or your team respond to similar situations?
3. Use the Internet to find more information about ethics and communication. Print this information for future study material.

Chapter 3

Property and Casualty Insurance on Land, Sea, and Air

Section 3.1
Automobile Insurance

Section 3.2
Marine and Aviation Insurance

Reading Prep. Before reading this chapter, look at the chapter title. What does this title tell you about what you will be learning? Compare and contrast the information to be presented with information you already know about the subject matter from sources such as videos and online media.

College and Career Readiness

As you learned in Chapter 2, property and casualty insurance protects policyholders against financial loss associated with property damage or injury to others. In addition to homes and businesses, property and casualty insurance also covers cars, ships and their cargo, and an odd assortment of other property. This chapter discusses property and casualty insurance that covers cars, watercraft, and aircraft.

As environmental issues become more important in our society, a growing segment of the insurance industry is focusing on environmental liability risks. This type of insurance protects a business from financial loss associated with correcting environmental damage it caused.

Check Your Insurance IQ

Before you begin this chapter, see what you already know about insurance by taking the chapter pretest.

www.m.g-wlearning.com
www.g-wlearning.com

Section 3.1
Automobile Insurance

Terms

automobile insurance
motorcycle insurance
bodily injury liability insurance
property damage liability insurance
property damage insurance
collision coverage
totaled
comprehensive coverage
financial responsibility laws
uninsured liability coverage
underinsured liability coverage
credit score
underwriter

Objectives

After completing this section, you will be able to:
- Describe automobile insurance.
- Discuss what states typically require for automobile insurance coverage.
- Explain what criteria insurers use to determine premiums.
- Identify ways to reduce automobile insurance premiums.

What Is Automobile Insurance?

Of all insurance products on the market, automobile insurance is probably the one people are most aware of. Why? Because it has historically been the only type of insurance many states *require* people to carry. **Automobile insurance** covers passenger vehicles and protects against the financial aspects of a traffic accident. Different types of insurance cover other vehicles. For example, **motorcycle insurance** covers any two- or three-wheeled motor vehicle that a person rides on roads and highways.

As with all types of insurance, the policyholder pays a premium to an insurance carrier. The company, in turn, agrees to pay for losses the policy covers. Automobile insurance has a deductible, which varies by policy. Generally, a higher deductible results in a lower premium.

Automobile insurance protects against the financial losses of an accident.

Source: Shutterstock (jcpjr)

Careers in Finance
Insurance Services

What Does an Insurance Appraiser Do?

An **insurance appraiser** assesses the cost to repair damaged vehicles for insurance purposes. He or she works directly with insurance policyholders and insurers. An appraiser:
- examines damaged vehicles and estimates the cost to repair them;
- negotiates with auto repair shops on the cost of repair;
- settles claims with policyholders;
- prepares insurance forms; and
- determines whether to repair it or total it if a vehicle is badly damaged.

What Is It Like to Work as an Insurance Appraiser?

Insurance appraisers have varied hours and often work from home. Sometimes, they work on the weekends. Appraisers may work directly for an insurance company or for an independent appraisal company. In any event, the insurance appraiser must follow accepted guidelines for use of e-mail, social networking, blogs, and texting.

When they are working in their home office, appraisers can dress as they please. However, when meeting policyholders or repair personnel, their attire must reflect the professional spirit of their work. The specific attire is determined by the situation.

What Education and Skills Are Needed to Be an Insurance Appraiser?
- a high school degree; some college-level education is often preferred
- strong negotiating skills
- sound judgment
- keen ability to think critically
- ability to use math to solve problems
- good verbal and written communication skills

Insurance companies typically write automobile policies that last six months or one year. In most cases, the policyholder can pay the premium in installments.

Automobile insurance is not a one-size-fits-all type of coverage. It is made up of many components. Generally, it breaks down into two broad categories: liability and property damage.

History of Insurance

In the late 1800s, Ohio was the center of automobile manufacturing. In fact, the first automobile policy was issued in Dayton in 1897. A Mr. Gilbert Loomis bought a policy from the Travelers Insurance Company. Travelers protected Mr. Loomis in the event his car killed or injured someone or damaged the property of others.

www.m.g-wlearning.com
www.g-wlearning.com

Liability Coverage

If a person is injured or killed in a traffic accident, **bodily injury liability insurance** protects the person who caused the accident against financial claims. If the injured person sues the policyholder, the coverage also pays for legal defense. Many states require a minimum $100,000 of bodily injury liability coverage per injured person, up to $300,000 per accident. This is known as 100/300 coverage in the insurance business.

Property damage liability insurance generally pays for damages the policyholder's vehicle caused to another's property. The property can belong to a person or an entity, such as a company or municipality. It also covers the damage the vehicle caused to other vehicles in a traffic accident. However, it does not cover damage to the policyholder's vehicle. For example, if you back out of your driveway and into your neighbor's fence, this insurance covers the cost of fixing or replacing the fence. But, it does not cover repairs to your car.

Property damage liability insurance covers damage caused by the policyholder's vehicle for the policyholder or anyone he or she allows to drive the car. Experts commonly suggest carrying at least $50,000 of property damage liability coverage. If this coverage is carried in addition to the suggested bodily injury liability insurance, the policy would state coverage as 100/300/50.

Real World Case

Jacob was driving over to Maria's house one day, when his cell phone rang. He glanced down at it to see who was calling as he was coming to a stoplight. That was a bad idea. Not only did he run into the car in front of him, but the driver of the other car suffered an injury. His automobile insurance paid for the repair of both cars, as well as the other driver's medical bills. But, his parents were not as accommodating. They took away his license and his cell phone for a month.

Property Damage

Property damage insurance covers physical damage to the policyholder's car. This insurance can include *collision coverage, comprehensive coverage,* or both.

Remember that fence you ran into backing out of your driveway? Property damage liability coverage pays to fix the fence. **Collision coverage** pays for the damage to your car as the result of the collision. States do not require collision coverage. But, if the policyholder has a loan to buy the car, the lender will require this coverage be carried.

Have you ever heard someone say a car was totaled? For insurance purposes, **totaled** means the insurer decided repairs to the car would cost more than the car is worth or that the car simply cannot be repaired. The term is short for "total loss." The insurer will take the car for recycling and pay the policyholder what the car is worth, minus the deductible. For this reason, somebody driving an older car probably does not need collision coverage. Compare the cost of insurance and the deductible to the car's value to decide if collision coverage makes sense.

The primary source for determining a car's value is the Kelley Blue Book. A blue book for the industry has been around for nearly a century. However, the consumer version only became available in hardcopy and online (www.kbb.com) in the 1990s.

Comprehensive coverage pays for car damages that result from causes other than collisions. For example, if a policyholder's car is pummeled by hail, then comprehensive coverage pays to fix the damage. Other causes of damage covered by comprehensive coverage include fire, flood, theft, explosions, and even riots. As a car ages and loses its value, the consumer may not want to carry comprehensive coverage for the same reasons he or she may not want to carry collision coverage.

Source: Shutterstock (Jonathan Lenz)

Property damage liability insurance pays for damages your vehicle causes to property, including other vehicles, but not for damages to *your* car.

State Coverage Requirements

States regulate the insurance industry. Each state sets rules that insurance companies must follow concerning policies providing coverage in the state. Many states also have financial responsibility laws. **Financial responsibility laws** require licensed drivers to buy a minimum amount of automobile liability insurance. These laws are intended to ensure that drivers can pay claims for accidents they cause. In the states with these laws, a driver generally cannot register a car without proof of the minimum coverage.

States typically require minimum liability limit coverage for these three areas:
- each injured person
- the payout for all injured persons per accident
- property damage per accident

Figure 3-1 shows the minimum liability limits for three states. You can typically find information about minimum coverage requirements in your state by visiting the state's insurance department website.

If a driver in Maine purchases the minimum amount, as shown in Figure 3-1, the policy would list coverage as 50/100/25. Some drivers

	Bodily Injury per Person	Bodily Injury per Accident	Property Damage per Accident
Maine	$50,000	$100,000	$25,000
Texas	$30,000	$60,000	$25,000
Pennsylvania	$15,000	$30,000	$5,000

Figure 3-1. Minimum State-Required Auto Coverage: Examples from Three States

may think the state minimum is enough insurance coverage, but it typically is not. For example, as noted earlier, some experts suggest carrying bodily injury liability insurance of at least $100,000 for each injured person, up to $300,000 per accident. If the minimum required coverage in your state is below this amount, you would need to purchase more coverage to meet what experts recommend.

Many states also require insurance companies to offer **uninsured liability coverage** or **underinsured liability coverage.** Generally, if an uninsured or underinsured driver injures the policyholder, the insurance carrier will pay for treating the beneficiary's injuries, up to the limits on the policy. Some states require that insurance carriers offer this insurance, but not that it be purchased. Other states require that drivers purchase either un- or underinsured motorist coverage, or both.

Figure 3-2 shows un- and underinsured motorist coverage rules in the same three states as in Figure 3-1. While drivers do not have to buy this coverage in Texas and Pennsylvania, insurance companies must offer it.

How Insurers Determine Premiums

The premiums people pay for automobile insurance can vary widely. When somebody applies for automobile insurance, he or she must provide information, including his or her:
- age;
- gender (depending on your state);
- residence location;
- car make, model, and year;
- driving history (accidents and tickets);
- miles driven annually; and
- expected vehicle usage (personal versus business).

The insurance carrier may also check the applicant's credit score. Your **credit score** is a numerical value that reflects your credit history. You will learn more about credit scores and other assessment tools insurers use in Chapter 10.

Each piece of information factors into the premium. For example, younger drivers are inexperienced and statistically cause the most car accidents. Their higher premiums reflect this risk. Additionally,

	Uninsured Coverage Required	Underinsured Coverage Required
Maine	Yes	Yes
Texas	No	No
Pennsylvania	No	No

Figure 3-2. Uninsured and Underinsured Coverage Requirements: Examples from Three States

the premium will be higher if the consumer lives in an urban or suburban area because those areas have more traffic. This increases the likelihood of an accident.

An insurance **underwriter** uses the information supplied on the application to figure out what level of risk the person represents to the company. It is up to the underwriter to determine what premium the company should charge. The underwriter can even recommend declining the application.

Real World Case

Jacob and Maria are only a few months apart in age. They got their driver's licenses on the same day, and they are both insured under their parents' automobile insurance policy. Both even drive their family's minivans. But, Jacob's insurance premium is twice the cost of Maria's premium! What gives? It is all about statistics.
- The Insurance Institute for Highway Safety finds that teenage boys are twice as likely as teenage girls to die in a car accident.
- A National Highway Traffic Safety Administration survey of driver attitudes found that men report much higher incidences of engaging in unsafe driving behavior than are reported by women.
- Teen drivers are less experienced and have a tendency toward risky driving behavior, like speeding. The Highway Loss Data Institute reports higher costs for vehicle damage for cars driven by teens versus cars driven by adults.

Ways to Reduce the Premium

Automobile insurance premiums will be high for young and inexperienced drivers. Some insurance companies reduce premiums if a student driver keeps good grades. It can also help to take driver-education and defensive-driving courses.

Many insurers offer discounts if more than one vehicle is insured or the family purchases other insurance policies from the company. This is often called a multicar or multipolicy discount. Features on a vehicle like antilock brakes and antitheft devices may also be eligible

Source: Shutterstock (Lisa F. Young)

Successfully completing driver-education or defensive-driving classes may qualify you for discounts on your automobile insurance premium.

AAA, which once stood for the American Automobile Association, has been around for over 100 years. If you were ever a school safety patrol, thank AAA. It created the program in the 1920s. Today, AAA provides roadside assistance to members, discounts on several types of insurance, traveler assistance, and other benefits.

www.m.g-wlearning.com
www.g-wlearning.com.

for discounts on the premium. Additionally, the insurer may provide discounts for memberships in organizations like AAA.

Another way to lower the premium is by increasing the deductible. Remember, the deductible is how much the policyholder pays before insurance takes over. If the deductible is $500, the policyholder could lower the premium by increasing it to $1,000. Also, if the car is worth less than $2,000, the policyholder should consider dropping collision and comprehensive insurance coverage. These are often the largest part of the premium.

Claims Process

Most claims against an automobile insurance policy are for vehicle damages, rather than injuries. In fact, 63% of the cost of every claim goes to fixing a car. If you are in an accident, follow these steps for preparing the insurance claim.
1. Make sure no one is injured. If anybody is injured, call emergency services. If you have a minor injury that does not require an ambulance, you should still have it checked out by a doctor. You want to make sure it is a limited injury that will not come back to haunt you.
2. Trade insurance and personal information with the other driver. Ask for his or her name, address, phone number, and insurance card. Note the company name and phone number. Provide your information to the other driver.
3. Ask any witnesses for their names and contact information. The insurer may need to hear their accounts of the accident.

4. File an accident report with the police. If an officer is not on the scene, contact your local police department to find out how to file the report. This will help when you file your claim.
5. Contact your insurance company to report the accident, and find out what steps you need to take. It is important to make this call soon following the accident. Otherwise, you could run into a time limit.

The insurer may send an appraiser to assess the damage. The appraiser will view and photograph the damage, investigate the claim if necessary, and determine which driver was at fault. If you are not at fault, you can have your own insurance company pay for the damages. If you file with your own insurer in this case, you may have to pay your deductible. Otherwise, you can pursue payment from the other driver's insurer. If you have any problems receiving payment from the at-fault driver's insurer, use your own insurer as your advocate. Your carrier will help you get your claim paid.

Checkpoint 3.1

1. What does automobile insurance cover?
2. If an automobile policy states bodily injury liability as 100/300, what does this mean?
3. What kind of automobile insurance would pay for damages caused by a tree falling on your parked car?
4. In states with financial responsibility laws, what minimum liability limit(s) are generally required?
5. How can you reduce your automobile insurance premium?

Build Your Vocabulary

As you progress through this course, develop a personal glossary of insurance terms and add it to your portfolio. This will help you build your vocabulary and prepare you for a career in insurance. Write out a definition for each of the following terms, and add it to your personal insurance glossary.

automobile insurance
motorcycle insurance
bodily injury liability insurance
property damage liability insurance
property damage insurance
collision coverage
totaled
comprehensive coverage
financial responsibility laws
uninsured liability coverage
underinsured liability coverage
credit score
underwriter

Section 3.2
Marine and Aviation Insurance

Terms

ocean marine insurance
marine cargo policy
hull policy
cargo war risk policy
yacht policy
personal watercraft (PWC)
inland marine insurance
aviation insurance
aircraft hull insurance
aircraft liability insurance
war risk insurance

Objectives

After completing this section, you will be able to:
- Explain what ocean marine insurance covers.
- Describe inland marine insurance.
- Describe the primary aviation insurance products.

Ocean Marine Insurance

Marine insurance dates back centuries. It was originally used to insure ships and their cargo. The issuers were individuals (not companies) willing to take the risk in return for a premium. Today, marine insurance is broken out into two broad categories: ocean marine insurance and inland marine insurance.

Just like in the old days, **ocean marine insurance** provides coverage for ocean-going ships and the cargo they carry. The first American insurance company to offer marine insurance was the Insurance Company of North America (CNA). It began writing policies in 1794 and remains in business today. Four types of ocean marine insurance policies are available: **marine cargo policy, hull policy, cargo war risk policy,** and **yacht policy.** Figure 3-3 describes each of these policies.

Cargo war risk policies are typically written with marine cargo policies. While cargo war risk insurance covers cargo from the perils of war, it may exclude certain locations. Also, it only covers war risk when the cargo is at sea, not when it reaches land.

Yacht insurance covers more than just yachts. A motorboat or a sailboat, for example, is covered through yacht insurance. This insurance would likely pay for damages if the boat is run aground, but would not pay if someone steals a camera from the boat while it is docked.

On the other hand, a **personal watercraft (PWC),** like a Jet Ski™ or WaveRunner™, is covered with hull insurance. The policy covers physical damage and provides liability coverage as well. Homeowner's insurance policies provide limited coverage for personal watercraft. So, it is usually a good idea to buy a hull policy specifically for the PWC. States do not require owners to insure PWCs, however.

Policy Type	What It Is	What It Covers
Marine Cargo	Covers ocean-shipped cargo from where it is picked up (by truck or train, for example) through its arrival at the buyer's location.	• Perils of the sea (sinking, stranding, collision, etc.). • Fire. • Piracy. • Goods thrown overboard to protect the ship. • Actions of the ship's master that violates the insured's trust. • Explosions. • Ship defects that cause damage.
Hull	Covers the ship (not the cargo) for the benefit of the ship owner or the shipper.	• Protects the ship against damages for all but excluded perils. • Provides legal liability protection to the insured.
Cargo War Risk	Add-on to a cargo policy to protect the insured in a time or place of war.	• Protects the ship and its contents when on the ship.
Yacht	Covers pleasure craft like yachts, sailboats, and motorboats. Offers both property and liability protection.	• Specifically excludes wear and tear, gradual deterioration, and petty theft.

Figure 3-3. Ocean Marine Insurance Policy Types

Source: Shutterstock (devi)

Personal watercraft may have limited coverage under a homeowner's insurance policy. Carrying hull insurance is a good idea.

Ethical Insurance Practices

The insurance profession has developed a set of seven guidelines for ethical behavior: act in the public interest, undertake continuing education, abide by laws and regulations, be diligent, aspire to raise ethical standards of the industry, maintain dignified relationships, and promote public understanding of insurance and risk management.

Inland Marine Insurance

Based on its name, you might guess that inland marine insurance has something to do with insuring shipments that travel on water. Traditionally, it was insurance for cargo that shipped on inland waterways, like rivers and canals. However, the definition expanded in the early 1900s to include shipments across land and even property at fixed locations.

Today, **inland marine insurance** covers risks that frequently change. This applies to construction, where, for example, a building reaches a new stage of completion each day. It also applies to personal and commercial property that gets moved around a lot. A work of art is protected by inland marine insurance as it travels from one museum to another, for example. Even electronic data fall under inland marine insurance.

Businesses and individuals purchase inland marine insurance as a supplement to another policy. For example, if a homeowner's insurance policy does not cover jewelry, an inland marine policy can be purchased to cover the collection.

Interestingly, bridges, tunnels, and radio- and television-transmitting equipment are insured by inland marine policies. The reasoning is that these properties are subject to the perils of transportation.

Real World Case

Jacob's dad works in construction. He uses a lot of heavy tools on each site. He typically leaves them at the site under lock and key. Last year, he spent several weeks working on new home construction across town. He arrived at the site early one morning to find that someone had broken in and stolen his equipment. Fortunately, the company he contracted with carried inland marine insurance. The insurance carrier paid to replace his stolen equipment.

Building construction is covered by inland marine insurance because it represents risks that may change daily.

Source: Shutterstock (stefanolunardi)

Aviation Insurance

Aviation insurance protects against financial loss involving aircraft. It is available for commercial airlines and private aircraft. In the commercial market, the risk to insurers of major loss is significant. For example, the terrorist attacks on September 11, 2001, produced $4.6 billion in losses for the aviation insurance industry. The industry shares risk across insurers to limit the impact of huge losses. More than 100 insurers may share the risk of covering one major airline.

In the early days of flight, few insurers were willing to write aviation policies. The risks were simply too great. But, as regulations and improved engineering reduced risk, the aviation insurance industry got off the ground.

Insurance for aircraft generally falls into three categories:
- hull insurance
- liability insurance
- war risk insurance

Aircraft hull insurance covers the aircraft and all parts permanently attached to it. This includes such parts as the engine and propeller. An all-risk policy covers the aircraft in all circumstances. It covers all losses aside from any listed exceptions.

Hull insurance can also specify when it will cover a loss. It could cover only loss occurring while the aircraft is on the ground and not in motion. Or, it may cover loss only when the aircraft is on the ground and in motion. It could also only cover loss when the aircraft is in flight. The term *hull* was brought over from the marine insurance industry. In fact, marine insurers wrote the earliest policies.

Aircraft liability insurance protects the insured if an accident causes injury or death to passengers or others. It also protects against third-party claims for property damage. Say for example, a pilot clips the wing of a parked aircraft on take off. Aircraft liability insurance would cover the damage.

Owners of both commercial and private aircraft carry aviation insurance.

Source: Shutterstock (Margo Harrison)

History of Insurance

Lloyd's of London wrote the first aviation insurance policies in 1911 when the company agreed to provide legal liability insurance to some planes that were participating in an air meet. The demand for aviation insurance remained low through World War I. It picked up in 1919, as the civil air transportation industry began to grow.

www.m.g-wlearning.com
www.g-wlearning.com

War risk insurance is a major insurance issue facing the aviation industry. It provides coverage for acts of terrorism and war. Following the terrorist attacks that occurred on September 11, 2001, aviation insurers withdrew war risk coverage. Since then, they have reinstated partial coverage, but at higher premiums. To help make this insurance available, the federal government stepped in. The Terrorism Risk Insurance Act of 2002 (TRIA) limits insurance industry losses from a terrorist attack. Under TRIA, the government will pay 85% of insured losses up to $100 billion. It kicks in when the entire industry experiences $100 million in losses. Also, the agency that regulates the US aviation industry, the Federal Aviation Administration, now offers lower-cost war risk coverage.

Checkpoint 3.2

1. What are the broad categories of marine insurance?
2. Under which type of policy would a sailboat or motorboat be covered?
3. Under which type of policy would a personal watercraft be covered?
4. What is the basic purpose of inland marine insurance?
5. What is aircraft hull insurance?

Build Your Vocabulary

As you progress through this course, develop a personal glossary of insurance terms and add it to your portfolio. This will help you build your vocabulary and prepare you for a career in insurance. Write out a definition for each of the following terms, and add it to your personal insurance glossary.

ocean marine insurance
marine cargo policy
hull policy
cargo war risk policy
yacht policy
personal watercraft (PWC)
inland marine insurance
aviation insurance
aircraft hull insurance
aircraft liability insurance
war risk insurance

Chapter Summary

Section 3.1 Automobile Insurance
- Automobile insurance protects a policyholder against the financial losses of an accident and includes liability and property damage coverage.
- Many states have financial responsibility laws, which require drivers to carry a minimum amount of insurance.
- Automobile insurance premiums depend on your age, your gender (in some states), what kind of car you drive, and where you live.
- There are many ways to reduce automobile insurance premiums, from increasing the deductible to qualifying for various discounts.

Section 3.2 Marine and Aviation Insurance
- Ocean marine insurance covers ships and cargo from the point at which it originates to the point at which the buyer receives it.
- Even though inland marine insurance sounds like it only covers shipments transported by water, it can be used to cover much more, such as personal jewelry, art, or even a construction site.
- Hull insurance, liability insurance, and war risk insurance are aviation insurance products that seek to manage the risk involved with owning and operating aircraft.

Check Your Insurance IQ
Now that you have finished this chapter, see what you know about insurance by taking the chapter post test.
www.m.g-wlearning.com
www.g-wlearning.com

Review Your Knowledge

On a separate sheet of paper or in a word processing document, match the following terms with the definition that fits best.

A. automobile insurance
B. hull policy
C. property damage liability insurance
D. inland marine insurance
E. totaled
F. yacht policy
G. comprehensive coverage
H. war risk insurance
I. financial responsibility laws
J. ocean marine insurance

1. Covers the cost of repairing or replacing your car if you have an accident.
2. The kind of insurance you would carry on a sailboat.
3. Provides coverage for acts of terrorism.
4. State laws that require drivers to carry automobile insurance.
5. Automobile insurance that covers damages caused by the vehicle, other than injuries.
6. Marine insurance that covers the ship rather than its cargo.
7. When a car is deemed damaged beyond repair by the insurance carrier.
8. Insurance that covers things like jewelry and power tools.
9. Car insurance that covers damages that are not the result of an accident.
10. Type of insurance that protects ships and their cargo.

On a separate sheet of paper or in a word processing document, answer each of the following questions.

11. What are the two broad categories of automobile insurance?
12. What is often suggested as the minimum amount of bodily injury liability insurance that an automobile policy should have?
13. Which type of automobile insurance pays for damages to your car as the result of an accident?
14. Which type of ocean marine insurance covers the perils of the sea?
15. Why is radio- and television-transmitting equipment covered by inland marine insurance?

Apply Your Knowledge

16. Investigate the average automobile insurance rates for teens in your state. Create a chart showing the number of accidents per year based on age. Create another chart including data for drivers in their 30s, 50s, and 70s. Compare and contrast the data. Then, draw a conclusion that the data support.
17. Research the financial responsibility laws in your state. If your state does not have these laws, select a neighboring state. Using PowerPoint or other electronic presentation software, create a slide show illustrating the different laws and explaining the insurance requirements of the law.
18. Select three different vehicles, such as a compact car, sports car, and full-size SUV. Next, contact an insurance agent, explain that you are a student and ask if you can discuss how these three vehicles will impact your automobile insurance premium. If there is a difference in premiums for you, ask if the difference is the same for an older driver, such as one of your parents. Then, write a one-page paper explaining your findings.
19. An extended warranty is a way to manage the risk of having to pay for a costly repair or having to replace a valued item, such as a car. Investigate extended warranties offered by automobile manufacturers. Evaluate the cost over time associated with purchasing an extended warranty and having to pay for repairs out of pocket. What do an extended warranty and an insurance policy have in common? Do you think that purchasing an extended warranty is a good idea? Why or why not?
20. Research inland marine insurance as it relates to businesses in your area. Identify at least three local businesses that you think should carry inland marine insurance. Write a three-page paper that describes each of the businesses and explains why you think each should carry inland marine insurance.

Working in Teams

Working with a classmate, conduct research into insurance companies that specialize in environmental liabilities. Create a chart that illustrates several companies and their insurance offerings. How does this type of insurance help lead to a greener society?

G-W Learning Mobile Site

Visit the G-W Learning mobile site to complete the chapter pretest and post test, to review the History of Insurance articles, and to practice vocabulary using e-flash cards. If you do not have a smartphone, visit the G-W Learning companion website to access these features.

G-W Learning mobile site: www.m.g-wlearning.com
G-W Learning companion website: www.g-wlearning.com

Common Core

College and Career Readiness

Reading. Research a current event that affects the insurance industry. Read closely to determine what the text says. Write several paragraphs, citing the events that impact the insurance industry. Then, create a visual display that shows how a specific condition discussed in the text can help or hinder the insurance business.

Writing. You are ready to open a business, and you need to purchase insurance as a part of your risk-management plan. Compose an informative letter or e-mail that you might send to an insurance company. Convey the information clearly and accurately through the effective organization of the content. Describe your business and your product or service. Ask for a quote for insurance. Be sure to follow the rules of writing a letter or e-mail.

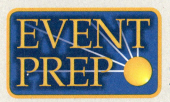

Public Speaking

Public speaking is a competitive event you might enter with your organization. This event allows you to showcase your communication skills of speaking, organizing, and making an oral presentation. This is usually a timed event you can prepare for prior to the competition. You will have time to research, prepare, and practice before going to the competition. Review the specific guidelines and rules for this event regarding topics and props you will be allowed to use. To prepare for the public speaking event:

1. Read the guidelines provided by your organization. Make certain you ask any questions about points you do not understand. It is important that you follow each specific item outlined in the competition rules.
2. Your speech will be judged by a panel of professionals. Practice your speech in front of your peers until you are comfortable.

Source: Shutterstock (Condor 36)

Doctors' bills are just one facet of the total cost of health care.

Chapter 4
Health Insurance

Reading Prep. Before reading this chapter, review the highlighted technical terms and definitions. As you read the chapter, investigate the meaning of each term until you comprehend it.

Y ou or your family likely knows someone who has suffered an illness or injury that required a hospital stay. Even one day in a hospital costs a lot. Without health insurance, a hospital stay, no matter how short, could financially devastate a family. This chapter takes a look at insurance products that protect against financial losses related to your health and your ability to work.

Section 4.1
The High Cost of Health Care

Section 4.2
Private Health Insurance

Section 4.3
Protection When Group Coverage Is Lost

Green companies are always looking for energy-efficient equipment, and the Energy Star label is one indication of energy efficiency. The US Environmental Protection Agency and the Department of Energy have created the Energy Star program to rate products. The Energy Star label guarantees the product meets a certain level of energy efficiency. By looking for this label, business owners and consumers can be confident that the product meets environmental standards. See the EPA and Energy Star websites for more information.

Check Your Insurance IQ

Before you begin this chapter, see what you already know about insurance by taking the chapter pretest.

www.m.g-wlearning.com
www.g-wlearning.com

Section 4.1
The High Cost of Health Care

Terms

health insurance
adverse selection
defensive medicine
chronic disease
Patient Protection and Affordable Care Act

Objectives

After completing this section, you will be able to:
- Describe some reasons for the high cost of health insurance.
- Identify the major health reform law that passed in 2010.

Health Insurance Costs

Health insurance, just like other insurance products, seeks to protect you from financial risk. It helps pay for doctor visits, tests and procedures, hospital stays, and medications. Health care is expensive, and so is health insurance.

One reason for the high cost of health insurance is because people who need care are typically those who purchase it. This is a concept known as adverse selection. **Adverse selection** is a situation in which those purchasing insurance represent a greater risk than the population as a whole. If everyone carried health insurance, then the premiums for those who are healthy would help to offset the higher costs for those who need care.

Technological advances in the health industry have also spurred increased costs. Companies that create and use new technologies have to recoup their costs. Also, new medical technology tends to increase demand for services that may not be cost-effective.

Some analysts point to the cost of defensive medicine as a driver of high health costs. The theory is that doctors are at high risk of being sued by patients who feel their care was substandard. So, doctors who practice **defensive medicine** order more tests and procedures than patients really need to protect themselves from lawsuits.

Another reason for the high cost of health insurance is chronic disease. A **chronic disease** is one that lasts for a long time or recurs. Estimates put the cost of caring for people with chronic disease at 75% of what the nation pays for health care. Because we are living longer, chronic diseases play a larger role in our health-care needs.

Administrative costs are another factor in the high cost of health insurance. Administrative costs for insurance companies include marketing, billing, legal costs, and costs associated with state and federal regulations. At least 7% of health-care spending is administrative costs.

Reform of the US health-care system has long been the subject of intense disagreement among policymakers. Rising costs have spiraled

Source: Shutterstock (stefanolunardi)
The cost of health care is high, and health insurance can be expensive.

out of control, and nearly 50 million Americans do not have health insurance. But, politicians have very different ideas on how to address the problems.

Patient Protection and Affordable Care Act

In 2010, Congress passed the Patient Protection and Affordable Care Act, Figure 4-1. The **Patient Protection and Affordable Care Act (PPACA)** was a major reform effort intended to address the problems in the health-care system. The law intends to reduce costs, make delivery of care more efficient, and provide health insurance to those who are not otherwise insured.

Lawmakers vigorously debated the legislation. Some provisions have been put in place, while many others are slated to become law by 2014. However, some lawmakers are attempting to repeal some or all of the provisions of the act. One major point of contention is that PPACA requires individuals to buy health insurance. Another point of contention is the extent of government involvement in the health-insurance market.

Ethical Insurance Practices

It is certainly not unethical to seek health insurance if you know you have a condition that requires medical care. However, it is unethical to knowingly omit information from your application. Not only is it the wrong thing to do, but the insurer can drop you from coverage if it finds out you lied on the application.

Goal	Provisions
Utilize Existing Public Programs	• Expands Medicare and Medicaid coverage.
Increase Access	• Prohibits insurers from canceling health-insurance coverage except for instances of fraud. • Extends dependent coverage up to age 26. • Provides assistance for those who are uninsured because of a preexisting condition. • Levies penalties on certain employers if they do not offer health insurance to their workers.
Improve Affordability and Price	• Eliminates lifetime and annual limits on benefits. • Facilitates administrative simplification to lower health-system costs. • Creates state-based health-insurance exchanges through which small employers and individuals can compare and purchase health insurance.
Boost Prevention Programs	• Requires coverage of preventive services and immunizations. • Increases access to preventive care and strengthens disease-prevention programs.
Add Individual Accountability	• Requires most individuals to purchase health-insurance coverage or pay a penalty.

Figure 4-1. Major Provisions of the Patient Protection and Affordable Care Act

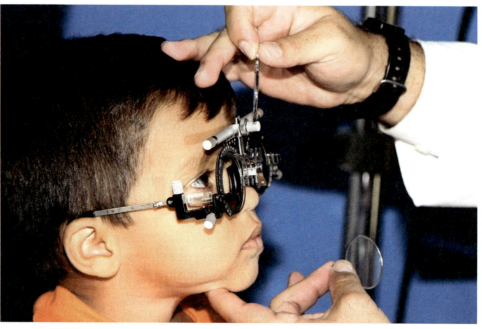

Preventive services, such as vision screenings for young children, must be covered under health-care plans as provided in the Patient Protection and Affordable Care Act (PPACA).

Source: Shutterstock (Reflekta)

Checkpoint 4.1

1. What is the basic purpose of health insurance?
2. What is adverse selection?
3. Approximately how much of what the nation pays for health care is for chronic diseases?
4. What is the basic intent of the Patient Protection and Affordable Care Act?
5. By what year are all of the provisions of the Patient Protection and Affordable Care Act scheduled to go into effect?

Build Your Vocabulary

As you progress through this course, develop a personal glossary of insurance terms and add it to your portfolio. This will help you build your vocabulary and prepare you for a career in insurance. Write out a definition for each of the following terms, and add it to your personal insurance glossary.

health insurance
adverse selection
defensive medicine
chronic disease
Patient Protection and Affordable Care Act

Section 4.2
Private Health Insurance

Objectives

After completing this section, you will be able to:
- Identify the elements of group health insurance.
- Explain the difference between individual and group insurance.
- Describe fee-for-service health plans.
- List the types of managed-care health plans.
- Explain how consumer-driven health plans function.

Group Health Plans

The majority of people with health insurance are in group health plans, Figure 4-2. **Group health plans** take a group of people and assess the risk for the group as a whole, instead of looking at the risk for each individual person in the group. A **group** is a set of people who have an interest in jointly sharing risk. Employer-offered plans are the main example of group health plans, covering 157 million Americans. These plans cover the employer's workers and usually the workers' immediate family members and dependents.

Source: Shutterstock (mangostock)

Terms
group health plans
group
preexisting condition exclusion
individual health plan
fee-for-service health plan
deductible
out-of-pocket maximum
lifetime limits
managed-care plan
provider network
preferred provider organization (PPO)
copayment
out-of-network
health maintenance organization (HMO)
primary care provider (PCP)
point-of-service (POS) plans
consumer-driven health plans
health savings account

Most people who purchase individual health insurance are self-employed.

Plan	Summary
Group Health Plans	Assess the risk for the group as a whole.
Individual Health Plans	Assess the risk of an individual person or family; purchased directly from an insurance company by the participant.
Fee-for-Service Plans	"Traditional plans"; can choose any care provider; must meet a deductible before coverage begins each year.
Managed-Care Plans	Insurance company enters into contracts with hospitals, doctors, and other providers of care; may be HMO, PPO, or POS plan.
Consumer-Driven Health Plans	High deductible with HSA; participant pays directly for services.

Figure 4-2. Overview of Health-Insurance Plans

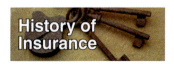

During World War II, the federal government limited wage increases employers could offer, but it permitted them to offer employee insurance plans. This led to an increase in employer-provided health plans.

www.m.g-wlearning.com
www.g-wlearning.com

Often, the employer pays for some of the health-insurance premium. The employee's share of the premium is handled as a paycheck deduction. Premium payments are not taxable to the employer or employee. This creates an incentive for employers to offer health insurance and for employees to enroll.

Employees and family members with preexisting conditions are eligible for the health plan. However, the insurer may not cover costs related to the preexisting condition for a stated period of time. This is known as a **preexisting condition exclusion.**

Individual Health Plans

Employers do not have to offer health insurance. Many small businesses do not offer health insurance because of costs and administrative challenges. People who do not have access to a group health plan may buy an individual health plan. An **individual health plan** is health insurance for a single person or family purchased directly from an insurance company by the participant. Only about 14 million people purchase health insurance in the individual market. The majority of individual health plans are sold to the self-employed.

Individual health insurance policies typically charge higher premiums and limit coverage more than group plans. This is partly because the two types of plans operate under different laws that vary by state. Also, insurers have less opportunity to spread risk in the individual market.

Those with preexisting conditions have historically been denied coverage in the individual market. However, PPACA eliminates this practice for individual health plans beginning in 2014.

Real World Case

Two years ago, Jacob got hurt at the skateboard park. Even though he wore a helmet, he landed a jump badly and was knocked unconscious. He awakened to find himself in the back of an ambulance. Once in the hospital, he underwent a scan of his brain, had blood work done, and received intravenous fluids to keep him hydrated. He stayed one night and was released the next morning with just a mild concussion. Total cost: $33,000. Fortunately, the health insurance purchased by Jacob's parents through his dad's employer paid most of the bill.

Fee-for-Service Plans

For decades, fee-for-service health plans made up the majority of health insurance policies. For this reason, they are often referred to as *traditional plans.* These plans allow the insured person to choose any doctor or specialist.

In a **fee-for-service health plan,** the plan participant (the insured person) pays a premium, but must also meet a deductible before coverage begins each year. The **deductible** is what you have to pay before the insurance kicks in. After the deductible is met, the insurance plan pays a percentage of health-care costs. The participant is responsible for the remainder of the cost. Fee-for-service plans commonly pay 80% of the usual and customary health-care costs; the remaining 20% is the insured person's responsibility.

Fee-for-service plans set an annual out-of-pocket maximum. Very simply, the **out-of-pocket maximum** is the maximum dollar amount the participant will have to pay in a given year. If the insured person hits this limit, the plan pays for 100% of health-care costs for the rest of the year.

Historically, plans have also set **lifetime limits.** This is the maximum amount the plan will pay out over the life of the participant. If the cost of care exceeded this amount, the insured person would be responsible for 100% of the costs. However, lifetime limits are no longer allowed.

Traditional fee-for-service plans often come with a lot of paperwork. The insured person typically pays the full cost of a doctor visit, for example, and then files paperwork with the insurance company to receive reimbursement.

Consumer Laws

The Patient Protection and Affordable Care Act prohibits insurance companies from setting lifetime limits.

Managed-Care Plans

The traditional form of health insurance (fee-for-service plans) is being replaced by managed-care arrangements. In a **managed-care plan,** the insurance company enters into contracts with hospitals, doctors, and other providers of care. Types of managed-care plans include preferred provider organizations (PPOs), health maintenance organizations (HMOs), and point of service (POS) plans. The hospitals, doctors, and other providers of care that are under contract with the plan make up what is called the plan's **provider network.**

Preferred Provider Organizations

A **preferred provider organization (PPO)** establishes a network of providers that the insurer encourages plan participants to use. In a PPO, participants pay a premium and may have an annual deductible.

If the participant uses providers in the network, there is a copayment at the time of service. The **copayment,** or copay, is a fee to help the insurer defer some of the cost. It may be around $10 or $20, depending on the plan. The copayment may be higher for certain services, such as emergency room visits or prescription drugs.

The fee structure of a PPO encourages the participant to use members of the provider network. However, participants can use an out-of-network care provider. A care provider is considered an **out-of-network** provider if he or she is not under the provider network contract. This option is more expensive. The participant typically has to meet a separate deductible for out-of-network care and pays more for each service. In-network care providers file claims for the participant, reducing the administrative burden of the coverage. Often, a participant has to file a claim on his or her own to seek reimbursement for out-of-network services.

Managed-care plans range from PPOs to HMOs, each with advantages and disadvantages.

Source: Shutterstock (Monkey Business Images)

Health Maintenance Organizations (HMOs)

A **health maintenance organization (HMO)** is a more restrictive managed-care plan. It was actually the first form of managed care in the US. The HMO typically consists of a provider network that participants *must* use for their health-care needs. The insurance company does not pay for out-of-network care. Sometimes the doctors and other providers in these plans are employees of the HMO. Other times, the insurance company forms a network of providers that participants must use.

HMO participants need to select a **primary care provider (PCP).** All health care for the participant is managed through the PCP. For example, before seeing a specialist, you need to see your PCP to get a referral. Participants make a copayment at the time services are received. Copayments are typically lower in HMOs than in other forms of insurance, and there is no deductible.

Point-of-Service (POS) Plans

Point-of-service (POS) plans mix features of HMOs and PPOs. These plans are like HMOs in that participants have to choose a PCP who coordinates all of their care. On the other hand, these plans are like PPOs in that participants can choose an out-of-network provider, paying more for those services. There is no deductible for in-network care, and copayments are low. Out-of-network care requires the participant to first meet a deductible, and copayments are higher.

Consumer-Driven Health Plans

In the early 2000s, health insurance companies began to market **consumer-driven health plans,** which are plans with high deductibles. The idea behind these plans is that individuals would pay more attention to the cost of care if they paid directly for the services. In this way, more cost-conscious consumers would help drive down rising health-care costs.

Consumer-driven health plans come with an annual deductible of at least $1,000

Source: Shutterstock (Kzenon)

Consumer-driven health plans are designed for consumers to take better control over how their health-care money is spent.

for individuals and $2,000 for families. As with other health plans, the participant has to pay the full deductible before insurance covers any care. Premiums tend to be lower for consumer-driven health plans versus other insurance plans.

To help pay the deductible, consumer-driven plans come with a tax-free health savings account (HSA). Money deposited into a **health savings account** can be used to pay for health-care costs until the deductible is met, as well as copayments and other health expenses. This money is not taxed. Therefore, tax law limits how much money the participant can deposit in an HSA each year. Additionally, tax law places restrictions on what qualifies as an acceptable use of money withdrawn from an HSA.

Checkpoint 4.2

1. What is the main example of group health plans?
2. What is an out-of-pocket maximum?
3. What is a managed-care plan?
4. What was the first type of managed-care plan in the United States?
5. Describe the features of a consumer-driven health plan.

Build Your Vocabulary

As you progress through this course, develop a personal glossary of insurance terms and add it to your portfolio. This will help you build your vocabulary and prepare you for a career in insurance. Write out a definition for each of the following terms, and add it to your personal insurance glossary.

group health plans
group
preexisting condition exclusion
individual health plan
fee-for-service health plan
deductible
out-of-pocket maximum
lifetime limits
managed-care plan
provider network
preferred provider organization (PPO)
copayment
out-of-network
health maintenance organization (HMO)
primary care provider (PCP)
point-of-service (POS) plans
consumer-driven health plans
health savings account

Section 4.3
Protection When Group Coverage Is Lost

Objectives
After completing this section, you will be able to:
- Explain the intent of COBRA as it relates to health-care coverage.
- Identify how HIPAA addresses preexisting condition exclusions.
- Describe how the uninsured affect society.

Terms
portability
COBRA
HIPAA
elimination period
uncompensated care

COBRA

Even though a group health plan has many advantages over an individual plan, a downside is that you cannot take it with you. **Portability** is continued access to health insurance regardless of employment. If you leave your employer, you leave the health-insurance coverage you had. Two laws, known as COBRA and HIPAA, are intended to reduce the risk of being uninsured if you lose your employer coverage.

Do not let the name fool you. The term COBRA has nothing to do with snakes or even health care. **COBRA** stands for the Consolidated Omnibus Budget Reconciliation Act. This is a federal law that includes a provision to extend health-plan coverage in certain circumstances. These provisions in COBRA, enacted in 1986, were a federal response to inconsistent state attempts to provide continuing health care for those who lost group coverage.

Refer to Figure 4-3. In companies with 20 or more employees, an individual can continue employer-based health-insurance coverage if:
- an individual leaves the job (whether by choice or circumstance, except in the case of gross misconduct);
- an individual experiences a reduction in hours to below what is needed to be in the health plan;
- a spouse carries the coverage and the couple divorces; or
- a spouse who carries the coverage dies.

Qualifying Event	Maximum Length of Coverage
Involuntary termination of job	18 months
Voluntary termination of job	
Reduction in work hours	
Divorce or legal separation	36 months
Death of a spouse who carries the coverage	

Figure 4-3. Overview of COBRA

When an individual is eligible for COBRA coverage, he or she stays with the same health plan at group plan rates. However, if the employer paid part of the premium, it will stop doing so. This usually makes the COBRA premiums higher for the individual. But, paying this higher premium may be cheaper than purchasing an individual health-insurance plan.

COBRA continuation coverage lasts for up to 18 months in the case of job loss. In the event of divorce or other qualified events, coverage can extend up to three years. COBRA is covered in more detail in Chapter 13.

HIPAA

The Health Insurance Portability and Accountability Act (HIPAA) of 1996 includes provisions that make it easier for people with preexisting conditions to obtain health insurance. **HIPAA** does not guarantee health-care coverage, but it reduces some obstacles for obtaining it. One of the goals behind HIPAA is to help individuals obtain health coverage once their COBRA eligibility expired.

One example of how HIPAA works is what happens during a job change. Say you had insurance under your old employer, and you have diabetes. Since your diabetes was covered under your previous insurance, HIPAA says your new health plan cannot deny services for your diabetes, nor can it deny you coverage because of it. The new health plan can impose a waiting period (or **elimination period**) before it will cover costs related to your condition. But, the period typically cannot last more than one year. The length of your prior coverage can reduce or eliminate this waiting period. HIPAA is covered in more detail in Chapter 13.

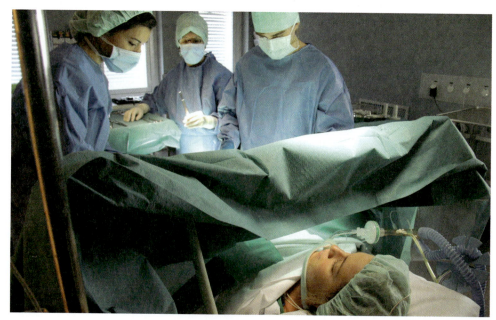

Hospital emergency rooms are required to stabilize and treat patients even if the patient cannot afford to pay for the care.

Source: Shutterstock (olly)

Impact of the Uninsured

It is important for each of us to carry health insurance to protect ourselves from financial risk. However, carrying health insurance is important for a broader reason, too. One of the reasons health costs are skyrocketing is uncompensated care. **Uncompensated care** is medical care provided to people who have no insurance and are unable to pay for the care on their own.

Careers in Finance
Insurance Services

What Does a Health Insurance Claims Examiner Do?

A **health insurance claims examiner** reviews health-insurance claims to ensure costs are reasonable given the diagnosis. He or she consults guides that identify the average period of disability, hospital stays, and treatments for various ailments. He or she also verifies information on claims applications and authorizes claims approval or denial. A claims examiner:

- reviews claims for accuracy and completeness;
- interviews medical specialists;
- consults policy files to verify information reported on a claim;
- authorizes or denies payment for claims; and
- may refer a claim to an investigator for further research.

What Is It Like to Work as a Health Insurance Claims Examiner?

A **health insurance claims examiner** typically works in a fixed office location. He or she may spend extended time on the phone interviewing medical specialists or sitting at a desk using a computer. The **health insurance claims examiner** must follow accepted guidelines for use of e-mail, social networking, blogs, and texting.

Work dress is determined by office policy. Often, business-casual attire is acceptable. However, some offices may require business-professional attire.

What Education and Skills Are Needed to Be a Health Insurance Claims Examiner?

- college degree is preferred, but not required
- solid communication skills
- knowledge of computer applications
- good analytical skills
- medical background is useful, but not required

For example, when someone goes to the emergency room following a heart attack, the hospital has to provide treatment. Federal law requires hospital emergency departments to stabilize and treat patients, regardless of their ability to pay. If the patient has no insurance, how does the cost of his care get paid? According to the Kaiser Family Foundation, as much as a third of the cost is paid by the uninsured person. Often, the result is financial devastation for that person. As taxpayers, we end up paying the remaining bill for uncompensated care. The cost of uncompensated care is in the tens of billions of dollars each year.

If everyone were insured, insurance companies would be able to spread risk across a wider group of people, both those who are healthy and those who are unhealthy. In theory, this would allow for lower insurance premiums. Also, uncompensated-care costs would no longer be a burden to taxpayers because everybody would have insurance. Plus, studies show that people with health insurance generally take better care of themselves. This also reduces health-care costs. PPACA requires everyone to carry health insurance beginning in 2014. This is projected to greatly reduce uncompensated-care costs.

Checkpoint 4.3

1. What is the basic purpose of COBRA, as related to health insurance?
2. COBRA applies to health-care insurance provided by employers with at least _____ employees.
3. What is the basic purpose of HIPAA?
4. Medical care provided to people who have no insurance and are unable to pay for the care on their own is called _____.
5. About what percentage of the cost of uncompensated care is paid for by the patient?

Build Your Vocabulary

As you progress through this course, develop a personal glossary of insurance terms and add it to your portfolio. This will help you build your vocabulary and prepare you for a career in insurance. Write out a definition for each of the following terms, and add it to your personal insurance glossary.

portability
COBRA
HIPAA
elimination period
uncompensated care

Chapter 4 Health Insurance

Chapter Summary

Section 4.1 The High Cost of Health Care
- Health insurance helps pay for medical care.
- A major reform of health care was passed in 2010 as the Patient Protection and Affordable Care Act.

Section 4.2 Private Health Insurance
- In a group health plan, risk is spread across a large number of people.
- Individual health insurance is purchased directly from an insurance company by the participant.
- A fee-for-service plan is considered traditional health insurance and includes an annual deductible.
- A managed-care plan may be a preferred provider organization, health maintenance organization, or point-of-service plan.
- Consumer-driven health plans include a health savings account that allows the policyholder to save money on a tax-free basis to pay for the deductible and other health costs.

Section 4.3 Protection When Group Coverage Is Lost
- If you lose group health insurance coverage, COBRA can extend the coverage.
- HIPAA allows coverage of existing conditions to continue once you obtain new insurance.
- PPACA requires everyone to carry health-insurance coverage beginning in 2014.

Check Your Insurance IQ

Now that you have finished this chapter, see what you know about insurance by taking the chapter post test.
www.m.g-wlearning.com
www.g-wlearning.com

Review Your Knowledge

On a separate sheet of paper or in a word processing document, match the following terms with the definition that fits best.

A. HIPAA
B. deductible
C. defensive medicine
D. copayment
E. uncompensated care
F. out-of-network
G. primary care provider (PCP)
H. Patient Protection and Affordable Care Act
I. adverse selection
J. COBRA

1. The amount a patient pays at the time of a doctor visit when in a managed-care health-insurance plan.
2. A law that allows an individual to continue employer-offered group health-insurance coverage in certain situations.
3. Describes health care provided by a doctor who is not one of the plan's approved providers.
4. A law that prevents insurers from denying coverage for a preexisting condition that was covered by previous insurance.
5. Describes when the people who are more likely to have claims than the population as a whole are those purchasing insurance.
6. The amount of money an individual must pay before his or her health insurance begins to pay for coverage.
7. The doctor through which all medical care is managed in an HMO.
8. A major reform effort passed in 2010 and intended to address problems in the health-care system.
9. Health care that is provided to those unable to pay for the care.
10. When doctors order unneeded tests and other diagnostic procedures in an effort to protect themselves from lawsuits.

On a separate sheet of paper or in a word processing document, answer each of the following questions.

11. What is the purpose of health insurance?
12. Why is group health insurance often less expensive than individual health insurance?
13. What is an out-of-pocket limit in a health-insurance policy?
14. What is the premise behind consumer-driven health plans?
15. How long may COBRA coverage last?

Chapter 4 Health Insurance

Apply Your Knowledge

16. Research the Patient Protection and Affordable Care Act. List several points in the act, and describe how you think each point will affect the health-insurance industry.
17. Talk to several people you know (such as parents, aunts/uncles, and cousins) who have health insurance through an employer. Ask them to explain what type of health insurance they have and how it works. Create a spreadsheet comparing and contrasting the features of the insurance plans.
18. Contact a local insurance agent. Explain that you are a student and would like to discuss individual insurance options. If possible, ask for some examples of premiums. Write a paper describing your findings.
19. If you have health insurance through your job and you lose that job, COBRA is the federal law that allows you to retain your insurance for a period of time. Research the law and list other events that can trigger coverage.
20. Anna's sister is diabetic. Research the federal law that protects her from denial of coverage if she changes health insurance. Describe how the law applies to Anna's sister.

Working in Teams

Using a flip chart or whiteboard, develop a chart with columns for each of the types of health insurance covered in this chapter. Working as a team, list the features of these health plans. Then, put a check mark in each column for the features offered by the plans. As a team, decide which plan you feel is the best value for the consumer. Justify your team's opinion to the class.

G-W Learning Mobile Site

Visit the G-W Learning mobile site to complete the chapter pretest and post test, to review the History of Insurance articles, and to practice vocabulary using e-flash cards. If you do not have a smartphone, visit the G-W Learning companion website to access these features.

G-W Learning mobile site: www.m.g-wlearning.com
G-W Learning companion website: www.g-wlearning.com

College and Career Readiness

Common Core

Reading. Locate an article explaining either COBRA or HIPAA. As you read the article, analyze how the author has structured the text. Determine how the author used major sections to organize the material and help the reader understand the material.

Writing. Investigate the Patient Protection and Affordable Care Act. Select at least one part of the act you think should be retained and one part you think should be repealed. Write a paper arguing to support your position.

Insurance Concepts

Many competitive events for career and technical student organizations (CTSOs) require students to take a test as a portion of the event. The test may count as 30% to 50% of the total score, or it may be the entire event. It is important that you are prepared to take a written or oral test focusing solely on subject content.

The insurance competitive event may include an objective test that covers multiple topics. Participants are usually allowed one hour to complete the event. One of the topics that may be included on the test is basic insurance concepts. To prepare for the concepts portion of the insurance event:

1. Review the checkpoint activities at the end of each section of the text.
2. Review the end-of-chapter activities in this text for additional practice.
3. Ask your instructor to give you practice tests for each chapter of this book. It is important that you are familiar with answering different question types. Have someone time you as you take a practice test.
4. Visit the organization's website, and look for tests that were used in previous years. Many organizations post these tests for students to use as practice for future competitions.
5. Create flash cards of the terminology from each chapter in this text.
6. Create a study routine. Spend 15–20 minutes each week reviewing test questions, flash cards, and other study materials.
7. Stay up-to-date. Check the organization's website for information about what will be on the test. Many websites will update test information many months before the competition is scheduled.

Chapter 5

Disability, Long-Term Care, and Life Insurance

 **Reading Prep.** Before reading this chapter, review the highlighted terms within the body. Determine the meaning of each term.

College and Career Readiness

In this chapter, you will learn about insurance products that cover disabling illnesses or injuries and chronic conditions that require special care. You will also read about a product that protects the policyholder's family in the event of his or her death. There is a wide variation of policy types for each of these insurance products. This chapter will cover the most well-known policy types.

Section 5.1
Disability Insurance

Section 5.2
Long-Term Care Insurance

Section 5.3
Life Insurance

 Many businesses, including insurance companies and agent offices, use green cleaning for their facilities. The crews that clean the building use green products rather than those containing toxic chemicals. Toxic chemicals in cleaning products can pollute water sources and damage equipment and other assets of a business.

Check Your Insurance IQ

Before you begin this chapter, see what you already know about insurance by taking the chapter pretest.

www.m.g-wlearning.com
www.g-wlearning.com

Section 5.1
Disability Insurance

Terms
disability insurance
short-term disability
long-term disability
workers' compensation insurance
renewability
cost-of-living adjustment
future purchase option
Social Security Disability Insurance (SSDI)

Objectives
After completing this section, you will be able to:
- Explain the role of disability insurance in financial security.
- Describe why disability insurance is important.
- Define terms related to a disability insurance policy.
- Discuss the Social Security Disability Income program.

Insuring Against Disability

Has it ever occurred to you that somewhere down the line you might suffer a disabling injury or illness? Probably not—who thinks about those things, anyway? But, according to the Social Security Administration, about 30% of men and 25% of women will become seriously disabled before they retire. In the United States, a disabling injury occurs every second. A fatal injury occurs every four minutes. Progress in the field of medicine has made it so we are living longer. However, we may be living with chronic illness, which yesterday may have been fatal, but today may be disabling. More people are disabled by illness than by injury.

Disability insurance pays the beneficiary a percentage of his or her income if he or she becomes ill or injured and is unable to work. In return for premium payments, the insurer pays an agreed-to percentage of the income the beneficiary was earning at the time of disability.

The most common type of disability coverage for American workers is group disability insurance. Employers often offer group coverage and may pay the premium as well. Group plans have two distinct components: short- and long-term disability.

Short-term disability pays a portion of the worker's income for up to three months. In fact, maternity leave typically

Source: Shutterstock (Lloyd Paulson)

Some jobs present more hazards than others, but you can be injured while working any job. Disability insurance helps replace part of your income if you are injured and cannot work.

falls under the category of short-term disability. Employers typically offer short-term disability benefits at no cost to employees.

Long-term disability kicks in after short-term disability expires. It typically replaces 40% to 60% of the worker's pre-disability income. The policy defines how long payments will last.

Beyond group coverage, long-term disability insurance can also be purchased on the individual market. Short-term disability policies generally are not available to individuals. Premiums for long-term disability policies can vary widely. Generally, you can expect to pay from 1% to 3% of your income on a disability policy in the individual market.

Why Disability Insurance Is Important

In the case of a job-related illness or injury, workers are typically covered by **workers' compensation insurance.** For example, if a window washer slips and breaks a leg, workers compensation would replace part of his or her income. Workers' compensation insurance usually replaces about one-third of the worker's income while he or she is disabled. Employers pay premiums into state insurance funds, which then pay the disabled worker. There is more on this in Chapter 7.

You may think that job-related illness or injury is the most common type of disability. But, in fact, this only accounts for about 10% of disability cases. In other words, about 90% of disability cases are not work related and, therefore, not covered by workers' compensation insurance. This is why it is so important to financially protect you and your family by purchasing disability insurance. However, the Social Security Administration reports that only 30% of working Americans carry it.

Workers should carry disability insurance coverage if they depend on their own income to live. The younger a worker is when he or she purchases a policy, the lower the premium will be.

Policy Definitions

What qualifies as a disability depends on how the insurer defines it in the policy. It is important to understand the insurer's definitions.

Some policies cover the policyholder if he or she is unable to engage in his or her occupation due to illness or injury. Others provide coverage only if the policyholder is unable to engage in *any* occupation. Still others provide coverage for loss of income due to illness or injury, focusing on the economic impact of a disability rather than its cause. Many policies will provide partial coverage for a disability that has a partial effect on the policyholder's income.

Ethical Insurance Practices

Genetic testing—an examination of a person's DNA—presents an ethical dilemma to the disability-insurance industry. Genetic testing can be used to find out if a person carries genes that may represent a higher risk of certain illnesses or diseases. The question is whether disability insurance providers should be able to use this information to limit or deny disability insurance. The debate over this issue will continue as genetic testing becomes more common.

Illness and injury definitions vary from one policy to another. Some policies require a hospital stay to label an accident or injury as a disability, for example. Many policies will only cover an illness if it did not exist when the policy was originally written.

Another important factor in disability-insurance policies is renewability. **Renewability** describes the requirements to renew the policy. Some types of policies may allow premiums to go up if you switch to a riskier job or as you get older, for example. Others may guarantee that you can renew the policy, but will not guarantee the same premium rate.

In addition to knowing a policy's definitions of disability, injury, illness, and renewability, you should understand the policy's definition of the terms in Figure 5-1.

Some optional features that are worth considering, even though they increase your premium, are a cost-of-living adjustment and a future purchase option. With a **cost-of-living adjustment,** your benefit payment will adjust when the cost of living goes up. Cost of living refers to what it costs to buy basic necessities (food, clothing, and shelter). A **future purchase option** gives you an opportunity every three years to increase your policy's benefit amount without having to take a medical exam.

Social Security Disability Income

Some workers who find themselves disabled may be eligible for the federal **Social Security Disability Insurance (SSDI)** program. SSDI is a social insurance program that pays benefits to disabled workers who cannot work for a year or more. Funding for the program comes from payroll taxes.

The definitions of disability under SSDI are stringent. The worker must be able to show that he or she is unable to work in any capacity to be eligible for SSDI benefits. And, the disability must last from at least one year to the life of the applicant. Only about one-fourth of applicants end up qualifying for the benefit. For people who do qualify for SSDI, they receive a monthly payment adjusted for the cost of living.

Term	Typical Policy Definition
Coverage Amount	Maximum amount of income the policy will cover. Typically ranges from 40% to 80%.
Elimination Period	Period between the start of disability and when the insurer will begin paying benefits. Longer elimination periods result in lower premiums.
Benefit Period	How long the policy will pay benefits. Typically two to five years, but some policies will pay until the policyholder turns 65.
Portability	Allows you to continue the policy if you switch jobs.

Figure 5-1. Important Terms in Disability Policies

Chapter 5 Disability, Long-Term Care, and Life Insurance

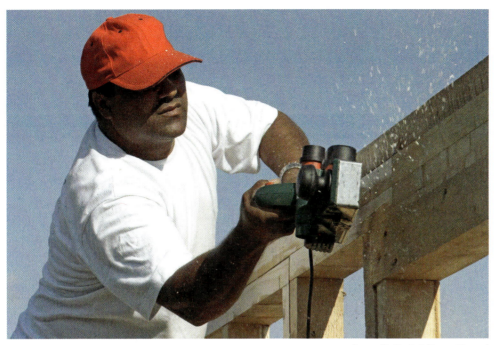

If a worker was unable to work for a year or more because of a qualifying health condition, he or she could apply for Social Security Disability Insurance (SSDI).

Source: Shutterstock (George Muresan)

Checkpoint 5.1

1. How does disability insurance protect you financially?
2. What percentage of people in the US will become seriously disabled before they retire?
3. Why is it important to carry disability insurance?
4. What is renewability in terms of disability insurance?
5. What is the SSDI program?

Build Your Vocabulary

As you progress through this course, develop a personal glossary of insurance terms and add it to your portfolio. This will help you build your vocabulary and prepare you for a career in insurance. Write out a definition for each of the following terms, and add it to your personal insurance glossary.

disability insurance
short-term disability
long-term disability
workers' compensation insurance
renewability
cost-of-living adjustment
future purchase option
Social Security Disability Insurance (SSDI)

Section 5.2
Long-Term Care Insurance

Terms
long-term care
long-term care insurance
Medicare
Medicaid
indemnity policy
expense-incurred policy
pooled-benefit policy
partnership long-term care policy

Objectives
After completing this section, you will be able to:
- Explain the benefit of carrying long-term care insurance.
- Identify the role of Medicare and Medicaid in long-term care coverage.
- Name the four types of long-term care insurance policies and describe the main features of each.

Benefit of Carrying Long-Term Care Insurance

On average, somebody in Ancient Greece lived 18 years. American boys born in 2010 will, on average, live to age 76, while girls will live on average to age 81.

Take a guess at what the fastest growing population in the US is today. It is not children or immigrants. It is those age 65 and over. This population is growing *four* times as fast as the rest of the population as a whole.

Many people will face needing long-term care, especially as they become elderly. Long-term care insurance can help ease the financial burden of the care.

Source: Shutterstock (James Steidl)

It is really hard to imagine this now in our youth, but as we age many of us will need help with our daily activities. A lot of us will need intensive and ongoing care because of health challenges. Care needs can range from help managing household chores to living in a nursing home. This type of care is called **long-term care.**

Most recipients of long-term care are older Americans. But, young and middle-aged people who have been in an accident or have a chronic illness receive long-term care, as well. Long-term care can be received at home, in an assisted-living facility, or in a nursing home.

The financial impact of needing long-term care is phenomenal. Based on the national average cost in 2010, a private room in a nursing home was over $80,000 for the year. Figure 5-2 shows 2010 averages for various types of long-term care.

Millions of families today manage the care of an older relative at home without compensation. Family members reduce work hours or stop working entirely to devote themselves to care giving. Unfortunately, the financial impact on the care provider can be as great as the emotional impact of experiencing the decline of an aging mother or father. **Long-term care insurance** protects both the policyholder and the immediate family from the financial impact of needing care. This prevents the policyholder from having to spend all of his or her assets on the cost of needed care.

Policies vary on what they cover and on how long benefits will last. As with other types of insurance, the policyholder pays a premium in exchange for financial benefits when long-term care services are needed. In general, the premium will be higher the older you are when you purchase long-term care insurance.

Each state maintains an Office on Aging that helps older residents find services they may need. You can learn about the services available to older residents in your community through the eldercare locator (www.eldercare.gov).

Service	Average Cost
Semiprivate Room in a Nursing Home	$205/day
Private Room in a Nursing Home	$229/day
One-Bedroom Unit in an Assisted-Living Facility	$3,293/month
Home Health Aide	$21/hour
Homemaker Services	$19/hour
Adult Day Health Care Center	$67/day

Figure 5-2. National Average Cost of Long-Term Care Services

> ### Real World Case
>
>
>
> Jacob's grandma was diagnosed with Alzheimer's disease two years ago. The disease has progressed slowly, starting with small episodes of forgetfulness that his family could handle. But, last month his grandma was heating some food on the stove and walked off, forgetting her task. The hot burner melted the pot, which exploded into shards of metal. It caused a lot of damage to the kitchen and could have caused a fire. Jacob's mom looked at her mother's long-term care policy and found it would cover the cost of an in-home aide. Eventually, Jacob's grandmother will need institutional care, but for now she gets to stay in her home.

Role of Medicare and Medicaid in Long-Term Care Coverage

A lot of older people assume that if they need long-term care, Medicare will cover it. Unfortunately, this is a bad assumption. **Medicare** is the federal health-benefits program for retired workers. It helps pay for doctor appointments, prescriptions, and hospital visits. Medicare is not intended for long-term care needs. It helps pay the cost of short nursing home stays and some in-home care following a hospitalization. It does not cover the ongoing assistance that many older Americans need. Medicare is covered in more detail in Chapter 8.

Another public health-care program, Medicaid, does provide long-term care payments. But, **Medicaid** is a social safety net and covers only low-income Americans. Quite often, an individual without long-term care insurance will spend all of his or her assets for care and then will qualify for Medicaid.

Long-Term Care Policy Types

Four types of long-term care policies are currently on the market. They are indemnity, expense-incurred, pooled-benefit, and partnership policies. The next sections describe each of these policies.

Chapter 5 Disability, Long-Term Care, and Life Insurance

Most people think long-term care is only for the elderly, but even young people may need long-term care in some situations.

Source: Shutterstock (Rob Marmion)

Indemnity Policy

An **indemnity policy** sets a fixed benefit amount that it pays regardless of actual costs. For example, the policy may state it will pay $250 a day for skilled nursing care. Say the facility charges $200 a day. With this policy, the beneficiary pockets the difference ($50). On the other hand, if the facility charges $300 a day, the policy still only pays $250. The beneficiary needs to pay the rest.

Expense-Incurred Policy

With an **expense-incurred policy,** the insured selects a maximum benefit amount upfront. Say you select a policy benefit limit of $200 a day. The policy will fully cover a stay at a facility that charges $200 a day. If the facility charges less than $200, the policy will pay the lesser amount. The beneficiary does not pocket the difference. If the facility charges more than $200, the beneficiary pays the additional charges.

Pooled-Benefit Policy

A **pooled-benefit policy** pays the actual cost of care up to the maximum daily benefit stated in the policy. If the maximum daily benefit is more than what is needed to pay for your care, the remaining money goes toward extending the benefit. So, if the benefit is $200 a day and the cost of care is $150 a day, then the extra $50 gets added to the benefit policy.

Partnership Long-Term Care Policy

Older Americans often end up spending all of their money on long-term care, and then they become eligible for Medicaid. However, with a **partnership long-term care policy,** an older person can qualify for Medicaid without first wiping out his or her assets. For every dollar the policy pays in benefits, a dollar of assets is protected. Say a woman purchases a long-term care policy with a maximum benefit of $300,000. If she uses all $300,000 of the benefit and still needs care, she can apply for Medicaid. At that time, Medicaid will not count $300,000 of her assets when it determines her eligibility.

Partnership long-term care policies are sold through state partnerships with select insurance carriers. The states see this as a way to increase long-term care insurance coverage, which will reduce the growing financial burden of Medicaid costs.

Checkpoint 5.2

1. What is long-term care?
2. How does long-term care insurance benefit the policyholder?
3. Who is eligible for long-term care services through Medicaid?
4. What is the difference between an indemnity policy and an expense-incurred policy?
5. How does a partnership long-term care policy work?

Build Your Vocabulary

As you progress through this course, develop a personal glossary of insurance terms and add it to your portfolio. This will help you build your vocabulary and prepare you for a career in insurance. Write out a definition for each of the following terms, and add it to your personal insurance glossary.

long-term care
long-term care insurance
Medicare
Medicaid
indemnity policy
expense-incurred policy
pooled-benefit policy
partnership long-term care policy

Careers in Insurance
Insurance Services

What Does a Life Insurance Claims Examiner Do?

A primary role of a **life insurance claims examiner** is to review the cause of death in life insurance claims. This is especially true in the case of accidents, because most policies pay additional benefits in the event of accidental death. A **life insurance claims examiner** also reviews new applications for life insurance to make sure the applicants have no serious illnesses that would make them a high risk. A claims examiner:
- reviews claims;
- interviews claimants;
- approves or denies claims;
- works with attorneys and witnesses to defend the insurer's position if claim is denied; and
- refers claims to an investigator if fraud is suspected.

What Is It Like to Work as a Life Insurance Claims Examiner?

A **life insurance claims examiner** typically works in a fixed office location. Extended time may be spent on the phone interviewing claimants or sitting at a desk using a computer. In addition, the life insurance claims examiner must follow accepted guidelines for use of e-mail, social networking, blogs, and texting.

Work dress is determined by office policy. Often, business-casual attire is acceptable. However, some offices may require business-professional attire.

What Education and Skills Are Needed to Be a Life Insurance Claims Examiner?

- college degree is preferred, but not required
- solid communication skills
- knowledge of computer applications
- good analytical skills

Section 5.3
Life Insurance

Terms
life insurance
proof of insurability
insurable interest
term life insurance
permanent life insurance
cash value component
surrender value
rate of return
dividend
guaranteed minimum interest rate
stock
bond
mutual fund

Objectives
After completing this section, you will be able to:
- Explain what a life insurance death benefit provides.
- Define insurable interest.
- Describe the main difference between term and permanent life insurance.
- Determine an appropriate amount of life insurance to purchase.
- Describe the role of life insurance as an investment.

How Life Insurance Works

When a family member dies, it is emotionally devastating. Unfortunately, it can be a financial catastrophe, too. If the person who died was an important income source for the family, the surviving family members may suffer financially. The right amount of life insurance coverage can provide financial stability to the surviving family members and is an element of estate planning.

Life insurance pays a benefit to beneficiaries when the policyholder dies. This is the only type of insurance where the person covered does not receive the benefit. The amount depends on the life

Life insurance can provide financial stability to those left behind by someone's passing.

Source: Shutterstock (Gina Sanders)

insurance policy in place at the time of the policyholder's death. The policyholder pays a monthly premium in return for the promised death benefit.

Since everybody dies some day, how do insurance companies make money? They are able to profit from life insurance sales by spreading risk across many lives. Based on their expertise in determining risk, companies can bring in more money in premiums than they will pay out in death benefits.

To purchase life insurance, you need to get a medical exam, answer a battery of questions, and sign an application stating the information is true and accurate. This process provides the company with **proof of insurability.** Rates may vary based on your weight and if you use tobacco. People with significant health problems may be turned down for coverage.

Insuring Another Person

In addition to buying life insurance on your own life, you may be able to buy insurance to cover other people. You cannot just choose some person at random and take out a policy, however. You have to demonstrate insurable interest. **Insurable interest** is receiving a benefit from the person, such as financial support.

You have an insurable interest in your own life to provide funds to your beneficiaries if you die. You can also show an insurable interest in another person. For example, spouses have insurable interest in their own lives, each others' lives, and the lives of their dependents. In another example, if you open a business and have a partner, you have an insurable interest in that person. Therefore, you could carry life insurance on your business partner's life.

History of Insurance

Life insurance in the US began to appear in the mid-1700s. But, back then, a wife could not buy a policy on her own life or her husband's life. At that time, women were not permitted by law to enter into contracts. Plus, women were deemed not to have an insurable interest in their husband's life. It would not be until the mid-1800s that a woman could take out life insurance on her husband.

Types of Life Insurance

The two broad categories of life insurance are term and permanent or whole insurance. But, it is not that simple; the variations are almost limitless. The next sections describe the basics of the two types of life insurance.

Term Life Insurance

As its name suggests, you purchase **term life insurance** to cover you over a set period of years. The time period is typically between one and 30 years. During this period, your premiums remain the same. At the end of the period, you have to apply again for insurance, and your premium will rise. Each time you apply for term life insurance, you need to fill out an application and get a medical exam.

www.m.g-wlearning.com
www.g-wlearning.com

Source: Shutterstock (Juan Carlos Tinjaca)

Life insurance provides protection to those who depend on you financially.

Term life insurance is the most affordable and straightforward type of life insurance. The catch is that you have to reapply at the end of the term. By then, you will of course be older, so your premium will go up. Plus, you may have developed health issues that will cause a higher premium.

The life insurance industry has developed online technology that allows an individual to estimate a premium in seconds. Your annual premium is estimated based on your age, gender, and smoking history. A 45-year-old, nonsmoking female living in Virginia, for example, may receive an instant quote in the range of $900 a year for a $500,000 term life insurance policy. You can also find free life insurance calculators online. These calculators help you figure out how much you need, versus the quote tools that tell you how much the premium will cost.

Permanent Life Insurance

Permanent life insurance, also known as *whole life insurance,* pays a death benefit and has a savings component. Permanent life insurance policies are just that; they can last for life, rather than end after a set term. These policies have higher premiums than term policies, and the premiums do not rise over time.

The savings-account portion of a permanent life policy is called the **cash value component.** Over time, the policy builds up cash value on a tax-deferred basis. This means you do not pay tax on your account's growth until you withdraw the money. Instead of withdrawing the money, the amount can be paid out as an additional death benefit. If used in this way, the money is never taxed.

Alternatively, you can use the cash value as collateral for a loan. Collateral is something of value that you borrow against. If you fail to repay the loan, the lender gets the collateral.

If you decide to discontinue a permanent life policy, you will receive the cash value (minus certain expenses) as a payout. This is the policy's **surrender value.**

Permanent life insurance comes in many varieties. The main types are whole life, universal life, and variable life. They all provide a death benefit and a savings feature.

Straight Whole Life

For a straight whole life policy, the premium starts out higher than term policies, but it does not go up as the policyholder ages. Part of the premium goes to fund the death benefit. The death benefit stays the same throughout the duration of a standard whole life policy. The other part goes into the cash value account, which offers a low, but guaranteed rate of return.

Rate of return refers to the amount of money an investment makes. The policyholder may also receive dividends into the cash value account. A **dividend** is an amount the insurer may pay to policyholders out of its profits.

Universal Life

Two key differences separate a universal life policy from a whole life policy. First, the universal life policyholder earns a **guaranteed minimum interest rate** on the cash value account. This means the money in the account will earn at least the specified rate of return.

Second, the policyholder can change the death benefit and premium payments on a universal life policy from time to time. This feature is not available in traditional whole life or term policies.

Variable Life

A variable life policy is more of an investment account than the others. The policyholder can use the cash value account to invest in stocks, bonds, and mutual funds. A **stock** is ownership of a small piece of a company, called a share. When a company's stock price rises, it earns money for the investor. When the stock price falls, it loses money for the investor. A **bond** is a loan to a company or government entity. Bonds earn interest for the investor. With a **mutual fund,** many investors contribute money to a fund that is made up of many stocks, bonds, or other investments.

These investment options can help your money grow, but they also carry risk. In other words, just as you can make money investing in stocks, bonds, and mutual funds, you can lose money, too. When your investments do well, your cash value account grows. But, if they do poorly, your cash value account will drop. The cash value account is not protected by state insurance guarantees, so if you lose money, there is no way to reclaim it.

History of Insurance

The Dutch East India Company was the first company to allow outside investors to purchase shares of the company in return for a fixed percentage of the company's profits. It was also the first company to issue stocks and bonds to the general public. The year? 1602.

www.m.g-wlearning.com
www.g-wlearning.com

Guaranty Funds

State guaranty funds back the cash value component of a permanent life policy, as well as the death benefit on both term and permanent life policies. States require insurance companies to pay into the guaranty fund. This fund protects policyholders in the event the insurer goes out of business. The most common coverage amount is $300,000 for a life insurance death benefit and $100,000 for the cash value component of a life policy. State guaranty funds are discussed in detail in Chapter 12.

How Much Life Insurance Is Enough?

The amount of the life insurance death benefit is critical for those who will receive the benefit—the beneficiaries. In deciding on the dollar amount of the death benefit, the policyholder needs to consider the following points.

- The immediate costs of the funeral and related expenses. The average cost of a funeral in the US is around $8,000. This amount does not include the cemetery plot or headstone.
- The amount of debt the policyholder may leave behind. This should include credit card debt, mortgage balance, and any other outstanding loans.
- College costs, if the policyholder has children and intends to pay for their college education.
- Requirements to maintain the standard of living of the beneficiaries.

While it is important to figure out how much is enough for your family's specific circumstances, a general rule is to buy a policy with a death benefit of 10 to 15 times your annual income. So, if you make $40,000 a year, this general guideline means you should carry between $400,000 and $600,000 in life insurance.

$40,000 annual salary × 10 = $400,000 in life insurance
$40,000 annual salary × 15 = $600,000 in life insurance

Role of Life Insurance as an Investment

The primary role of life insurance is to financially protect loved ones when the policyholder dies. However, many people also use their policies as a long-term financial investment. In fact, variable life insurance policies are sold as investment products.

Whether or not to use life insurance as an investment depends on an individual's own circumstances and preferences. Some people who purchase a whole life insurance policy see it as forced saving, since part of the premium goes into a savings account. This could be attractive to people who otherwise might not get around to long-term saving.

Others believe it is a better idea to separate life insurance from investing. The philosophy here is that you only buy life insurance for the death benefit. Any other money you would have paid for a whole life premium could be saved and invested separately.

Source: Shutterstock (auremar)

When purchasing life insurance, it is important to purchase an amount that will provide enough of a benefit for your beneficiaries.

Real World Case

At 17, Maria is the oldest of her three brothers and sisters. Her dad works part-time in construction, and her mom is a business professional earning $100,000 a year. They still owe $150,000 on the mortgage. Maria's mom has a life insurance policy of $500,000. This appears to be insufficient coverage. By the general guideline of 10 to 15 times her annual salary, Maria's mom should carry $1 million to $1.5 million in coverage.

Some life insurance products can be used as a means of investing for the future as well as a way to protect beneficiaries.

Source: Shutterstock (Morgan DDL)

Checkpoint 5.3

1. What is the purpose of life insurance?
2. What is an insurable interest?
3. What is the primary difference between term and permanent life insurance?
4. What should be considered when deciding how much life insurance to purchase?
5. How can permanent life insurance serve as an investment?

Build Your Vocabulary

As you progress through this course, develop a personal glossary of insurance terms and add it to your portfolio. This will help you build your vocabulary and prepare you for a career in insurance. Write out a definition for each of the following terms, and add it to your personal insurance glossary.

life insurance
proof of insurability
insurable interest
term life insurance
permanent life insurance
cash value component
surrender value
rate of return
dividend
guaranteed minimum interest rate
stock
bond
mutual fund

Chapter Summary

Section 5.1 Disability Insurance
- Disability insurance provides some income if you cannot work due to illness or injury.
- About 90% of disability cases are not work related and, therefore, not covered by worker's compensation insurance.
- When looking for a disability insurance policy, know how disability and renewability are defined in the policy.
- In some cases, Social Security Disability Insurance may cover a disability.

Section 5.2 Long-Term Care Insurance
- Long-term care insurance helps protect the policyholder and family from the cost associated with long-term care.
- Medicare does not cover long-term care expenses. However, Medicaid will cover such costs but only after the patients have deleted their financial assets to the point where they meet eligibility requirements.
- The types of long-term care policies are indemnity, expense incurred, pooled benefit, and partnership long-term care.

Section 5.3 Life Insurance
- Life insurance provides a financial payment when the policyholder dies.
- You can purchase life insurance on somebody else if you can prove an insurable interest in that person.
- Life insurance can be either term or permanent.
- In general, you should carry life insurance in an amount equal to 10 to 15 times your annual salary, but be sure to look at your specific situation when determining the amount.
- Some people use permanent life insurance as a long-term financial investment, but some people believe that life insurance should be used only for the death benefit.

Check Your Insurance IQ

Now that you have finished this chapter, see what you know about insurance by taking the chapter post test.
www.m.g-wlearning.com
www.g-wlearning.com

Review Your Knowledge

On a separate sheet of paper or in a word processing document, match the following terms with the definition that fits best.

A. surrender value
B. rate of return
C. short-term disability
D. dividend
E. cost-of-living adjustment
F. life insurance
G. future purchase option
H. proof of insurability
I. indemnity policy
J. long-term care

1. The benefit payment will adjust when the cost of living goes up.
2. An amount the insurer may pay to policyholders out of its profits.
3. Intensive and ongoing care needed because of health challenges.
4. An opportunity every three years to increase a disability policy's benefit amount without having to take a medical exam.
5. A long-term care insurance policy that sets a fixed benefits amount it pays regardless of actual costs.
6. The amount of time you elect in a disability or long-term care policy between when you qualify for benefits and when they actually begin.
7. Cash value minus expenses paid after a permanent life policy is discontinued.
8. Background information that an insurance company uses to determine if you are eligible for a policy.
9. Insurance that pays a benefit to the policyholder's beneficiaries when the policyholder dies.
10. The amount of money an investment makes.

On a separate sheet of paper or in a word processing document, answer each of the following questions.

11. How does disability insurance protect you financially?
12. When does long-term disability insurance kick in?
13. What are three examples of where long-term care may be received?
14. What must be proven to take out a life insurance policy on somebody other than yourself?
15. Which type of life insurance is the most affordable and straightforward?

Apply Your Knowledge

16. Investigate long-term care indemnity policies. Also, contact several facilities in your area that provide long-term care, and find out what the average daily expenses are. What benefit amount would you consider to be enough given the cost of long-term care in your area?
17. Some types of insurance can or do come with cost-of-living adjustments. Explain the risk of *not* including this provision in a long-term care or disability policy.
18. Identify a highly specialized field, such as a musician or movie reviewer. Describe what you think should be included in the definition of disability for a disability insurance policy covering this profession.
19. Review the difference between a whole life policy and a term life policy. Select one and list your reasons for choosing it.
20. Research using permanent life insurance as an investment. Using PowerPoint or other presentation software, create a slide show illustrating pros and cons of using life insurance as an investment.

Working in Teams

Working with a classmate, create a flowchart of the step-by-step process of applying for Social Security Disability Income. Collect or print out the needed forms and applications. Create a packet of information for the class, and make a presentation on how to apply for SSDI.

G-W Learning Mobile Site

Visit the G-W Learning mobile site to complete the chapter pretest and post test, to review the History of Insurance articles, and to practice vocabulary using e-flash cards. If you do not have a smartphone, visit the G-W Learning companion website to access these features.

G-W Learning mobile site: www.m.g-wlearning.com
G-W Learning companion website: www.g-wlearning.com

Common Core

Reading. Read a magazine, newspaper, or online article about determining the amount of life insurance that is appropriate. Analyze the author's purpose for providing this explanation.

Writing. Research a topic related to insurance that is currently being debated in the news media. Follow the topic for three weeks. Each day, take five minutes to write a summary of your findings related to the discussion. Also, over the entire three-week span, record your thoughts on the overall discussion in a blog or journal.

Community Service Project

Many competitive events for career and technical student organizations (CTSOs) include a community service project. This project is usually carried out by the entire CTSO chapter and spans a number of months. There will be two parts of the event: written and oral. The local chapter will designate several members to represent the team at the competitive event.

1. Contact the association immediately after the state conference to prepare for next year's event.
2. Go to the website of your organization for specific information. Visit the site often as information may change.
3. Print a copy of the event so that you may highlight important information.
4. Closely read all the guidelines. These rules and regulations must be strictly followed or disqualification can occur.
5. Ask your instructor for guidance in assigning roles to team members in order to execute the community project.
6. The plan for the project should be based on direction from the CTSO and created during regular chapter meetings.

Chapter 6
Additional Types of Insurance

Reading Prep. Before reading this chapter, flip through the pages and make notes of the major headings. Analyze the structure of the relationships of the headings with the concepts in the chapter.

College and Career Readiness

This unit has covered the standard insurance products on the market today. There is a whole host of other kinds of insurance that can serve important roles in managing risk, too. This chapter provides an overview of them. The first question someone should ask when considering one of these products is if the risk can be managed without insurance.

Section 6.1
Insurance That Plugs the Holes

Section 6.2
Other Insurance for Homeowners

Section 6.3
Medical Malpractice Insurance

Section 6.4
Trends in Insurance Products

Insurance companies, insurance agents, and others in the insurance businesses who have brick-and-mortar establishments occasionally need to paint the walls in their buildings. When given an opportunity, many companies choose green products that are safe for the environment. Companies can contribute to an overall smaller carbon footprint by using wall paint that contains zero volatile organic compounds (VOCs), which cause indoor pollution.

Check Your Insurance IQ

Before you begin this chapter, see what you already know about insurance by taking the chapter pretest.

www.m.g-wlearning.com
www.g-wlearning.com

Section 6.1
Insurance That Plugs the Holes

Terms
umbrella liability policy
net worth
deductible
gap insurance policy
depreciation
lease
loan term

Objectives
After completing this section, you will be able to:
- Describe how an umbrella liability insurance policy provides protection.
- Explain what gap insurance protects against.

Umbrella Liability Insurance

Just as its name implies, an **umbrella liability policy** provides coverage on top of other insurance. It financially protects the policyholder in the event other policies do not cover a given loss. The policy has a maximum coverage limit, but this is much higher than the maximum coverage limit on other policies. For example, a typical automobile insurance policy may have a maximum liability limit of $100,000 per person. On the other hand, an umbrella policy may have a total maximum limit of $1 million or more.

Umbrella policies offer important protections for people who have significant financial assets. A person's **net worth** is the total of assets minus the total of liabilities (debt). The more a person is worth, the more likely he or she will be a target for lawsuits. But, even people with moderate financial assets should consider umbrella coverage.

An umbrella insurance policy kicks in for a traffic accident, as an example, if the claim exceeds the limits of the automobile insurance policy.

Source: Shutterstock (Tramper)

For example, say you think you have your insurance needs covered by your auto and homeowner's policies. Then, one day, you try to beat a red light and end up hitting an expensive car. No one was badly injured, but the cost to fix the car you hit is much more than your insurance will cover. Plus, the owner wants to sue you for negligence since you were trying to beat a red light. If you had an umbrella policy, it would cover the cost of repairing the car and any settlement from the lawsuit, up to the limit of the policy.

Umbrella policies are not expensive. The cost of a policy is generally $200–$300 a year, depending on the coverage and risk. But, these policies typically do not begin to cover losses until a high deductible is met, usually around $300,000. The **deductible** is how much you have to pay out of pocket before the insurance begins to pay. In this case, the deductible for the umbrella policy will be met by the payout from another policy. So, it is important to coordinate the umbrella coverage with the coverage limits of all other policies.

Real World Case

In Chapter 2, you read about Jacob's cousin Ellie, who was badly injured in a boating accident. A family friend was driving the boat when the accident occurred, and his homeowner's insurance was responsible for Ellie's medical bills. His coverage was not enough to pay for all of her care, though. Fortunately, he carried an umbrella policy. It covered the medical costs incurred after the limit was reached on his homeowner's policy. Without this coverage, he would have needed to pay Ellie's medical bills out of his pocket.

Gap Insurance

Gap insurance pays the difference between the cash value of a car and the balance on the loan for the vehicle. This coverage is a good idea whenever more is owed on the car than it is worth. This may be the case, for example, if the buyer uses a low down payment to buy the car. If a larger down payment is used, the loan amount will be less, and gap insurance may be unnecessary.

For example, say you have your eye on a new car with a sticker price of $28,000. You have saved $5,000, so you need to take out a loan for the rest. With the down payment, taxes, title, and registration factored in, the loan amount is $24,680. You purchase collision coverage, as required by the lender. Three months later, you encounter a worst-case scenario; you end up in a collision in which your new car is totaled. Well, at least you have automobile insurance. But, is the automobile insurance enough to cover how much you still owe on the loan?

It is a startling fact to most new car buyers that a car's value drops by about a third soon after first driving it. **Depreciation** is the reduction in value of an item over time, such as a car. So, the car that cost $28,000 new has depreciated and is worth about $19,600 three months later. The auto insurance pays $19,600 to the bank to pay off the loan. That leaves a balance of $3,705 on the loan, counting the three payments you have made.

loan amount = $24,680
monthly payments = $425 (× 3 = $1,275)
loan balance after three months = $24,580 − $1,275 = $23,305
auto insurance payout = $19,600
remaining loan balance for which you are responsible = $23,305 − $19,600 = $3,705

This is where gap insurance comes into play. It will cover this difference. If you do not carry gap insurance, you now owe more than $3,700 on a car you no longer own.

Experts suggest gap insurance for these situations:
- The vehicle is leased, instead of purchased. A **lease** is a contract for rental of a car for a specified term, usually three or more years. The car is returned at the end of the term.
- The loan term is five or more years. The **loan term** is the length of time over which the loan is repaid.
- The down payment is less than 20% of the purchase price.
- The vehicle has a high rate of depreciation (it loses its value faster than other vehicles).

Gap insurance can be purchased through the auto dealer. Insurance carriers, however, may offer better terms.

Checkpoint 6.1

1. How does an umbrella liability policy offer protection?
2. What is a person's net worth?
3. What is a common deductible for an umbrella liability policy?
4. What type of insurance combines with a gap policy?
5. What is a way to eliminate the need to buy gap insurance?

Build Your Vocabulary

As you progress through this course, develop a personal glossary of insurance terms and add it to your portfolio. This will help you build your vocabulary and prepare you for a career in insurance. Write out a definition for each of the following terms, and add it to your personal insurance glossary.

umbrella liability policy **depreciation**
net worth **lease**
deductible **loan term**
gap insurance policy

Section 6.2
Other Insurance for Homeowners

Objectives
After completing this section, you will be able to:
- Describe what earthquake insurance policies cover.
- Explain what title insurance protects against.

Terms
earthquake insurance
California Earthquake Authority
title
title defect
lien
title insurance

Earthquake Insurance

A standard homeowner's policy does not cover earthquake damage. However, these policies cover fire or water damage that *results* from earthquakes. **Earthquake insurance** covers the damage that the shaking ground causes to buildings, such as cracked foundations or collapsed walls. Federal aid may or may not be available to help cover the cost of earthquake damage. When it is available, federal aid is often in the form of low-interest loans, not cash payouts.

Earthquake insurance can be added to a standard homeowner's policy, or it can be purchased as a separate earthquake policy. The deductible for earthquake insurance ranges from 2%–20% of the policy value. Premiums vary widely based on the property's location, age, and building materials used in construction.

Source: FEMA News Photo

The Northridge earthquake hit California on January 17, 1994. It damaged or destroyed about 114,000 residential and commercial structures.

You may be surprised to learn how many earthquakes have occurred in the US, and where. While the US only has 2% of the world's earthquakes, 90% of our population lives in areas of seismic activity. When you think of earthquakes in the US, you probably first think of California.

Homeowners in California can purchase coverage through the California Earthquake Authority (CEA). The **California Earthquake Authority** is a privately funded, publicly managed organization through which homeowners in the state can purchase earthquake insurance. CEA's primary mission is to provide California homeowners with affordable earthquake insurance. Private insurers participate in the program to offer the coverage. However, according to the Insurance Information Institute of California, only 12% of homeowners and businesses carry earthquake insurance.

Title Insurance

A house's **title** is a public record that lists who owns the property. When a house is purchased, the title is transferred to the new owner from the previous owner. Sometimes, a title comes with defects. A **title defect** is an issue that disputes the legal ownership of the property, such as deed errors, omissions, or forgery. These can cost a lot of money to correct and may even throw ownership of the property into question.

Unpaid real estate taxes are a common title defect. This might lead the government to place a lien on the house. A **lien** is a legal claim of debt against property, such as real estate or a car. If the government places a lien on the house for taxes, the taxes have to be paid before the house can be sold.

A mortgage lender requires a borrower to pay for title insurance as a standard part of the home-buying process. **Title insurance** provides lenders with coverage for losses and legal fees in the event of a title defect. The insurance is backward-looking. It covers the lender against defects that were unknown prior to the home's sale. The home buyer typically pays a one-time premium for title insurance. The insurance remains in effect until the homeowner repays the loan in full or sells the property.

Homeowners can carry title insurance to protect themselves, as well. A policy covers the homeowner just as it would the lender, and it remains in effect as long as that person owns the home. Sometimes the home seller pays for title insurance for the buyer, but processes vary by location.

History of Insurance

When the Northridge earthquake struck southern California in 1994, it caused an estimated $25 billion in insured losses. The insurance industry paid out more in claims for this earthquake than it collected in earthquake premiums over the prior 30 years.

www.m.g-wlearning.com
www.g-wlearning.com

Ethical Insurance Practices

A standard of "utmost good faith" exists in the insurance industry. It is intended to ensure an ethical relationship between insurers and the insured. This means the insurance professional is expected to act with integrity, be trustworthy, have a sense of fairness, and accept personal accountability.

Chapter 6 Additional Types of Insurance 113

Title insurance is required when taking out a mortgage to buy a house. This insurance protects you and the lender against title defects.

Source: Shutterstock (Andy Dean Photography)

Checkpoint 6.2

1. What type of damage does earthquake insurance protect against?
2. What type of earthquake-related loss is covered by a standard homeowner's policy?
3. What is the purpose of the California Earthquake Authority?
4. What coverage does title insurance provide?
5. Why does a mortgage lender require the borrower to buy title insurance?

Build Your Vocabulary

As you progress through this course, develop a personal glossary of insurance terms and add it to your portfolio. This will help you build your vocabulary and prepare you for a career in insurance. Write out a definition for each of the following terms, and add it to your personal insurance glossary.

earthquake insurance
California Earthquake Authority
title
title defect
lien
title insurance

Section 6.3
Medical Malpractice Insurance

Terms
medical malpractice
misdiagnosis
damages
medical malpractice insurance
patient compensation funds
joint underwriting associations

Objectives
After completing this section, you will be able to:
- Define medical malpractice.
- Explain what a common medical malpractice insurance policy provides.

What Is Medical Malpractice?

Medical malpractice occurs when a health-care provider fails to provide appropriate care and as a result causes injury to the patient. One example of malpractice is misdiagnosis.

Misdiagnosis is when a physician makes an error in identifying an illness. Take, for example, an emergency room doctor who sends home a patient experiencing chest pain with a diagnosis of a pulled chest muscle. If the patient is actually having a heart attack, that is an example of misdiagnosis. Other types of malpractice include surgical errors, prescription errors, and anesthesia errors.

When a patient claims medical malpractice, he or she can sue. When a medical practitioner is sued for malpractice and loses the case, he or she may have to pay damages. **Damages** are financial compensation, and there are three types: compensatory, noneconomic losses, and punitive. Figure 6-1 defines these terms. A malpractice settlement may include any or all of these damages.

How Medical Malpractice Insurance Works

Most states require medical providers to carry medical malpractice insurance to protect against medical malpractice lawsuits. **Medical malpractice insurance** protects physicians and other medical care

Type of Damages	Definition
Compensatory	Economic loss to the patient, including medical care and lost wages.
Noneconomic losses	Pain and suffering caused by the malpractice incident.
Punitive	Punishment for a care provider who has shown disregard for the patient's well-being.

Figure 6-1. Types of Medical Malpractice Damages

providers from the financial risk associated with malpractice lawsuits. In return for premium payments, the insurer typically agrees to investigate claims and pay damages up to a specified limit. The most common insurance coverage pays $1 million per incident or $3 million per year.

Malpractice insurance premiums vary widely based on geography and medical specialty. For example, a primary care physician in Minnesota may pay around $3,800 a year in premiums, while a surgeon in Florida may pay nearly $175,000 a year. Figure 6-2 shows how often malpractice claims are brought based on the physician's specialty. The frequency of claims does not represent the number of errors, though. A majority of claims are dropped or closed without payment. In 2008, for example, only 5% of claims went to trial.

The reasons for the high cost of medical malpractice insurance are hotly debated. Some say the cost is high because too many people bring illegitimate lawsuits and that claims awards are too high. Others say it is because too few insurers offer malpractice insurance, which drives up premiums. Yet another camp believes medical professionals practice defensive medicine for fear of being sued. An example of defensive medicine is ordering multiple tests to rule out all possible causes of an illness. The additional, and some would say unnecessary, testing drives up medical costs.

Several states run **patient compensation funds** (PCFs) as a way to address unaffordable malpractice insurance. These funds cover higher-end losses. Funding for PCFs comes generally from provider assessments and investment returns. Some states also have **joint underwriting associations** (JUAs) through which insurers join together to offer medical providers affordable malpractice insurance.

Specialty	Physicians ever sued
Pediatrics	27%
General/family practice	39%
Anesthesiology	42%
Emergency medicine	50%
General surgery	69%
Obstetrics/gynecology	69%

Figure 6-2. Frequency of Medical Malpractice Claims by Specialty

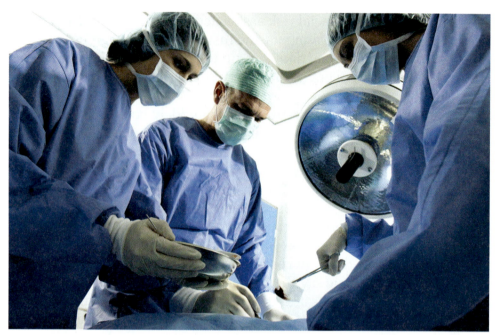

Medical malpractice insurance provides protection against financial loss arising from malpractice claims brought against healthcare providers, such as surgeons.

Source: Shutterstock (stefanolunardi)

Checkpoint 6.3

1. What is medical malpractice?
2. What are damages, as related to malpractice?
3. What purpose does medical malpractice insurance serve?
4. Why do some states sponsor patient compensations funds?
5. What is the purpose of state joint underwriter associations?

Build Your Vocabulary

As you progress through this course, develop a personal glossary of insurance terms and add it to your portfolio. This will help you build your vocabulary and prepare you for a career in insurance. Write out a definition for each of the following terms, and add it to your personal insurance glossary.

medical malpractice
misdiagnosis
damages
medical malpractice insurance
patient compensation funds
joint underwriting associations

Section 6.4
Trends in Insurance Products

Objectives
After completing this section, you will be able to:
- Define what protections identity theft insurance offers.
- Explain why companies might purchase hacker insurance.

Terms
identity theft
identity fraud
phishing
identity theft insurance
credit report
hacker
hacker insurance

Identity Theft Insurance

Identity theft and fraud are among the fastest growing crimes. The US Federal Trade Commission estimates that as many as 10 million Americans have their identities stolen each year. **Identify theft** involves stealing someone's personal information and using it to impersonate them. **Identity fraud** is using the victim's personal information to do things like withdraw money from bank accounts and rack up credit or debit card charges.

Someone's identity can be stolen in many ways. The traditional means are stealing purses or wallets and dumpster diving. Dumpster diving is when somebody goes through trash to find bank statements, credit applications, and the like. Identity thieves also have success in tricking people to share sensitive information over the phone.

Shredding personal documents can help protect against identity theft.

Source: Shutterstock (yelo34)

Careers in Insurance
Insurance Services

What Does an Insurance Investigator Do?

An **insurance investigator** researches claims that may be false. This is an important function for an insurance company both as a way to control costs and to ensure ethical practices. An investigator:
- researches the claimant to determine if there is a history of insurance fraud;
- interviews claimants and witnesses;
- visits the scene to take pictures and inspect the facilities;
- conducts surveillance of suspects;
- works with lawyers; and
- may testify in court cases.

What Is It Like to Work as an Insurance Investigator?

An **insurance investigator** works some of the time in an office and some of the time in the field. Work in the office may involve using computers to conduct database searches and recording data collected during field work. Time is also spent on the phone communicating with claimants, witnesses, and lawyers. In all business communication, the **insurance investigator** must follow accepted guidelines for use of e-mail, social networking, blogs, and texting. In the field, an **insurance investigator** may interview people, examine a scene, and conduct surveillance.

Some offices require business-professional attire when working in the office. Others may allow business-casual attire. When working in the field, dress should be appropriate to what is being done, keeping in mind that the **insurance investigator** is a representative of the insurance company.

What Education and Skills Are Needed to Be an Insurance Investigator?

- minimum of a two-year degree
- persistence and assertiveness
- solid verbal and written communication skills
- good interviewing skills
- good conflict management skills
- strong computer skills
- background in law enforcement or private investigation preferred

Identity thieves enjoy great success online. Hacking into people's computers is easy if they are left unprotected. Other online efforts involve activities like phishing. **Phishing** is the use of fraudulent e-mails and copies of legitimate websites to trick people into providing personal, financial, and other data.

Identity theft insurance is intended to address the financial losses that often come with identity theft and fraud. Identity theft coverage may be included in a homeowner's insurance policy. This coverage will likely provide reimbursement for costs related to restoring one's identity and credit. Stand-alone identity theft insurance policies also exist.

The best defense against identify theft and fraud is vigilance. Never toss out paperwork that contains sensitive data without first shredding it, for example. Do not leave the receipt at the ATM machine after a transaction. Keep computers protected with updated antivirus software and firewall software. These software products protect computers and data from outside attacks that can damage the computer or access personal data.

Every person should also monitor his or her credit report. A **credit report** contains information about a person's credit history, such as what credit cards the person has and the payment history. It also reports where the person has lived and worked for the past 10 years. Lenders and employers use this information for background checks. A credit report can help you see if someone has tried or succeeded in using your identity. For example, if the report shows a new credit card account that you did not open, somebody may have stolen your identity.

Three credit bureaus maintain credit information. Each bureau can show different activity for the same individual. You can request a free copy of your credit report once a year through www.annualcreditreport.com. Many companies try to sell you your credit report, but you can get it for free through this website. You can view your information more frequently than once a year for a small fee.

Real World Case

Last year, Maria's Aunt Lisa fell victim to identity theft. In retrospect, she believes the thief got hold of her personal information from her recycling bin. By the time she noticed something was amiss and ordered her credit reports, the damage was done. The thief opened up ten credit card accounts and a dozen bank accounts. Bounced checks and overdue credit card bills were being sent to twenty different addresses the thief made up. A year later, Maria's aunt is still trying to restore her good credit.

Consumer Laws

The Fair and Accurate Credit Transactions Act became law in 2003. It allows consumers to order free credit reports once a year from the three national credit-reporting agencies. These agencies are Experian, Equifax, and TransUnion.

Hacker Insurance

You may hear stories in the news about computer hackers causing mayhem for individuals and businesses. The specific definition is debated, but one definition of a **hacker** is someone who has expertise in manipulating computer technologies. Not all hackers are malicious people out to cause harm or steal data or money. However, those who act with malice are subject to criminal penalties. In fact, private businesses and the federal government employ tens of thousands of hackers to help protect sensitive systems. But, the hackers that are up to no good are those who cause concern for everybody.

Source: Shutterstock (Edw)

Not all hackers are out to steal, but hacker insurance can provide protection from losses caused by those who are.

General liability policies may not cover losses associated with hacking activities. Businesses can, however, purchase hacker insurance. **Hacker insurance** protects the policyholder from losses and liability caused by hackers. This is a developing market, so insurers may approach the coverage in different ways. The types of activities hacker insurance may cover include:
- loss caused by malicious or fraudulent acts against computer systems, programs, and electronic data;
- loss caused by virus attacks that shut down or hinder operations;
- penalties charged by the federal government for breaches of certain types of private data; and
- liability protection from claims by the company's clients or other third parties as a result of a hacking event.

Ethical Insurance Practices

Insurance professionals should take care to uphold the highest standards of integrity and ethics when working with electronic data and computing systems. Terms of use that accompany software should be strictly adhered to as should all safeguards and practices established to protect client and corporate data.

Checkpoint 6.4

1. What is the difference between identity theft and identity fraud?
2. What does identity theft insurance offer?
3. What is a credit report?
4. What is a hacker, in general terms?
5. Explain how a business can protect itself from the financial impact of hacker attacks.

Build Your Vocabulary

As you progress through this course, develop a personal glossary of insurance terms and add it to your portfolio. This will help you build your vocabulary and prepare you for a career in insurance. Write out a definition for each of the following terms, and add it to your personal insurance glossary.

identity theft
identity fraud
phishing
identity theft insurance
credit report
hacker
hacker insurance

Chapter Summary

Section 6.1 Insurance That Plugs the Holes

- An umbrella liability policy financially protects the policyholder after other policies have reached their coverage limits.
- Gap insurance pays the difference between the cash value of your car and the balance on your car loan.

Section 6.2 Other Insurance for Homeowners

- Earthquake insurance covers the damage that shaking from the earthquake causes to buildings.
- Title insurance protects the policyholder in the event defects in a home's title are discovered.

Section 6.3 Medical Malpractice Insurance

- Medical malpractice occurs when a health-care provider fails to provide appropriate care and as a result causes injury to the patient.
- Medical malpractice insurance protects physicians and other medical care providers from the financial risk associated with malpractice lawsuits.

Section 6.4 Trends in Insurance Products

- Identity theft insurance reimburses policyholders for costs incurred in restoring their identity and credit.
- Hacker insurance may cover malicious assaults against computer systems, losses caused by virus attacks, penalties charged by the government for breaches of certain types of private data, and claims by clients or third parties.

Check Your Insurance IQ

Now that you have finished this chapter, see what you know about insurance by taking the chapter post test.
www.m.g-wlearning.com
www.g-wlearning.com

Review Your Knowledge

On a separate sheet of paper or in a word processing document, match the following terms with the definition that fits best.

- A. medical malpractice insurance
- B. identify theft
- C. depreciation
- D. umbrella liability policy
- E. loan term
- F. title insurance
- G. credit report
- H. hacker insurance
- I. damages
- J. lien

1. Protects against defects in the history of ownership of a property.
2. Shows your history of paying credit card bills and other financial information.
3. A policy that covers losses exceeding other insurance the policyholder has.
4. The length of time over which you agree to repay a loan.
5. A legal claim of debt against property.
6. Covers losses associated with claims of medical damages.
7. An example would be a thief stealing a Social Security number to pretend to be that person.
8. Insurance that protects against losses associated with malicious computer activities.
9. The reduction in value over time of, for example, a vehicle.
10. Financial compensation for losses incurred.

On a separate sheet of paper or in a word processing document, answer each of the following questions.

11. How does gap insurance work?
12. What kind of damage resulting from an earthquake is covered under a homeowner's policy?
13. Describe a title defect.
14. What coverage does medical malpractice insurance provide?
15. Describe the difference between identity theft and identity fraud.

Chapter 6 Additional Types of Insurance

Apply Your Knowledge

16. When you are ready to buy your first new car, do you think it is better to have money saved for a 20% down payment or to buy gap insurance? Explain your reasoning.
17. Only about one in eight California home and business owners carry earthquake insurance. Why do you think they take this financial risk?
18. Why do you think the federal government hires hackers?
19. Research health-care providers in your state. Identify the three health-care professions most likely to be sued for malpractice in your state. Indicate the percentage of health-care providers in each profession that are sued each year.
20. Three credit reporting agencies collect data on your credit activity, addresses, and employers: Experian, Equifax, and TransUnion. Go online, and research each agency. Find out how much it costs to request a copy of a credit report. Also, identify how each agency takes steps to prevent unauthorized access to a person's credit information.

Working in Teams

Working in a team, conduct research on identity theft. What new identity theft schemes did you find? Create a step-by-step plan on how to avoid potential identity theft, and describe how insurance can play a role in protecting you from identity theft.

G-W Learning Mobile Site

Visit the G-W Learning mobile site to complete the chapter pretest and post test, to review the History of Insurance articles, and to practice vocabulary using e-flash cards. If you do not have a smartphone, visit the G-W Learning companion website to access these features.

G-W Learning mobile site: www.m.g-wlearning.com
G-W Learning companion website: www.g-wlearning.com

Common Core

College and Career Readiness

Reading. Read a magazine, newspaper, or online article about the importance of leadership in the workplace. Determine the central ideas of the article and review the conclusions made by the author. Provide an accurate summary of your reading, making sure to distinguish among facts, reasoned judgment based on research findings, and speculation.

Writing. Conduct research on effective management strategies. Select either positive or negative management strategies as your focus. Write a clear and coherent informative report consisting of several paragraphs to describe your findings of the implications of positive or negative management strategies in the workplace.

Role Playing and Interviews

Some competitive events for career and technical student organizations (CTSOs) require entrants complete a role-playing or interview event. Those who participate in role playing will be provided information about a company or situation and given time to practice. A judge or panel of judges will review the presentations. To prepare for the role-playing or interview event, complete the following activities.

1. Visit the organization's website and look for role-playing and interview events that were used in previous years. Many organizations post these tests for students to use as practice for future competitions. Also, look for the evaluation criteria or rubric for the event. This will help you determine what the judge will be looking for in your presentation.
2. Using tests from previous events, write your response to the situation or questions. Time yourself to see if you are within the allotted time frame. Repeat this several times so that you are comfortable with preparing the presentation.
3. Practice in front of a mirror. Are you comfortable speaking without reading directly from your notes?
4. Ask a friend or teacher to listen to your presentation. Give special attention to your posture and how you present yourself.
5. Concentrate on the tone of voice. Be pleasant and loud enough to be heard, but do not shout.
6. Make eye contact with the listener. Do not stare, but engage the person's attention.
7. After you have made your presentation, ask for constructive feedback.

Unit 1 Summative Assessment

On a separate sheet of paper or in a word processing document, use what you have learned in this unit to answer the questions that follow.

True/False Questions

1. *True or False?* The best insurance is the insurance with the lowest premium.
2. *True or False?* Any homeowner can purchase flood insurance.
3. *True or False?* Aircraft hull insurance covers the aircraft and all parts permanently attached to it.
4. *True or False?* In a managed-care plan, the participant must contract with individual hospitals, doctors, and other providers of care to negotiate the best price.
5. *True or False?* Long-term care is intensive and ongoing treatment needed because of health challenges.

Multiple Choice Questions

6. What are the kinds of life decisions that can affect your insurance coverage?
   A. Engaging in dangerous activities, such as skydiving or riding a motorcycle.
   B. Leading an unhealthy lifestyle, such as being overweight or using tobacco.
   C. Getting married and having children.
   D. All of the above.
7. What is adverse selection?
   A. When somebody purchases insurance that does not meet their needs.
   B. When somebody pays too much for insurance.
   C. When somebody has to pay more for insurance because of a past history of high claims.
   D. When somebody buying insurance represents a greater risk than the population as a whole.
8. What are four ways to manage risk?
   A. Transfer risk, eliminate risk, reduce risk, and ignore risk.
   B. Reduce risk, avoid risk, retain risk, and transfer risk.
   C. Retain risk, eliminate risk, avoid risk, and ignore risk.
   D. Avoid risk, eliminate risk, transfer risk, and ignore risk.
9. What is a credit report?
   A. A report that indicates the correctness of facts on a person's application for a loan.
   B. Information about a person's available credit and payment history.
   C. An application for loan or credit card that lists all outstanding credit balances.
   D. A report on the ability of a person to avoid moral hazard.
10. How can you reduce your automobile insurance premium?
    A. By taking driver education and defensive driving courses.
    B. By dropping collision and comprehensive coverage.
    C. By increasing the deductible.
    D. All of the above.

Unit 2: Social Insurance

The insurance products covered in Unit 1 are all part of the private insurance industry. That is, people buy the products from private insurers and receive certain protections in return for premium payments. Unit 2 covers social insurance. These are programs run by the federal or state governments to protect a given population from a particular risk. Program funding comes from taxes on employers, workers, or both. Social insurance programs are typically compulsory. This means companies or individuals are required by law to participate.

Chapter 7
Worker Protections

Chapter 8
Public Health Insurance Programs

Chapter 9
Social Security

Chapter 7
Worker Protections

Reading Prep. Scan this chapter and look for information presented as fact. As you read this chapter, try to determine which topics are fact and which ones are the author's opinion. After reading the chapter, research the topics and verify which are facts and which are opinions.

Two social insurance programs provide benefits to injured workers and to people who lose their jobs. These programs are workers' compensation insurance and unemployment insurance. Both programs are run by the states and are primarily funded by taxes on employers. This chapter discusses them.

Section 7.1
Workers' Compensation Insurance

Section 7.2
Unemployment Insurance

Go Green

Some insurance companies may encourage consumers to be eco-friendly by offering special rates for fuel-efficient cars or environmentally-friendly housing. By offering these special rates, insurers can help customers reduce their carbon footprint. From a business standpoint, think about how the insurers can justify offering these reduced rates.

Check Your Insurance IQ

Before you begin this chapter, see what you already know about insurance by taking the chapter pretest.

www.m.g-wlearning.com
www.g-wlearning.com

Section 7.1
Workers' Compensation Insurance

Terms
workers' compensation insurance
ergonomics
schedule
self-insure

Objectives
After completing this section, you will be able to:
- Discuss how workers' compensation programs function.
- Identify how state rules govern workers' compensation insurance.
- Describe how to make a claim against workers' compensation insurance.

Basics of Workers' Compensation

Workers' compensation insurance is a state-mandated program intended to provide medical and financial support for workers who are injured or made ill on the job. About 90% of workers in the US are covered by workers' compensation insurance. The policy provides benefits to workers, such as:
- paying for medical treatment to address the illness or injury, including rehabilitation;
- cash payments to replace lost wages if the worker cannot work; and
- death benefits to the surviving family if the worker dies.

Some jobs are more dangerous than others. Regardless of the danger, workers' compensation covers most workers injured on the job.

Source: Shutterstock (Mark William Richardson)

Careers in Insurance
Insurance Services

What Does an Insurance Underwriter Do?

Insurance underwriters review insurance applications to determine if the company should issue policies to applicants. They also determine what premium to charge. Insurance underwriters are the link between insurance agents and the insurance company. An underwriter:
- discusses insurance applications with the agent who submits them;
- uses software called "smart systems" to analyze risk;
- uses online databases to assess risks an applicant might pose to the company;
- reviews other available resources to identify risk;
- accepts or rejects insurance applications; and
- writes policies.

What Is It Like to Work as an Insurance Underwriter?

An insurance underwriter makes important decisions everyday that have a direct impact on the profitability of the company. To work as an underwriter, you have to be able to analyze data and make these decisions.

An insurance underwriter spends most of the time in an office, working on a computer and talking on the phone. Therefore, the insurance underwriter must follow accepted guidelines for use of e-mail, social networking, blogs, and texting. Underwriting is typically a 40-hour-a-week job, but additional time may be required during periods of high volume. Underwriters normally work out of a company's regional branch office.

What Education and Skills Are Needed to Be an Insurance Underwriter?

- at least a bachelor's degree, along with industry certifications
- strong computer skills
- good judgment
- excellent analytical skills
- solid communication skills

Covered injuries at work can be accidental, like one caused by tripping over a power cord. Or, coverage can relate to the work being done. For example, a worker in a restaurant kitchen slices a finger while preparing food. If the worker happens to lose that finger in the process, the state probably has a schedule that shows the value of a given limb. A **schedule,** as related to workers' compensation, is a list of injuries each with a corresponding dollar value. What is a finger worth, anyway? A federal government worker would receive two-thirds of normal income for 46 weeks for the first lost finger.

Most claims against workers' compensation insurance are for medical costs only. The biggest costs to the system, though, are payments for claims that include lost wages as well as medical costs. Insurers pay the claims, and, in some cases, will investigate if the worker's claim is questionable. Though most claims are found to be valid, experts estimate the cost of workers' compensation fraud to be $16 billion a year.

The cash benefit typically equals two-thirds of the injured employee's income, up to a state-determined time limit. In general, a worker cannot sue the employer for the injuries once he or she accepts workers' compensation payments unless significant negligence can be proved. This protection from lawsuits is an important benefit to employers.

Employers pay the premiums for workers' compensation insurance. Premiums are based on the type of work employees do. Premiums are higher for high-risk jobs, like window-washing on tall buildings, and lower for low-risk jobs, like administrative work. An employer's safety record also factors into the premium. An employer with a history of workers' compensation claims will pay higher premiums than others.

Workers' Safety

Workplace safety in the US has continuously improved since the beginning of the 20th century. Workplace injury, death, and illness have declined due to a change in the nature of work we do today and improved safety precautions. Many workers now spend extended periods of time in front of computers. This can result in injury that leads to a workers' compensation claim. **Ergonomics** is the science of adapting the workstation to fit the needs of the worker and lessen the chance of injury. Figure 7-1 depicts the best way for a worker to sit at a computer workstation.

OSHA

In 1970, Congress passed the Occupational Safety and Health Act. The Occupational Safety and Health Administration (known as OSHA) was established a year later. This federal agency enforces safety and health regulations in the workplace. OSHA's efforts have led to a significant decline in workplace injuries and deaths since the 1970s.

State Rules

State programs vary in terms of who is eligible to provide workers' compensation coverage, which injuries or illnesses it covers, and the level of benefits. Most states require employers to purchase insurance or prove they are financially able to self-insure. To **self-insure** means the business assumes the risk on its own and pays claims. Texas is

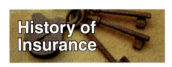

History of Insurance

Before workers' compensation insurance in the US, an injured employee had to prove employer negligence in the courts. While employers often won the cases, they were frustrated with the unpredictable nature of the situation. Ultimately, both employers and employees supported the formation of workers' compensation laws.

www.m.g-wlearning.com
www.g-wlearning.com

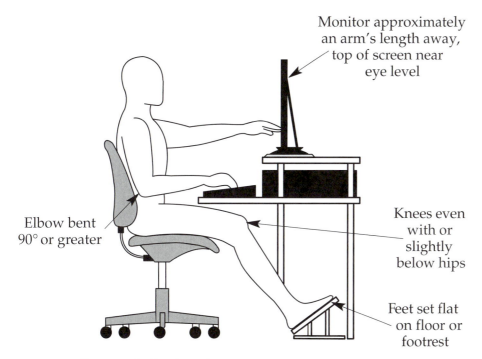

Figure 7-1. Ergonomic Workstation

the only state that does not require employers to purchase workers' compensation insurance. However, many Texas companies still opt for the insurance because of the protection it provides against lawsuits.

In about half of the states, companies can purchase workers' compensation insurance through a state-run fund or private insurers. Four states—North Dakota, Ohio, Washington and Wyoming—exclude private insurers from offering the coverage.

Source: Shutterstock (Andresr)

Ethical Insurance Practices

The insurance system relies not only on the ethical behavior of insurance professionals, but also on the honesty of people who file claims. Filing false claims for workers' compensation is unethical. Doing so is also punishable by fines and even jail in some states.

When a worker is injured on the job, when practical, the employer must be notified before a workers' compensation claim is filed.

Making a Claim

Filing requirements for a workers' compensation claim vary by state. Typically, the employer must first be notified of a work-related injury or illness. Then, either the employee or the employer files a claim with the state workers' compensation office or the insurer. The insurance carrier reviews the claim, then approves or denies it.

If a claim is denied, the decision may be appealed with the state's workers' compensation office. If the claim is still denied, the employee may be able to seek payment through legal action.

Checkpoint 7.1

1. What percentage of workers are covered by workers' compensation insurance?
2. What is the purpose of workers' compensation insurance?
3. How are workers' compensation benefits funded?
4. What is the typical benefit paid for workers' compensation?
5. What does it mean to self-insure?

Build Your Vocabulary

As you progress through this course, develop a personal glossary of insurance terms and add it to your portfolio. This will help you build your vocabulary and prepare you for a career in insurance. Write out a definition for each of the following terms, and add it to your personal insurance glossary.

workers' compensation insurance
ergonomics
schedule
self-insure

Section 7.2
Unemployment Insurance

Objectives
After completing this section, you will be able to:
- Define unemployment insurance.
- Discuss unemployment during the Great Recession.
- Describe how unemployment insurance is funded.
- Identify the roles of the federal and state governments in the unemployment insurance program.
- Explain how to file an unemployment claim.

Terms
unemployment insurance
recession
depression
jobless recovery
payroll tax
experience rating
quarter

Unemployment Insurance

When a worker experiences a job loss, he or she may be able to collect financial assistance from the state. The benefit replaces part of the worker's income while looking for another job. The benefits come through unemployment insurance. **Unemployment insurance** is a joint federal-state program that provides partial income replacement when people lose their jobs through no fault of their own. Those receiving payments have to actively seek employment in return for the benefit. Each state runs its own program, but must follow certain federal guidelines.

The purpose of the unemployment insurance program is not only to provide financial assistance to the unemployed, but also to support the economy. When workers lose their jobs and cannot afford to buy goods and services, then businesses suffer. This, in turn, causes more unemployment as companies cut more jobs or even close.

Generally, unemployed workers may collect unemployment benefits for up to 26 weeks. In times of significant and widespread unemployment, the benefit period can be extended by the federal government.

Source: Shutterstock (Alexander Raths)

During the Great Recession, many people faced unemployment as companies cut back and laid off workers.

Unemployment Insurance during the Great Recession

Anyone who lived through the Great Recession that began in late 2007 likely knows someone who was out of work at the time. A **recession** is marked by an overall decline in the economy that lasts for six months or more. In a **depression,** the economic decline is much steeper and lasts longer. The Great Depression lasted from the stock market crash in 1929 until near the beginning of World War II and had a world-wide scope.

Recessions and depressions usually involve significant unemployment. Unemployment occurs when somebody who is able to work does not have a job. In most cases, an unemployed person cannot find a job. However, some people considered unemployed are not actively seeking employment; for example, they have a job waiting for them, but have not yet started it. This type of unemployment is referred to as transient unemployment.

During the Great Recession, the unemployment rate rose significantly. Figure 7-2 illustrates the climb. Because the unemployment rate was so high for so long, Congress funded an

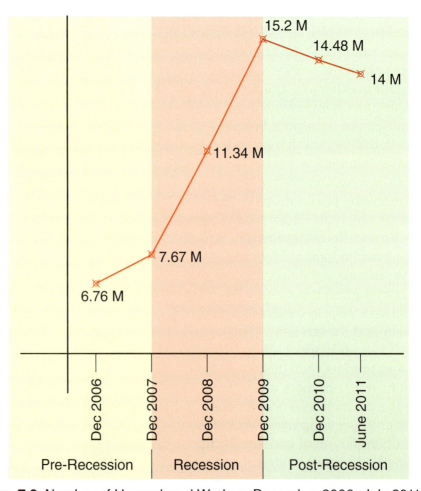

Figure 7-2. Number of Unemployed Workers December 2006–July 2011

extension for unemployment compensation. The total duration of benefits was 99 weeks. This was, by far, the longest extension of benefits during a recession in the nation's history.

Beginning in 2010, unemployment rates started to drop, but slowly. The country witnessed what economists call a jobless recovery. In a **jobless recovery,** the economy begins to improve, but employers are slow to hire. Unemployment does not decline as much as would be expected by the economic recovery.

Real World Case

Maria's Aunt Laura lost her job as a result of the Great Recession. Laura worked in middle management for a national retailer that slashed thousands of jobs during the economic downturn. She applied for and received unemployment insurance from her state. Despite a stellar work career and excellent credentials, Laura was still out of work in July 2011. Her unemployment insurance had run out some time ago.

Unemployment Insurance Funding

Employers are required to fund unemployment insurance through payroll taxes. A **payroll tax** is a fee an employer pays on the wages of each employee. In a handful of states, workers also pay taxes into the program. These funds pay cash benefits to the unemployed.

Employers pay federal and state unemployment taxes. The federal unemployment tax is 6.2% on wages up to $7,000. But, employers that pay on time receive a credit of 5.4%. This puts the yearly tax rate at .8%, making the per-employee tax $56.

.8% = .008
$7,000 × .008 = $56

Each state sets its own unemployment insurance tax rate. State rates are based on an employer's history of claims. So, an employer with a less-stable employment environment pays a higher tax rate than others. This history of unemployment claims is known as **experience rating.**

Program Administration

The US Department of Labor sets the general guidelines for unemployment insurance and administers the program. States collect taxes and make payments. Eligibility, the benefit amount, and its duration depend on each state's laws. Federal law requires a state to extend the length of benefits when its unemployment rates rise to a certain level.

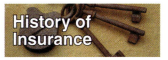

Unemployment insurance has been around since the Great Depression. It was enacted in 1935 to help stabilize the economy when millions of people were out of work.

www.m.g-wlearning.com
www.g-wlearning.com

Unemployment Insurance Tier		Who Pays	Duration
I.	Regular Unemployment Insurance	State	Up to 26 weeks
II.	Federal-State Extended Benefits*	State and Federal	Up to 13 more weeks
III.	Temporary Benefits	Federal	As determined by Congress during recessions

* Paid when the state hits an established rate of unemployment. In 2009, Congress passed a law that temporarily shifted the cost of extended benefits entirely to the federal government.

Figure 7-3. Three-tiered System of Unemployment Insurance

Both the federal and state governments pay unemployment insurance benefits. The program is set up in three tiers, as identified in Figure 7-3. The tier dictates whether the state or federal government pays.

Applying for Benefits

State laws vary as to who can apply for unemployment benefits. Generally, if you worked four of the last five quarters before you file a claim, you are eligible for benefits. A **quarter** is a three-month segment of a 12-month period. The year can be a fiscal year or a calendar year. The federal government and often state governments set unemployment benefits based on calendar quarters. The calendar year begins on January 1 and ends on December 31. A fiscal year is used by businesses for budgeting and financial reporting. It often starts on July 1 and ends the following June 30, but varies widely from business to business.

Unemployed workers can apply for benefits through the state's unemployment agency. Increasingly, states are allowing people to apply by phone or online. Once approved, benefits are paid weekly or twice a month. But, the claim needs to be filed again with the same regularity as payments to keep getting benefits. The state will also want to know about interviews or any job offers and may ask the person receiving benefits to register for state help in finding a job. In many cases, the person receiving unemployment benefits may be able to sign up for training for a different kind of job.

The state could deny a claim for unemployment benefits for a number of reasons. According to the US Department of Labor, reasons for denying a claim can include:
- choosing to leave a job without a good cause;
- being fired for misconduct;
- not being available or able to work;
- refusing an offer for work that suits the person's skills; and
- lying to get benefits.

Unemployment benefits typically last no more than 26 weeks.

Source: Shutterstock (Anita Patterson Peppers)

If a claim is denied, the applicant may appeal. The employer also has the right to appeal the approval of a claim. One reason an employer may decide to appeal the claim is due to the higher state tax rate it will pay. As unemployment insurance claims rise from former workers, the employer's rate increases. The state's laws govern the appeals process.

Checkpoint 7.2

1. What is the purpose of unemployment insurance?
2. How is unemployment insurance funded?
3. What is the state's role in administration of unemployment insurance?
4. What is the general eligibility requirement for unemployment benefits?
5. Why might an unemployed worker be denied benefits?

Build Your Vocabulary

As you progress through this course, develop a personal glossary of insurance terms and add it to your portfolio. This will help you build your vocabulary and prepare you for a career in insurance. Write out a definition for each of the following terms, and add it to your personal insurance glossary.

unemployment insurance
recession
depression
jobless recovery
payroll tax
experience rating
quarter

Chapter Summary

Section 7.1 Workers' Compensation Insurance

- Workers' compensation insurance is a state-mandated program that provides medical and financial support for workers who are injured or made ill on the job.
- Most states require employers to purchase workers' compensation insurance, although a business may be able to prove it can self-insure.
- To file a claim, typically the employer is first notified and then the state office is notified.

Section 7.2 Unemployment Insurance

- Unemployment insurance is a federal-state program that provides partial income replacement to workers who are out of work.
- During the Great Recession, unemployment was high.
- Unemployment insurance is a three-tiered system in which states and the federal government pay benefits.
- Unemployment insurance is funded through payroll taxes that the employers pay.
- A claim for unemployment insurance is filed through the state's unemployment agency and may be approved or denied.

Check Your Insurance IQ

Now that you have finished this chapter, see what you know about insurance by taking the chapter post test.
www.m.g-wlearning.com
www.g-wlearning.com

Chapter 7 Worker Protections

Review Your Knowledge

On a separate sheet of paper or in a word processing document, match the following terms with the definition that fits best.

A. quarter
B. recession
C. workers' compensation insurance
D. schedule
E. payroll tax
F. unemployment insurance
G. self-insure
H. depression
I. jobless recovery
J. experience rating

1. A period of economic decline that lasts for at least six months.
2. The history of unemployment claims against a company.
3. Economic expansion with continued high unemployment.
4. Fee an employer, employee, or both pay on wages.
5. When a company takes full financial responsibility for insuring against workplace injuries.
6. A list states maintain that specifies payments for certain types of workplace injuries.
7. A social insurance program that replaces a portion of wages of unemployed workers.
8. A social insurance program that compensates workers who get hurt or become ill on the job.
9. A long period of economic decline that can last for years.
10. One-fourth of a year, or three months.

On a separate sheet of paper or in a word processing document, answer each of the following questions.
11. Identify the purpose of workers' compensation insurance.
12. How do employers benefit from workers' compensation programs?
13. What is the purpose of unemployment insurance?
14. How is unemployment insurance funded?
15. Why might a worker be denied unemployment benefits?

Apply Your Knowledge

16. If you get hurt goofing around at work, you will typically be able to get workers' compensation benefits. Write a paragraph explaining why you think you should or should not be eligible in this situation.
17. Aside from helping unemployed workers pay the bills, what are the larger benefits to society of unemployment insurance?
18. Locate someone who lost his or her job during the Great Recession and who is willing to discuss the experience. Write a one-page paper describing how the person lost the job, how long he or she was unemployed, what had to be done to receive unemployment benefits, and how he or she found a new job.

19. It is illegal to employ undocumented workers, but those workers can file a workers' compensation claim if injured or made ill on the job. Some states are trying to enact policies to deny workers' compensation claims by undocumented workers. Research this topic using various sources. Draw a conclusion from your research and support your position in a one-page paper.

20. Go online and look up the unemployment rate of your state and three other states. How does your state compare to the rates of the other states? Can you draw any conclusions from the geographic location of the states?

Working in Teams

Working with a classmate, contact at least two insurance agents in your local community. Explain that you are students, and ask if you can make an in-person visit to discuss insurance for teenagers. Ask the agents about automobile insurance, specifically what options a teenager has for this type of insurance. Compare and contrast the premiums and any other information that a teenager should know to make a decision on automobile insurance. As a team, present your findings to the class.

G-W Learning Mobile Site

Visit the G-W Learning mobile site to complete the chapter pretest and post test, to review the History of Insurance articles, and to practice vocabulary using e-flash cards. If you do not have a smartphone, visit the G-W Learning companion website to access these features.

G-W Learning mobile site: www.m.g-wlearning.com
G-W Learning companion website: www.g-wlearning.com

Common Core

College and Career Readiness

Reading. Locate an insurance policy, such as an automobile or homeowner's policy your parents may have. Read the policy, paying attention to technical terms and concepts. Research the meaning of any terms and concepts that are not clear until you comprehend them.

Writing. Select one topic about the insurance industry. Come up with a question you have related to that topic, and conduct a short research project to answer it. Gather information from multiple sources, such as print magazines and online content. As you conduct your research, list other questions that come up and investigate the answers to those as well.

Written Events

Many competitive events for career and technical student organizations (CTSOs) require students to write a paper and submit it either before the competition or when the student arrives at the event. Written events can be lengthy and take a lot of time to prepare, so it is important to start early. To prepare for a written event, complete the following activities.

1. Read the guidelines provided by the organization. The topic to be researched will be specified in detail. Also, all final format guidelines will be given, including how to organize and submit the paper. Make certain you ask questions about any points you do not understand.
2. Do your research early. Research may take days or weeks, and you do not want to rush the process.
3. Set a deadline for yourself so that you write at a comfortable pace.
4. After you write the first draft, ask a teacher to review it for you and give feedback.
5. Once you have the final version, go through the checklist for the event to make sure you have covered all of the details. Your score will be penalized if you do not follow an instruction.
6. To practice, visit your CTSOs website and select a written event in which you might be interested. Research the topic and then complete an outline. Create a checklist of guidelines that you must follow for this event. After you have completed these steps, decide if this is the event or topic that interests you. If you are still interested, move forward and start the writing process.

Source: The National Archives and Records Administration

Then president, Lyndon B. Johnson signed the Social Security Act of 1965, establishing the Medicare and Medicaid programs. Harry S. Truman is by his side in recognition of the former president's leadership on the issue of health insurance.

Chapter 8
Public Health Insurance Programs

Section 8.1
Medicare

Section 8.2
Medicaid

Reading Prep. Before reading this chapter, preview the illustrations. As you read the chapter, cite specific textual evidence to support the information in the illustrations.

College and Career Readiness

In the US, most people can get private health insurance only if they are employed. This leaves people who are out of the workforce without health insurance. The federal and state governments have both public-health and economic reasons to want citizens to have health insurance. Public health insurance provides coverage to those who would otherwise be unable to obtain health care coverage.

Go Green

Insurance companies spend a lot of time and money in advertising costs. Online promotion is a green alternative to print advertising. But, some promotional materials are more effective in print form. Many companies are using environmentally friendly printing methods, such as paper made from by-products of sugar cane instead of wood. Sugar cane biodegrades faster than wood, and sugar-cane paper is cleaner to make.

Check Your Insurance IQ

Before you begin this chapter, see what you already know about insurance by taking the chapter pretest.

www.m.g-wlearning.com
www.g-wlearning.com

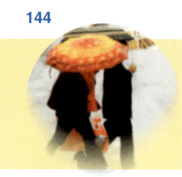

Section 8.1
Medicare

Terms

Centers for Medicare and Medicaid Services
Medicare
FICA
Medicare Part A
hospice care
custodial care
Medicare Part B
outpatient hospital care
physical therapy
occupational therapy
preventive services
Medicare Part D
Medicare Part C
Medicare Advantage plans
Medigap insurance

Objectives

After completing this section, you will be able to:
- Explain why it is important to have access to health insurance.
- Describe Medicare coverage under Parts A through D.
- Define Medigap insurance.
- Use an online tool to assist in selecting a Medicare plan.
- Discuss the impact of rising costs on Medicare.

Public Health Insurance

Good health care is important, as is being able to afford health care. When people get sick and do not seek treatment, they could spread illness to others. The spread of disease is a public health concern. On the economic side, part of the cost of health care for the uninsured is transferred to those who have insurance. The rest is picked up by governmental spending, which we all pay for in tax dollars.

Public health insurance provides coverage to those who would otherwise be unable to obtain it.

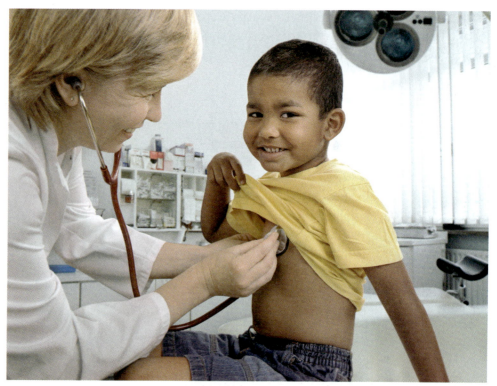

Source: Shutterstock (Alexander Raths)

In 1965, Congress enacted two public health programs aimed at insuring vulnerable populations. Medicare is public health insurance that generally insures people age 65 and older (retirees and their spouses). Medicaid is public health insurance that covers low-income families, the blind, and the disabled who otherwise have no access to health insurance. The **Centers for Medicare and Medicaid Services** administers the programs for the federal government. States share administration of Medicaid with the federal government, so the program is different from state to state.

The State Children's Health Insurance Program, commonly known as SCHIP, was established by the federal government in 1997. It provides insurance coverage to children who would otherwise be uninsured. The children covered by this program live in families with incomes that are too high to qualify for Medicaid and too low to afford private insurance coverage. The program was expanded in 2009.

Today, despite public and private health insurance, about 50 million Americans do not have health-care coverage. The Patient Protection and Affordable Care Act (PPACA) of 2010 was an effort to address the uninsured and rising health costs. The act calls for changes to private insurance, Medicare, and Medicaid. Many of the changes do not go into effect until 2014.

Politicians in Washington and the states continue to debate provisions of the law. Some of the provisions could be repealed. Repealed means overturned and removed from the law. If all of the original provisions remain intact, the Obama administration projects health-care costs will be reduced and health insurance will be provided to 32 million uninsured Americans.

President Lyndon Johnson signed Medicare and Medicaid into law in 1965. He stood next to former President Harry Truman at the signing to honor Truman's leadership on the issue. Truman first proposed public health insurance in 1945.

www.m.g-wlearning.com
www.g-wlearning.com

Overview of Medicare

Medicare is a public health insurance program run by the federal government. It provides health insurance for Americans aged 65 and older. The program also covers some disabled individuals and those with permanent kidney failure. In total, about 40 million Americans are covered by Medicare.

The program's funding comes from federal payroll taxes, direct government payments, and premiums that beneficiaries pay. All employers and workers pay Federal Insurance Contribution Act taxes, more commonly known as FICA. **FICA** taxes are payroll taxes that fund Social Security and Medicare. The portion that pays for Medicare, FICA-HI, is 1.45% of pay. HI stands for health insurance. Both the employee and the employer pay a 1.45% tax into the Medicare program.

At age 65, Americans can enroll in Medicare. The program has four components. Three of them provide health insurance for various needs, while a fourth component enables enrollees to select among Medicare-approved health plans offered by private insurers.

Medicare provides medical coverage to those age 65 and older.

Source: Shutterstock (Monkey Business Images)

Medicare Part A

Medicare Part A generally provides insurance benefits for hospital stays. A beneficiary does not pay a premium for Part A as long as he or she is at least 65 and he or she or a spouse worked for at least 10 years and paid into the system through FICA-HI taxes. People who do not meet these criteria can buy-in to Medicare by paying a premium.

Workers who begin collecting Social Security at age 65 are automatically enrolled in Medicare Part A. Those who delay Social Security benefits, for example, if they are still working, need to enroll.

Medicare Part A pays for a portion of care provided in:
- hospitals;
- skilled nursing facilities (but, not nursing homes);
- rehabilitation centers; and
- psychiatric care facilities.

Part A also pays for limited in-home health services and for hospice care. **Hospice care** is physical care and counseling for terminally ill patients. Hospice seeks to make the patient comfortable and to support the family.

Many people think Medicare covers custodial care, but it does not. **Custodial care** provides nursing home care or in-home care for people who need help with activities like bathing and dressing. Government data suggest that people who reach age 65 have a 40% chance of needing nursing home care at some point. The cost of long-term care is high. For this reason, aging Americans should consider buying long-term care insurance.

Medicare Part B

Medicare Part B coverage generally pays for doctor's visits and medical services. Part B comes automatically with Part A, but beneficiaries can opt out. Beneficiaries pay a premium for this coverage. Premiums vary based on the income of the beneficiary and whether or not the premium is automatically deducted from the beneficiary's Social Security benefit. Figure 8-1 shows the premiums for 2011.

In addition to doctor's visits, Medicare Part B covers outpatient hospital care. **Outpatient hospital care** is provided in a medical setting that generally does not require an overnight stay. Outpatient care can include certain types of medical testing, surgery, and counseling. Further, Medicare Part B pays for some in-home care as well as physical and occupational therapy. **Physical therapy** helps individuals with illness or injury to recover. **Occupational therapy** helps individuals live as independently as possible.

In 2011, Medicare Part B began to cover a range of preventive services that previously were not covered. This change was part of the Patient Protection and Affordable Care Act. **Preventive services** include certain vaccines, wellness visits, and tests that screen for cancer and other diseases.

Medicare Part D

Medicare Part D is a voluntary program that helps seniors pay for prescription drugs. It was enacted in 2003. Private, Medicare-approved insurers offer Part D coverage. Medicare beneficiaries that elect Part D pay monthly premiums and copayments for their prescriptions. Some plans charge an annual deductible.

The amount the beneficiary pays in premiums depends on the plan selected. Different plans cover different prescription drugs and at different costs. Also, premiums for Part D vary based on a beneficiary's income and whether the premium is deducted from that person's Social Security benefit, just as with Part B. Most plans require beneficiaries to meet a deductible before paying benefits. Most also require a copayment for each prescription.

Ethical Insurance Practices

Medicare fraud and abuse cost the system billions of dollars each year. Medicare fraud occurs when suppliers, medical providers, or individuals submit false claims for payments. Abuse occurs when care providers fail to follow good medical practices, resulting in unnecessary costs to Medicare. Medicare fraud and abuse are unethical, and fraud is illegal.

Beneficiary Status	Monthly Premium (in 2011)
Premium deducted from Social Security benefits	$ 96.40
Premium not deducted from Social Security benefits	$110.50
Premium for beneficiaries with higher incomes • More than $85,000 for singles • More than $170,000 for couples	$115.40

Figure 8-1. Medicare Part B Premiums

Medicare Part D provides coverage for prescription medications.

Source: Shutterstock (mangostock)

Medicare Advantage Plans

Medicare beneficiaries can choose to join a managed-care plan through **Medicare Part C.** A managed-care plan, as discussed in Chapter 4, delivers health care through provider networks with the aim of controlling costs. These plans are commonly known as **Medicare Advantage plans.**

These private Medicare Advantage plans provide Part A and Part B coverage and may include additional coverage like vision and hearing. Most Medicare Advantage plans include Medicare Part D coverage, as well.

Although all Medicare Advantage plans are Medicare-approved, the cost of coverage varies. Beneficiaries pay the monthly Part B premium and a monthly premium for other services the plan covers. This amount varies, as do copays and deductibles.

Consumer Laws

Under Medicare Part C, beneficiaries have the right to information, to participate in treatment decisions, to emergency services, and to file complaints. Some states provide additional consumer protections for Part C beneficiaries.

Medigap

Because of certain gaps in Medicare coverage, beneficiaries can choose to enroll in private Medigap insurance. **Medigap insurance** pays for costs Medicare does not cover, such as copays and deductibles. It is also known as *Medicare supplemental insurance.* These policies are available to beneficiaries who carry Medicare Parts A and B.

Private insurers offer Medigap policies, but policies are generally standardized under federal law, regardless of which company offers them. State laws govern what plans are available to residents. Premiums and other costs can vary widely. For example, some plans offer discounts to nonsmokers or to people who pay their premiums electronically.

Choosing a Medicare Plan

Choosing which Medicare coverage to carry is no easy task. To make the search for the right plan easier, the government has created an online tool called the Medicare Plan Finder. Users can input information such as where they live, their health status, and what medications they take. The tool then produces a list of plan options that meet the user's needs. Users can narrow their results based on deductibles and monthly premiums. Check it out at www.medicare.gov.

>
> ### Real World Case
> Maria's grandmother was an unwitting player in a $1.1 million Medicare fraud and identity theft scheme. Her podiatrist pleaded guilty to submitting false claims to Medicare for reimbursement. Most of the false claims were for services the podiatrist never rendered. He used the personal information of Maria's grandmother and about 200 other "patients" to submit the claims. He faces up to 10 years in prison and has to reimburse Medicare.

Rising Costs of Medicare

Medicare is affected by the growing cost of health care in the US. This coincides with a marked increase in the number of beneficiaries as the nation's Baby Boomers retire. Baby Boomers are those Americans born between 1946 and 1964. As Baby Boomers retire, fewer workers are left to pay into Medicare through FICA taxes. Estimates suggest the Medicare program will run out of funds by 2019. Analysts point to reducing services, cutting payments to medical providers, and raising payroll taxes as ways to address the funding imbalance.

The Patient Protection and Affordable Care Act of 2010 addresses some of the funding challenges for Medicare. It increases the FICA tax on earners with incomes over $250,000, imposes reforms on the delivery system to make it more efficient and less costly, and funds efforts to reduce Medicare fraud.

Checkpoint 8.1

1. What is the purpose of Medicare?
2. Which part of Medicare pays for doctor's visits and medical services?
3. What does Medigap insurance cover?
4. What is the government's online tool to help someone choose a Medicare plan?
5. How does the Patient Protection and Affordable Care Act of 2010 address funding challenges for Medicare?

Build Your Vocabulary

As you progress through this course, develop a personal glossary of insurance terms and add it to your portfolio. This will help you build your vocabulary and prepare you for a career in insurance. Write out a definition for each of the following terms, and add it to your personal insurance glossary.

Centers for Medicare and Medicaid Services
Medicare
FICA
Medicare Part A
hospice care
custodial care
Medicare Part B
outpatient hospital care
physical therapy
occupational therapy
preventive services
Medicare Part D
Medicare Part C
Medicare Advantage plans
Medigap insurance

Section 8.2
Medicaid

Objectives
After completing this section, you will be able to:
- Describe the purpose of Medicaid.
- Identify the eligibility requirements for Medicaid.
- Discuss the impact of rising costs on Medicaid.

Terms
Medicaid
mandate
assets

Overview of Medicaid

Medicaid is a federally mandated public health insurance program that helps low-income individuals and some others receive health care. A **mandate** is a requirement that carries the force of law. Medicaid is a safety net for low-income people who are unable to get health insurance through the private insurance system. Today, it covers 45% of poor Americans and about 25% of the near-poor. Prior to Medicaid, the poor could only barter or beg for health care, or do without.

The federal government sets broad guidelines for each state to run the Medicaid program, including mandating coverage for certain populations. The federal Medicaid mandate covers limited-income families with children, the disabled, and infants born to Medicaid-eligible mothers, for example.

Source: Shutterstock (Monkey Business Images)

Medicaid provides health care to low-income individuals and families.

History of Insurance

During World War II, policymakers became aware that poor Americans were not getting health care. This became obvious because of the state of men's health when they received physicals when being drafted into the war. It would take another twenty years before the federal government enacted legislation addressing health care for those who could not afford it.

www.m.g-wlearning.com
www.g-wlearning.com

Federal dollars account for about 57% of Medicaid funding. Medicaid reimburses medical providers directly for their services. Some states require small copayments for certain services.

Eligibility and Covered Services

Eligibility for Medicaid is generally based on an applicant's age, income, and assets. **Assets** are things that can be sold to produce income. However, an individual's home and car typically do not count as assets for Medicaid purposes. States set the rules for how income and assets are counted for determining eligibility.

The federal government requires state programs to cover certain services, like doctor visits, hospitalizations, and nursing home care. States can cover optional services, like prescription drugs and dental care. Most state Medicaid programs pay for long-term care services for older residents who have low income and few assets.

You may have heard of grandparents having to "spend down" assets to qualify for Medicaid to pay nursing home care. Once assets are reduced to a certain level set by the state, the person becomes eligible for Medicaid long-term care coverage. But, if the person sold an asset (like a house) in the previous three years, Medicaid counts it as a resource. This ends up delaying the point at which Medicaid payments kick in for nursing home care.

Rising Costs of Medicaid

Medicaid costs have skyrocketed in recent years. The Great Recession caused a surge in Medicaid enrollment as people lost jobs and stayed unemployed for long periods of time. At the end of 2010, Medicaid enrollment stood at 51.5 million individuals.

In order to qualify for Medicaid, certain conditions must be met.

Source: Shutterstock (Keith Bell)

The Patient Protection and Affordable Care Act of 2010 expanded Medicaid to cover more uninsured Americans, beginning in 2014. The change is estimated to add 16 million people to Medicaid rolls. The federal government will pay 96% of expansion costs over 10 years. This is expected to reduce state costs for health care for the uninsured.

The persistent unemployment that accompanied the Great Recession led to a great increase in those eligible for Medicaid.

Source: Shutterstock (Wrangler)

Checkpoint 8.2

1. What is the purpose of Medicaid?
2. How much of Medicaid funding comes from the federal government?
3. In general, what is Medicaid eligibility based on?
4. What typically does not count as an asset when determining eligibility for Medicaid?
5. How will the Patient Protection and Affordable Care Act of 2010 reduce state costs for Medicaid?

Build Your Vocabulary

As you progress through this course, develop a personal glossary of insurance terms and add it to your portfolio. This will help you build your vocabulary and prepare you for a career in insurance. Write out a definition for each of the following terms, and add it to your personal insurance glossary.

Medicaid
mandate
assets

Careers in Finance
Insurance Services

What Does a Customer Service Representative Do?

A **customer service representative** (CSR) works directly with sales agents (producers) and insurance companies in addition to performing customer-focused work. A CSR:
- processes insurance policy applications, changes, claims, and cancellations;
- handles continuing contact with clients;
- provides information on policies to potential clients; and
- may sell policies to existing clients.

What Is It Like to Work as a Customer Service Representative?

A **customer service representative** works directly with insurance customers. He or she may work in an office during normal business hours, or in a call center that serves customers 24-hours a day, seven days a week. The **customer service representative** must follow accepted guidelines for use of e-mail, social networking, blogs, and texting.

Attire varies based on the company. If the **customer service representative** works in a call center, the attire may be casual. On the other hand, if the CSR will have face-to-face contact with customers, business-professional attire may be required, although business-casual may be acceptable, depending on the company.

Most CSRs receive on-the-job training. If a **customer service representative** can speak another language, he or she may be asked to communicate with customers in that language.

What Education and Skills Are Needed to Be a Customer Service Representative?

- a high school degree; some college-level education is often preferred
- strong computer skills
- solid verbal and written communication skills
- ability to work independently
- licensing may be required by the state

Chapter Summary

Section 8.1 Medicare

- To maintain good health, access to health insurance is important.
- Medicare Part A pays for hospital care, Part B pays for doctor visits and outpatient care, Part C consists of Medicare-approved managed-care health plans offered by private insurers, and Part D offers prescription drug coverage.
- Medigap insurance pays for that which is not covered by Medicare coverage.
- The government's online tool, Medicare Plan Finder, can be used to help choose a Medicare plan.
- Rising health-care costs, more beneficiaries, and fewer workers paying into Medicare have put significant strain on the program.

Section 8.2 Medicaid

- Low-income individuals and some other qualified individuals receive health care through a federally mandated public health insurance program called Medicaid.
- To determine eligibility for Medicaid, the age, income, and assets of the individual are examined.
- During the Great Recession, millions of unemployed people joined the Medicaid rolls, which caused costs to skyrocket.

Check Your Insurance IQ

Now that you have finished this chapter, see what you know about insurance by taking the chapter post test.
www.m.g-wlearning.com
www.g-wlearning.com

Review Your Knowledge

On a separate sheet of paper or in a word processing document, match the following terms with the definition that fits best.

A. assets
B. Medicare
C. occupational therapy
D. mandate
E. preventive services
F. hospice care
G. custodial care
H. Medicaid
I. outpatient hospital care
J. Medigap insurance

1. The health insurance program for Americans age 65 and over.
2. A requirement that carries the force of law.
3. Care provided in a medical setting that generally does not require an overnight stay.
4. Care that involves activities like bathing and dressing.
5. Helps individuals live as independently as possible.
6. A health insurance program for low-income families.
7. Flu shots and mammograms are an example.
8. Care that focuses on making a terminally ill patient as comfortable as possible.
9. Things that can be sold to produce income.
10. Private insurance that pays for what Medicare does not.

On a separate sheet of paper or in a word processing document, answer each of the following questions.

11. How is Medicare funded?
12. What is the purpose of Medicaid?
13. How will the Patient Protection and Affordable Care Act affect Medicaid beginning in 2014?
14. What services did Medicare begin to pay for in 2011?
15. How would expanding Medicaid coverage benefit state budgets if the expansion adds enrollees to the system?

Apply Your Knowledge

16. Use the Medicare Plan Finder tool to see how it identifies Medicare options for users. Write one paragraph for each that summarizes their respective options.
17. Every state has an agency responsible for the administration of Medicaid. Find out what agency runs Medicaid in your state and list three things about the program you learn from the agency's website. A list of websites for state agencies is available on the Centers for Medicare and Medicaid Services website (www.cms.gov).

Chapter 8 Public Health Insurance Programs

18. Public health insurance is expensive and eats up a lot of state and federal budgets. Write a paper at least one page in length explaining why you think or do not think its benefits to society are worth the cost for taxpayers.
19. Research the preventive services covered by Medicare. Create a list of services covered and another list of services not covered. Explain how somebody on Medicare would pay for them.
20. Write a one-page paper explaining why it makes sense for Medicare and Medicaid to cover health screenings, like those that catch cancer in its early stages.

Working in Teams

Working with another classmate, research the Patient Protection and Affordable Care Act. Using PowerPoint or other presentation software, create a slide show to illustrate the main points of the act and how the act affects Medicare and Medicaid.

G-W Learning Mobile Site

Visit the G-W Learning mobile site to complete the chapter pretest and post test, to review the History of Insurance articles, and to practice vocabulary using e-flash cards. If you do not have a smartphone, visit the G-W Learning companion website to access these features.

G-W Learning mobile site: www.m.g-wlearning.com
G-W Learning companion website: www.g-wlearning.com

Common Core

College and Career Readiness

Reading. Go to the Medicare website and read about the steps for enrolling for coverage. Summarize the steps needed to enroll in Medicare.

Writing. Write a five-page paper (1000 to 1500 words) describing each of the four parts of Medicare coverage. The audience for the paper is an older person, such as a grandparent, seeking information on Medicare. Write a first draft, and then edit it as needed. Give the paper to a classmate and one of your parents for review. Then, based on the comments you receive, revise your paper. Finally, review your paper to make sure you have covered the topics and addressed the purpose and audience.

Team Presentation

Making a team presentation may be part of an insurance career and technical student organization (CTSO) competitive event. If so, the activity will be an industry scenario for which your team will provide a solution. You may be asked to interact with the judges as they ask you questions about the case. However, you may be asked to role-play and assigned a specific part to play. To prepare for this event:

1. Do an Internet search for "insurance case studies." Your team should select a case that seems appropriate to use as a practice activity.
2. Read the case and discuss it with your team members. What are the important points of the case?
3. So that you may practice your note-writing techniques, each team member should have two index cards. Make important notes on the card that will help with a presentation.
4. Team members should exchange note cards so that each evaluates the other person's notes. Are the cards accurate enough to help while presenting?
5. Assign each team member a role for the presentation.
6. Ask your teacher to play the role of competition judge. Ask a fellow student to be the timekeeper as the presentation is made.
7. Each team member should introduce themselves, review the case, make suggestions for the case, and conclude with a summary.
8. After the presentation is complete, ask for feedback from your teacher. You may consider also having a student audience to give feedback.

Chapter 9
Social Security

Reading Prep. Before you begin reading this chapter, review the introductory material preceding section 9.1. Based on this introduction, determine the central ideas that you anticipate being discussed in the chapter.

President Roosevelt signed the Social Security Act into law in 1935. At that time, most seniors had no other retirement income. The Social Security retirement program is the most successful social insurance program on the books. Without it, millions of older Americans would live in poverty. This chapter covers the Social Security program and its benefits.

Long before the economic blight of the depression descended on the Nation, millions of our people were living in wastelands of want and fear. Men and women too old and infirm to work either depended on those who had but little to share, or spent their remaining years within the walls of a poorhouse…The Social Security Act offers to all our citizens a workable and working method of meeting urgent present needs and of forestalling future need.
—President Franklin D. Roosevelt, August 14, 1938

Section 9.1
Social Security Retirement Benefits

Section 9.2
Other Social Security Benefits

Many insurance companies and agents purchase forms that are printed on recycled paper. Many of these forms are also printed with soy-based ink, which is more environmentally friendly than petroleum-based ink.

Check Your Insurance IQ

Before you begin this chapter, see what you already know about insurance by taking the chapter pretest.

www.m.g-wlearning.com
www.g-wlearning.com

Section 9.1
Social Security Retirement Benefits

Terms
Social Security
pension
401(k) plan
progressive
inflation
purchasing power
full-benefit age
spousal benefit
pay-as-you-go system
Social Security Trust Fund
privatize

Objectives
After completing this section, you will be able to:
- Describe what role Social Security retirement benefits should play in a person's retirement income.
- Explain how Social Security works.
- Discuss Social Security spousal benefits.
- Describe how Social Security benefits are funded.

Social Security: Just One Source of Retirement Income

Social Security is federal social insurance that replaces a portion of income in retirement for eligible Americans. It also pays some disability benefits. It was never intended to be the *only* source of retirement income. But, it is just that for nearly one in five seniors. About 53 million people currently receive Social Security retirement benefits.

Generally, you are eligible if you or your spouse has at least a 10-year work history. The Social Security program covers almost all workers. However, it does not cover public workers in about 15 states. This means they do not pay into the system through payroll taxes, and they do not receive a Social Security benefit in retirement.

Social Security is funded by payroll taxes.

Source: Shutterstock (Albert Lozano)

Real World Case

Jacob's family has "adopted" their next-door neighbor. Jacob calls her Aunt Louise. She's been widowed for 10 years and only has Social Security income to keep her afloat. Fortunately, she no longer has a mortgage on the house, and her kids are grown. But, her Social Security benefit is only about $1,000 a month. She finds it difficult to make ends meet. Jacob's mom often invites Aunt Louise to dinner and picks things up for her at the grocery store.

Recall, Social Security is only intended to be one source of retirement income. Some workers are able to rely on a traditional pension for retirement income. A **pension** is an employment-based plan that provides monthly income. The benefit amount depends on the length of the worker's service and on his or her income near retirement. However, over the last 30 years, the number of traditional pensions has dwindled as they are being phased-out of the business world. Only about 21 million workers today are covered by a traditional pension. By comparison, about 113 million people hold full-time jobs in the US.

Many more workers today are covered by a 401(k) or similar plan. In a **401(k) plan,** workers contribute part of their monthly earnings to an investment account. Employers typically contribute, too. Unlike with a pension, the employee must decide whether to participate in the plan, how much to contribute, and how to invest the money. Additionally, the income in retirement is not guaranteed. About 53 million workers participate in this kind of plan.

Saving when you are young can help you live comfortably in your retirement.

Source: Shutterstock (Blend Images)

Careers in Finance
Insurance Services

What Does an Actuary Do?

Actuaries use sophisticated modeling techniques to determine the likelihood of events occurring and what the cost of these events might be to the insurer. For example, a property and casualty **actuary** will assess the likelihood of auto accidents occurring based on the driver's age, gender, type of car, and other factors. This information is used to set a premium that will be enough to cover costs to the insurer, but at a level that is competitive with other insurers. An actuary:

- uses statistical, business, and finance knowledge to analyze data and determine the likelihood of certain events occurring, such as accidents, death, injury, and disasters;
- designs insurance policies and pension plans in a financially sound manner;
- helps determine what premiums to charge that will cover the insurer's cost, while remaining competitive in the insurance marketplace; and
- determines how the company or a client should invest resources.

What Is It Like to Work as an Actuary?

An **actuary** spends a lot of time in an office, working at a desk. He or she must follow accepted guidelines for use of e-mail, social networking, blogs, and texting. In this office environment, business-professional attire is usually required. In some cases, depending on the company, business-casual attire may be acceptable. Additionally, an **actuary** must be able to work at a desk for periods of time without much opportunity to move around the office.

What Education and Skills Are Needed to Be an Actuary?

- college degree in statistics, mathematics or actuarial science, or a business degree in finance, economics, or business along with industry certifications
- strong computer skills
- excellent analytical skills
- solid communication skills

Beyond work-based pensions and savings plans, workers can also save for retirement through banks or other financial institutions. Unfortunately, we are not a nation of savers. So many people end up relying on Social Security for most or all of their income in retirement. The earlier you begin saving for retirement, the better off you will be when you get there. When you enter the workforce, always look at benefits in addition to the salary when considering a job offer. Look for a traditional pension or a 401(k) plan as part of the compensation package.

How Social Security Works

In return for paying into the system over your working years, Social Security provides a monthly retirement benefit for life. The dollar amount depends on your earnings history. The Social Security Administration bases your benefit on the 35 highest years of your earnings. Beginning at age 25, you will receive an annual estimate of benefits statement from the Social Security Administration. You can also go online to the Social Security Administration's website to get a benefits estimate.

The Social Security program is progressive. **Progressive,** in this sense, means lower-income workers get a higher benefit relative to their income than higher-income workers do. Social Security replaces about 55% of income of the lowest-paid workers and about 27% of the highest paid.

Inflation poses a big risk to financial security in retirement. **Inflation** is the rise in prices that occurs over time. Annual inflation of just 3% will make $100 today worth only about $75 in today's dollars in ten years. If your income does not adjust with inflation, then your purchasing power goes down. **Purchasing power** is how much your money is worth as measured by how many goods and services it can purchase. To help with this, Social Security benefits adjust with inflation.

To determine your retirement benefit, Social Security uses a full-benefit age. The **full-benefit age** is the age at which you will receive your projected full retirement benefit. It is based on the year you were born. For people born in 1960 or later, the full-benefit age is 67. You can begin collecting benefits as early as age 62. However, your benefit amount will be smaller than the full projected benefit. You can also delay benefits up to age 70 to earn a higher monthly payment. The average Social Security retirement benefit is currently $1,174 per month. Figure 9-1 provides an example of how the benefit amount changes based on when it begins.

The reason benefits adjust based on your actual retirement age is a function of math. If you retire early, then you will likely receive benefits over a longer period of time. This is why early retirees receive a smaller monthly benefit. Likewise, people who wait to collect benefits (up to age 70) will likely receive benefits over a shorter period of time. This is why people who put off retirement receive a larger monthly benefit.

History of Insurance

In the 1930s, most large companies sponsored pension plans, but employees had no legal right to benefits. The Great Depression resulted in many companies dropping their pension plans or cutting benefits. Others began requiring employees to contribute to the plans.

www.m.g-wlearning.com
www.g-wlearning.com

Date of birth: January 1, 1965	
Current annual salary: $35,000	
Early benefit at age 62	$882
Full retirement age at 67	$1,288
Delayed retirement at age 70	$1,627

Benefits are shown in 2011 dollars, and they do not account for any future earnings or price increases.

Figure 9-1. Example of Social Security Benefits at Different Retirement Ages

Spousal Benefits

Workers' spouses who have low or no earnings may qualify for a spousal benefit from Social Security. A **spousal benefit** is generally half of the retired worker's benefit. Spousal benefits commonly go to wives who have worked fewer or no years while raising their families. The worker has to file for Social Security retirement benefits before his or her spouse can receive benefits based on his or her work record. Spousal benefits are available to divorced spouses if the marriage lasted at least 10 years.

Real World Case

Maria's Great-Aunt Rita raised three boys and two girls. She took part-time jobs here and there, but the rest of her time was devoted to the kids. When Aunt Rita's husband Kenny retired last year, she was able to claim a Social Security spousal benefit. The Social Security Administration determined which benefit—her own worker benefit or spousal benefit—would be higher. In Aunt Rita's case, the higher benefit was the spousal benefit. So that is the benefit Social Security sends her each month. If Aunt Rita and Uncle Kenny would have divorced, Aunt Rita could still have received the spousal benefit based on Kenny's work history as long as the marriage lasted at least 10 years.

Social Security's Funding

Social Security's funding comes mostly from payroll taxes workers and their employers pay. The taxes are known as FICA taxes, for the Federal Insurance Contributions Act. The Social Security portion of

Due largely to advances in health care, many Americans are living much longer than in years past.

Source: Shutterstock (Orange Line Media)

the FICA tax is 6.5% of pay up to a predetermined maximum amount, or cap. In 2011, the cap was $106,800. Both employers and employees pay this tax, for a total of 13% of compensation.

Social Security is known as a pay-as-you-go system. In a **pay-as-you-go system,** money coming in from taxes goes directly out as benefit payments. The taxes collected get credited to the Social Security Trust Fund. The **Social Security Trust Fund** is the source from which benefits are paid. The amount not paid as benefits (plus interest) is credited to the trust fund to pay future benefits.

The Social Security Trust Fund faces a shortfall. Many people may think they will never see a Social Security retirement benefit. One reason is that our nation's Baby Boomers have begun to retire. Baby Boomers number about 78 million. As they retire, more people will

Source: Shutterstock (Gina Sanders)

Many people rely on Social Security benefits as their sole source of retirement income.

collect benefits than will be working and paying into the system. Also, people live longer today than they did when Social Security first began. In 1935, if a person lived to age 65, he or she could expect to live 12 more years. Today, it is 18 more years. Since Social Security pays benefits until death, this means people are collecting benefits over longer periods.

Each year, the trustees of Social Security report on its financial well-being. A recent report estimates that by 2040 the Social Security Trust Fund will be out of money. At that time, Social Security revenue from taxes will only be able to pay about 75% of promised benefits.

To shore up funding, laws governing the Social Security program will have to be changed. This is the tricky part. Some advocate adjusting the existing system. This could include raising the retirement age, lowering benefits, increasing taxes, or a mix of these actions. Others think the system needs drastic change. This camp thinks we should privatize part of the system. To **privatize** the system would allow workers to contribute part of their Social Security tax to an investment account. This would allow people to do very well, if they make good investment decisions. On the other hand, people could lose much of their benefit, if they make bad investment decisions.

Checkpoint 9.1

1. How is Social Security intended to be used in retirement?
2. What is a person's Social Security benefit based on?
3. What is purchasing power?
4. Who can get a spousal benefit from Social Security?
5. How are Social Security benefits funded?

Build Your Vocabulary

As you progress through this course, develop a personal glossary of insurance terms and add it to your portfolio. This will help you build your vocabulary and prepare you for a career in insurance. Write out a definition for each of the following terms, and add it to your personal insurance glossary.

Social Security
pension
401(k) plan
progressive
inflation
purchasing power
full-benefit age
spousal benefit
pay-as-you-go system
Social Security Trust Fund
privatize

Section 9.2
Other Social Security Benefits

Objectives
After completing this section, you will be able to:
- Describe the purpose of Social Security Disability Income.
- Explain who Social Security Supplemental Security Income is intended to help.
- Discuss Social Security survivors benefits.

Terms
Social Security Disability Income (SSDI)

substantial gainful activity

Supplemental Security Income (SSI)

resources

survivors benefit

Social Security Disability Benefits

Today, most people know of Social Security for the retirement income it provides to older Americans. This is the largest part of the program. But, it also pays benefits to disabled workers and their families and to survivors of workers who die.

Social Security provides benefits to disabled people through the Social Security Disability Income (SSDI) program. This program came into effect in 1954. **Social Security Disability Income (SSDI)** pays benefits to individuals who are unable to work due to a serious medical condition. About 10 million people currently receive SSDI payments. Benefits are available to those who meet a very strict definition of disability and have worked enough years to qualify.

Disabled individuals who are unable to work depend on SSDI benefits.

Source: Shutterstock (Dean Mitchell)

The amount of the benefit depends on an individual's earnings history. Also, a person receiving SSDI benefits undergoes periodic review. This is a check to see if his or her medical condition continues to qualify for the program.

SSDI recipients are eligible for Medicare health insurance after two years of receiving disability benefits. SSDI benefits convert to retirement benefits at the Social Security full-benefit age. But, the amount of the benefit does not change.

Definition of a Disability

At its root, Social Security's definition of disability requires an individual to be unable to engage in any substantial gainful activity (SGA). **Substantial gainful activity** is any physical or mental activity that can be performed for compensation. A qualifying applicant needs to have a disability that has or will last for more than a year, or have a disability that is expected to result in death.

SSDI Funding

Like the retirement program of Social Security, the disability program has its own trust fund. Part of the FICA tax funds the disability program. Workers who have paid into the system through payroll taxes are eligible for disability benefits.

The SSDI trust fund is in much worse shape than the retirement program's trust fund. It could run out of money in 2018. Part of the reason is an expected rise in the number of beneficiaries, with a corresponding drop in tax receipts.

Lawmakers in Congress make decisions about SSDI funding and taxes.

Source: Shutterstock (EastVillage Images)

To address this, lawmakers could increase the share of revenue SSDI gets from the FICA tax. But, remember, the Social Security retirement trust fund faces its own funding problems. Another option is to reduce benefit payments. This could come through benefit reductions or by making work a more viable option for people on disability. Experts, however, say there is little evidence that this would have any effect.

Supplemental Security Income

Social Security **Supplemental Security Income (SSI)** is a federal program that pays extra income to certain people to help meet basic needs for food, clothing, and shelter. Beneficiaries are low-income people over age 65, the blind, and the disabled. About 8 million people receive SSI benefits. More than half of recipients are blind or disabled between the ages of 18 and 64.

The Social Security Administration also considers an individual's resources before granting SSI benefits. In terms of SSI, **resources** include assets like cash, bank accounts, life insurance, and personal property. A person must have less than $2,000 in assets to qualify for benefits.

The average benefit is $674 a month. While the basic monthly benefit is the same for all beneficiaries, some states pay additional benefits.

There is no trust fund for SSI like there is with the retirement and disability programs. General tax revenues, rather than FICA taxes, fund SSI.

Ethical Insurance Practices

People sometimes try to "beat the system" by collecting Social Security benefits they have not earned or do not qualify for. An example of this fraud might be someone who continues to collect SSDI benefits even though he or she has gone back to work. This is unethical and illegal. The Social Security Administration's Office of Inspector General prevents and detects fraud in the program. The office offers a fraud hotline for an individual to report fraud, waste, and abuse.

Eligible children with a deceased parent can receive Social Security survivors benefits typically until age 18.

Source: Shutterstock (rSnapshotPhotos)

Before SSI, states ran their own programs. The federal government helped with the funding. But, the benefits and rules varied widely. This prompted President Richard Nixon in 1972 to sign the SSI program into law. He stated SSI would "bring reason, order, and purpose into a tangle of overlapping programs."

Social Security Survivors Benefit

The Social Security **survivors benefit** helps replace a portion of family income if a spouse or parent dies. The benefit amount depends on the deceased worker's earnings history. If a widow or widower has children under age 16, survivors benefits can be taken right away. In most cases, children receive a benefit up until age 18.

If a widow or widower has no kids under 16, a reduced benefit can be taken starting at age 60. If he or she receives the survivors benefit, but has earned a higher retired-worker benefit, he or she can begin collecting a benefit as early as age 62. As with spousal benefits, survivors benefits may also be available to a divorced spouse if the marriage lasted at least 10 years.

Checkpoint 9.2

1. What is the purpose of Social Security Disability Insurance?
2. What does substantial gainful activity mean?
3. When is the SSDI trust fund estimated to be exhausted?
4. What is the purpose of Supplemental Security Income?
5. For children receiving survivors benefits, at what age does the benefit end in most cases?

Build Your Vocabulary

As you progress through this course, develop a personal glossary of insurance terms and add it to your portfolio. This will help you build your vocabulary and prepare you for a career in insurance. Write out a definition for each of the following terms, and add it to your personal insurance glossary.

Social Security Disability Income (SSDI)
substantial gainful activity
Supplemental Security Income (SSI)
resources
survivors benefit

Chapter Summary

Section 9.1 Social Security Retirement Benefits

- Social Security is social insurance intended to be a supplemental source of income for retired Americans.
- The Social Security monthly retirement benefit is based on your highest 35 years of earnings, and you receive the benefit for life once you start collecting it.
- A spousal benefit is also part of Social Security for those who qualify.
- Workers and employers pay a 6.5% payroll tax to pay for Social Security benefits.

Section 9.2 Other Social Security Benefits

- Social Security pays benefits to individuals who are unable to work due to a serious medical condition under the Social Security Disability Income (SSDI) program.
- Supplemental Security Income (SSI) is a federal program that provides income to low-income people over age 65, the blind, and the disabled to help meet basic needs for food, clothing, and shelter.
- The Social Security survivors benefit helps replace income for spouses and dependent children of deceased workers.

Check Your Insurance IQ

Now that you have finished this chapter, see what you know about insurance by taking the chapter post test.
www.m.g-wlearning.com
www.g-wlearning.com

Review Your Knowledge

On a separate sheet of paper or in a word processing document, match the following terms with the definition that fits best.

A. substantial gainful activity
B. Social Security Disability Income (SSDI)
C. progressive
D. full-benefit age
E. Social Security
F. privatize
G. purchasing power
H. survivors benefit
I. 401(k) plan
J. Supplemental Security Income (SSI)

1. The age at which you can receive your full Social Security benefit.
2. Any mental or physical activity that can be performed for compensation.
3. One proposal to reform Social Security in which workers can contribute to an investment account.
4. Goes down when inflation goes up.
5. Income retired workers receive from the federal government.
6. Social Security program that pays benefits to certain disabled workers.
7. The benefit Social Security pays to the family of a worker who dies.
8. Retirement savings in the form of an investment account that the employee contributes to, and often the employer contributes as well.
9. The lower a worker's income, the higher the percentage is replaced in retirement by Social Security.
10. Income from the federal government for people over age 65 with low income, the blind, and the disabled.

On a separate sheet of paper or in a word processing document, answer each of the following questions.

11. How many years do you need to work to be eligible for Social Security retirement benefits?
12. On what is the dollar amount of your Social Security benefit based?
13. How is Social Security a pay-as-you-go system?
14. What is Social Security's basic definition of a disability?
15. What must a person's asset level be in order to qualify for Supplemental Security Income?

Chapter 9 Social Security

Apply Your Knowledge

16. Go to the Social Security Administration's website. Use the search function to search for "impairments part a". Locate the search result for Adult Listings Part A and open it. Locate the respiratory system category and write down three types of respiratory diseases that qualify an adult for disability benefits.

17. What options might lawmakers consider to address the disability insurance trust fund's financial challenges?

18. When a parent takes time out of the workforce to care for family members (kids or aging parents, for example), credit is not being earned for Social Security. Do you think credit should be given? Why or why not?

19. Go to the Social Security Administration's website. Use the search function to search for "estimate retirement benefits". In the search results, select the quick calculator. Enter your birth date and a current earnings amount of your choice between $40,000 and $80,000. Write down the estimate of retirement benefits for ages 62, 67, and 70.

20. Research the issue of Social Security funding. Of the proposed solutions to the funding issues, what do you think is the best option? Write a one-page paper explaining and justifying your position.

Working in Teams

Working with one or two classmates, brainstorm solutions to the funding issues Social Security Disability Income faces. Present your ideas to the class.

G-W Learning Mobile Site

Visit the G-W Learning mobile site to complete the chapter pretest and post test, to review the History of Insurance articles, and to practice vocabulary using e-flash cards. If you do not have a smartphone, visit the G-W Learning companion website to access these features.

G-W Learning mobile site: www.m.g-wlearning.com
G-W Learning companion website: www.g-wlearning.com

Common Core

College and Career Readiness

Reading. Go to the Social Security website and use the search function to search for "glossary". In the search results, locate the glossary and open it. Read at least five terms and determine their meanings from the definition.

Writing. Research the issue of reforming the Social Security retirement system. Write a one-page paper describing what you believe to be the best option. Draw evidence from your research to support your position.

Extemporaneous Speaking

Extemporaneous speaking is a competitive event you might enter with your career and technical student organization (CTSO). You will be evaluated on verbal and nonverbal skills as well as the tone and projection of your voice. At the event, you will be given several topics from which to choose, a time limit for creating the speech, and a time limit for delivering the speech. To prepare for the extemporaneous speaking event, do the following.

1. Read the guidelines provided by your organization. Make certain to ask any questions about points you do not understand. It is important you follow each specific item that is outlined in the competition rules.
2. Ask your instructor for several topics on insurance so you can practice making impromptu speeches.
3. Practice, practice, practice. Your speech will be judged by a panel of professionals.
4. Ask your instructor to bring together a panel that will listen to your practice speech and provide feedback.

Unit 2 Summative Assessment

True/False Questions

1. *True or false?* About 57% of Medicaid funding comes from the federal government.
2. *True or false?* Social Security survivors benefits for children end in most cases at age 21.
3. *True or false?* Two-thirds of the worker's income for a specified time limit is the typical benefit paid for workers' compensation.
4. *True or false?* To be eligible to receive unemployment benefits, an individual must have purchased unemployment insurance.
5. *True or false?* Social Security is intended to be used by retirees as their sole source of income.

Multiple Choice Questions

1. What is the purpose of workers' compensation insurance?
   A. To provide financial support if a worker becomes unemployed.
   B. To provide medical and financial support for workers who are injured or made ill on the job.
   C. To provide medical support for workers and their families.
   D. To protect a company from being sued in cases of extreme negligence.
2. What is the purpose of unemployment insurance?
   A. To replace part of a worker's income when he or she is injured on the job and cannot work.
   B. To replace all of a worker's income if he or she is fired.
   C. To replace part of an unemployed worker's income while he or she looks for another job.
   D. To provide financial compensation to employers if they have to lay off workers.
3. What is the purpose of Medicare?
   A. To provide health insurance to those with low incomes.
   B. To provide health insurance to those age 65 and older.
   C. To provide health insurance to all Americans.
   D. To provide health insurance to the dependents (children) of those with low income.
4. What is the purpose of Medicaid?
   A. To provide health insurance to those age 65 and older.
   B. To protect the federal government against the increasing cost of Medicare.
   C. To help low-income individuals and some others receive health care.
   D. To provide health insurance to all Americans.
5. What is the purpose of Social Security Disability Insurance?
   A. To provide retirement income to all Americans.
   B. To provide a supplement to normal retirement savings.
   C. To provide income for those who have reached a specified age.
   D. To provide income to those who are unable to work due to a serious medical condition.

Unit 3: Nature of the Industry

The first two units of this text focused on the basics of insurance as a risk-management tool and the types of insurance products that help manage risk. Unit 3 focuses on the nature of the insurance industry. You will learn about insurance contracts and the claims process, as well as how insurance carriers manage the risk they assume. This unit also explains how insurance companies make money and how they are regulated.

Chapter 10
Nature of the Insurance Industry

Chapter 11
How Insurance Companies Make Money

Chapter 12
State Regulation of Insurance

Chapter 13
Federal Insurance Industry Regulations

Chapter 14
Legal Principles

Chapter 15
Ethics and Social Responsibility

Chapter 10
Nature of the Insurance Industry

Reading Prep. Before reading this chapter, look at the chapter title. Can you analyze the author's purpose for this chapter by studying the title?

At this stage, you know about the types of insurance we use to manage risk. Now you will learn how the insurance industry works, starting with the components of the fundamental insurance document. This document is the insurance contract, perhaps better known as the insurance policy.

Section 10.1
Insurance Contracts

Section 10.2
How Insurers Manage Risk

Section 10.3
Insurance Claims

Section 10.4
Consumer Resources

Most major insurance companies in the US are following strategies established by the US Green Building Council when they build or renovate their office facilities. The companies pursue Leadership in Energy and Environmental Design (LEED) certification to improve energy and water efficiency, reduce carbon emissions, as well as mindfully choose and use resources. While green building techniques may initially cost more, the long-term savings more than make up for it.

Check Your Insurance IQ

Before you begin this chapter, see what you already know about insurance by taking the chapter pretest.

www.m.g-wlearning.com
www.g-wlearning.com

Section 10.1
Insurance Contracts

Terms
insurance contract
legally binding
utmost good faith
insurance agent
Insurance Services Office, Inc. (ISO)
declarations
definitions
insuring agreement
named-perils policy
all-risk policy
conditions
exclusions
endorsements

Objectives
After completing this section, you will be able to:
- Explain the nature of insurance contracts.
- Identify the components of an insurance contract.

Overview of Insurance Contracts

As you have learned throughout this text, insurance products transfer risk from the consumer to the insurance company. When a consumer decides to transfer risk to an insurer and the company accepts it, both sides are entering into an insurance contract. The **insurance contract**, also called a *policy*, is a legally binding agreement. **Legally binding** means that both the customer and the insurance company accept and agree to the contract's provisions. If either party fails to keep their end of the deal, the other can sue.

Legal principles are discussed in Chapter 14. However, a central principle of insurance contracts is utmost good faith. **Utmost good faith** means that the consumer and the insurance agent have been honest with each other. An **insurance agent**, also called a *producer*, is the professional licensed to sell an insurance contract.

For example, when applying for an automobile insurance policy, the customer says he or she drives 15 miles to work, but really drives 50. The principle of utmost good faith has been broken because the customer was not truthful. In another example, the insurance agent sells somebody a policy that is more coverage than needed. The principle of utmost good faith has been broken because the agent did not have the customer's best interest in mind.

Buying and selling insurance has to rely on the utmost good faith of the parties. The insurer has no real way of knowing if the statements made by the customer, like the distance driven to work, are true. Likewise, it

Source: Shutterstock (Kateryna Larina)

A contract is central to an insurance agreement.

could be hard for a customer to tell if an agent is being truthful about the product. The very nature of an insurance contract makes mutual trust essential.

Basics of an Insurance Contract

Most insurance contracts are based on policy forms developed by Insurance Services Office, Inc. (ISO). **ISO** is an organization that advises the insurance industry and produces policy forms. So, contracts typically follow the same standard structure. These are the sections that make up a typical insurance contract:
- declarations
- insuring agreement
- named perils
- all-risk
- definitions
- exclusions
- conditions
- endorsements

Insurance contracts can seem overwhelming. In fact, many people just scan the main page of their policies and then file them away. They only find out after a loss whether or not they had the right coverage. Read through your contract before you sign it and again once you have it in hand.

Declarations

The **declarations** section lists a policy number, the name of the policyholder, and the insurance carrier. This section also identifies what the policy covers and the start and end dates of the coverage. It will include other information specific to the type of policy, too. For example, the declarations section on a life insurance policy lists the name and age of the person it covers.

Definitions

Insurers are careful to clearly define everything in a policy. If something in the contract is ambiguous and a policyholder sues, the courts will likely side with the policyholder. *Ambiguous* means there is more than one way to understand the meaning. So, policies include a **definitions** section to clearly define terms used in the contract. For example, this section defines who is insured under the policy ("the insured"). A homeowner's policy would define "the insured" as the policyholder, his or her spouse, the children, and any relatives who live with them.

It is important to understand the details of an insurance policy's terms and conditions.

Source: Shutterstock (Monkey Business Images)

Insuring Agreement

The **insuring agreement** identifies the commitment the insurance carrier has made to the policyholder. It outlines perils the policy does or does not cover. Some policies are named-peril policies. A **named-peril policy** means the contract only covers losses resulting from the causes listed in the insuring agreement. On the other hand, **all-risk policies** list perils it will not cover. If a peril is not listed, then the policy covers it.

Conditions

The **conditions** section describes the responsibilities the policyholder has when a loss occurs. Conditions may require the policyholder to contact the insurance carrier within a certain period following a loss. This section will also explain what happens when a claim is filed.

Exclusions

Exclusions are losses the insurance carrier will not cover. For example, homeowner's insurance may cover water damage caused by a pipe that breaks. But, it may not cover damage from a flood caused by a rainstorm. If this is the case, it will be stated as an exclusion on the policy.

Endorsements

Most policies are standard, but often the carrier needs to add information not found on the standard policy. The **endorsements** section details agreements that are not otherwise part of the policy. It may state, for example, that the contract covers your personal computer. It could also contain modifications to the contract that restrict coverage. For example, if it is not addressed in the policy, an endorsement might state that the policy does not apply for losses caused by an act of terrorism.

Checkpoint 10.1

1. What is the term for the mutual trust between a policyholder and an insurance carrier?
2. Which basic element of an insurance policy lists a policy number, the name of the policyholder, the insurance carrier, what the policy covers, and the start and end dates of the coverage?
3. What kind of information is included in the definitions section of an insurance policy?
4. What is the term for losses the insurance carrier will not cover?
5. What element of an insurance contract would need to be added to an existing homeowner's insurance policy to make sure a new 55-inch flat-panel television is covered if it was ever stolen or damaged?

Build Your Vocabulary

As you progress through this course, develop a personal glossary of insurance terms. This will help you build your vocabulary and prepare you for a career in insurance. Write out a definition for each of the following terms, and add it to your personal insurance glossary.

insurance contract
legally binding
utmost good faith
insurance agent
Insurance Services Office, Inc. (ISO)
declarations
definitions
insuring agreement
named-peril policy
all-risk policy
conditions
exclusions
endorsements

Section 10.2
How Insurers Manage Risk

Terms

law of large numbers
underwriting
adverse selection
smart systems
inspection report
Medical Information Bureau
credit score
insurance score
actuary
ratings bureau
reinsurance

Objectives

After completing this section, you will be able to:
- Explain the law of large numbers.
- Define the role of underwriting in insurance.
- Describe how reinsurance works.

Law of Large Numbers

Insurance allows individuals and businesses to protect themselves from financial loss by transferring risk to the insurance company. But, what does the insurance company do to manage the risks it assumes? The insurer must pay claims whenever a policyholder experiences a covered loss. An important way insurance companies manage the risks they take on is through the law of large numbers. The **law of large numbers** holds that the accuracy of a statistic increases with a greater sample size.

Insurance companies pool risk. That is, they cover a group made up of a large number of policyholders. The probability is that only a small number of the policyholders will experience a loss. So, the money coming in from premiums will likely be more than the money going out to pay covered losses.

A larger statistical sample creates the expected outcome of a coin landing heads-up 50% of the time.

Source: Shutterstock (jcjgphotography)

The law of large numbers is at play when you flip a coin. In a single flip, there is a 50% chance that the coin will land heads-up. This is the expected outcome. However, if you flip the coin only ten times, the outcome might be different from the expectation. The coin may land heads-up seven times and tails-up three times. The law of large numbers says if you flip the coin a thousand times, the outcome will approach the expected result. So, the larger the "pool" of coin flips, the more likely you are to achieve the expected outcome of the coin landing heads-up 50% of the time.

Here is an example of the law of large numbers in action. Suppose that in a pool of 100,000 people, statistics suggest each person faces a 2% probability of incurring a loss in a year. This means 2,000 people will likely experience a loss. Now, if each person in the pool pays $1,500 in premiums, the insurer collects $150 million. This gives the insurer enough money to pay $75,000 to 2,000 policyholders who experience a loss.

100,000 policyholders in pool × 2% chance of loss = 2,000 policyholders experiencing a loss
100,000 policyholders × $1,500 premium = $150,000,000 total revenue for insurance company
$150,000,000 revenue ÷ 2,000 policyholders with loss = $75,000 paid per claim

What if more than 2,000 policyholders experience a loss? Based on the law of large numbers, this is very unlikely. But, if it does occur, the insurance company may have to pay more in claims than it has collected in premiums.

Underwriting

Spreading risk across a large population is not the only way insurance companies manage the risks they assume. Insurance companies also analyze the risk of each policy applicant before approving the policy. They use information the applicant provides to determine the likelihood of that person or business experiencing a loss. For example, a chronic smoker who does not exercise or eat well represents a greater risk to a health or life insurance carrier than a physically fit nonsmoker.

Underwriting is the process of determining whether to accept the risk of an applicant and what premium to charge. Underwriting is a key factor in an insurance company's profitability. If the underwriter's decision results in high payouts, it will affect the company's bottom line.

The underwriter's job is to minimize adverse selection. **Adverse selection** happens when someone has a need for insurance because of a particular risk. For example, a young male who is otherwise healthy applies for a life insurance policy. Data show that young men typically do not buy life insurance policies. It may be that the applicant faces a terminal illness. In this case, he represents a poor risk to the carrier. If the insurance carrier approves him for a life insurance policy, adverse selection has occurred.

Ethical Insurance Practices

Everyone has a responsibility to use information technology in an ethical manner. Using material illegally downloaded from the Internet or software that you do not hold a lawful license for is not only unethical but illegal. Because trust is so central to the whole insurance industry, insurance professionals must take special care to avoid any appearance of impropriety in any area.

History of Insurance

Lloyd's of London was an early player in the insurance game. It is not actually a company, but an association of people willing to take on insurance risks. It started in the late 1600s when men with the means to underwrite shipments to the New World gathered at Lloyd's coffeehouse. The coffeehouse became known as the place for mariners to go to insure their cargo. Its history of insuring ships was evident in the writing of its first automobile policy in 1904. The automobile was described as "a ship navigating on land." Today, Lloyd's of London is known for the specialized insurance it offers. For example, it insures Bruce Springsteen's voice and other celebrity body parts.

www.m.g-wlearning.com
www.g-wlearning.com

Tools of the Underwriting Trade

How does an underwriter know whether an applicant poses a good risk or a poor one? The policy application, statistics, and other data sources are used to make the decision. For example, for medical insurance, the underwriter will look at the application to find out the person's age, occupation, medical history, and current physical health.

The underwriter also relies on the assessment of the insurance agent. The agent is the one who walks the person through the application process. Insurance companies rely on their agents for local knowledge about people, houses, and businesses to supplement the underwriting process.

Computer applications play a big role in the underwriting process. Smart systems help calculate risk. **Smart systems** are computer applications that can quickly analyze applications, recommend whether to deny or accept them, and adjust premiums based on the applicant's risk profile. The underwriter sets up what information the smart system should screen for, like credit scores, income, and health status. Smart systems are only guides. An underwriter can choose whether to accept the decision or reject it.

Sometimes, insurers require a medical exam or a physician's statement when considering an application. This is typical with life insurance policies. If the underwriter needs more information about the applicant, he can order an inspection report. The application will include a statement indicating that an inspection report may be requested.

An **inspection report** takes a more detailed look at the applicant's finances, health habits, occupation, and character. The process may involve phone interviews with colleagues, friends, and neighbors. Inspection report companies are independent. Insurance companies pay for their services.

Underwriters study various data sources to get more information about an applicant.

Source: Shutterstock (Stephen Coburn)

Careers in Finance
Insurance Services

What Does an Insurance Sales Manager Do?

Insurance sales managers oversee sales teams, including employee sales agents, independent sales agents, and sales supervisors. They have responsibility for ensuring their teams meet their sales goals. A sales manager:
- recruits sales agents;
- oversees all the work performed by sales agents;
- manages the operations of the sales function;
- prepares reports to support agents and to meet compliance requirements;
- develops training programs and delivers them to the team; and
- may handle customer service complaints.

What Is It Like to Work as an Insurance Sales Manager?

An **insurance sales manager** uses sophisticated computerized data systems to track sales and establish goals and quotas for the team of sales agents, often using smartphones and tablet computers. Well-developed communication and people skills are essential for a successful **insurance sales manager**. In any kind of communication, the agent must follow accepted guidelines for use of e-mail, social networking, blogs, and texting.

Insurance sales managers are responsible for the success of their sales teams. They are part leader, part motivator, part trainer, and part operations manager. The manager trains the sales team and continuously monitors its progress.

Insurance sales managers are usually based in an office but may work from home. They put in long hours, which include nights and weekends. **Insurance sales managers** often dress in business-professional attire. In some cases, business-casual attire is acceptable.

What Education and Skills Are Needed to Be an Insurance Sales Manager?
- an associate's or bachelor's degree
- strong project management skills
- broad technical expertise
- solid verbal and written communication skills
- excellent analytical skills

The underwriter may also consult the Medical Information Bureau (MIB). It is a corporation owned by insurance companies. The **Medical Information Bureau** maintains records of applications for life, health, disability, long-term care, and critical-care insurance. The MIB maintains information on an applicant that was previously reported to insurance companies. If this information is missing in a subsequent application for insurance, the MIB notifies the insurer. An underwriter can only consult the MIB with the applicant's consent. Also, an insurer cannot deny an applicant based solely on information obtained through the MIB.

Consumer credit scores are another information resource for underwriters. A **credit score** is a numerical value that reflects a person's credit history. If you pay your debts on time and do not have too many sources of credit available to you, your credit score should be high. Debts include credit cards, a home mortgage, other lines of credit, and rent. Likewise, your score will be low if you frequently miss payments or have too much credit available to you. The reason having a lot of credit available is a bad thing is because people are more likely to use available credit and increase their debt.

Insurance companies use an applicant's credit score as the basis for assigning an insurance score. Why? Research has shown that credit scores correlate with the frequency of claims. The **insurance score** is a numerical value that reflects the risk the applicant represents to the insurance carrier. The higher the insurance score, the better risk the applicant is to the insurer. Using insurance scores is controversial, and some states bar insurance companies from using them.

Role of the Actuary

An **actuary** uses statistics, math, computer science, and finance to determine risk for insurance companies. The actuary creates a model of the probability of accidents or other causes of loss to set insurance premiums. This model helps determine how much income an insurer needs in order to pay expected future claims while earning a profit. Therefore, the role of the actuary is critical to the success of an insurance company.

About 60% of actuaries work in the insurance industry. Others may work for pension funds or financial-services companies. Wherever they work, the role of the actuary in assessing risk is a critical business function.

Ratings Bureaus

Insurance companies look at their own claims and loss history when determining premiums. But, they can also turn to ratings bureaus. A **ratings bureau** collects loss and claims information from across the industry and sells it to insurance companies. These data help insurance companies determine what premiums to charge.

Several states have non-profit ratings bureaus that collect and disseminate data to insurance companies in those states. Some states require insurers to become members of the state's ratings bureau.

Reinsurance

Even insurance companies need insurance. What might happen if an insurer wrote too many policies at too low of a premium? Or, if many of its clients experienced catastrophic loss at the same time? The company may not be able to pay its clients' claims. This is where reinsurance comes in.

With **reinsurance**, an insurance company transfers some of its risk to another insurance company. For example, an insurer writes a $20 million property policy to cover a commercial building. It can work with another insurance company to share the risk. The first insurer could agree to pay damages up to $10 million. The reinsurer would be responsible for any losses above that, up to $20 million.

Reinsurance is a global business. This helps spread risk across markets worldwide. Reinsurance proved to be enormously important in 2011. In just the first six months of the year, policyholders around the world suffered $67 billion in insured losses. This was more than double the losses in the first half of 2010. From January through June, the world witnessed earthquakes, a tsunami and the threat of a nuclear accident in Japan, a massive earthquake in New Zealand, landslides in Brazil, and deadly storms and tornadoes in the US. Overall losses, not just insured losses, were estimated at $278 billion.

Checkpoint 10.2

1. What principle is based on the idea that the greater the pool of policyholders, the lower the risk is to the insurance company?
2. What essential process determines the risk an applicant poses to an insurance carrier?
3. From what source do insurance companies receive information regarding industry-wide claims and losses?
4. What insurance professional uses statistics, math, computer science, and finance to determine the probability of claims being made?
5. How do insurance companies transfer their risk?

Build Your Vocabulary

As you progress through this course, develop a personal glossary of insurance terms. This will help you build your vocabulary and prepare you for a career in insurance. Write out a definition for each of the following terms, and add it to your personal insurance glossary.

law of large numbers
underwriting
adverse selection
smart systems
inspection report
Medical Information Bureau
credit score
insurance score
actuary
ratings bureau
reinsurance

Section 10.3
Insurance Claims

Terms

claim
loss adjuster
arbitration
mediator

Objectives

After completing this section, you will be able to:
- Describe the basic process of filing an insurance claim.
- Identify potential pitfalls when filing a claim.

Nature of Insurance Claims

When a policyholder experiences a loss, he or she must file a claim with the insurance carrier. A **claim** is the process of documenting the loss against the policy. This typically involves either contacting the agent who sold the policy, going online to the insurer's website, or calling the insurance carrier directly. Depending on the complexity of the claim, it can be settled in a few weeks or it may take several years.

Most insurance claims are straightforward and quickly settled. When a more-complex claim arises, an insurance carrier will turn to loss adjusters for assistance. A **loss adjuster** is a specialist who visits with the policyholder to determine the cause of a loss and its extent, whether the policy covers the loss, and whether the amount claimed

A loss adjuster works toward settling a claim with a policyholder.

Source: Shutterstock (JHDT Stock Images LLC)

is reasonable. The loss adjuster is responsible for arriving at a final settlement with the policyholder.

The insurance carrier has to balance two competing interests when it receives a claim. It wants to provide good customer service and be perceived as fair by its policyholders. At the same time, the company wants to settle a claim at the lowest possible cost.

The way in which an insurance carrier processes claims is an important customer-relations activity. A company that is reasonable and efficient will earn more trust and respect than one readily denying claims or with a hard-to-use claims process.

Insurance companies typically have a stated claims-management philosophy that their claims professionals follow. A stated philosophy can be a useful marketing tool. Here are some examples of insurer claims philosophies:

> "Whether it's a life insurance claim, a long-term absence due to illness, a short-term maternity leave—or any other reason for a claim—we handle it all with sensitivity, attention to detail, accuracy and knowhow...Taking the time necessary to talk to employees, answer their questions and ease their minds really sets us apart. So do our speedy phone response time and prompt payments."
>
> —The Hartford Group Benefits Claims Philosophy

> "It is our policy to deal openly, ethically and promptly with our customers. We are devoted to achieving excellence by committing our efforts toward service, efficiency, teamwork and communication. Our goal is to be *The Company of Choice*® by providing superior customer service."
>
> —Golden Eagle Insurance Claims Philosophy (member of Liberty Mutual Group)

> "...We realize that policies issued by most insurance companies have basically the same coverages and features. While we do try to offer some special features to meet the needs of our members we know that the manner in which claims are handled can make the real difference in meeting those needs. We feel all of our customers should receive the best and most professional service we can offer..."
>
> —Missouri Farm Bureau Insurance Services Claims Philosophy

Claims-Filing Pitfalls

What happens if the insurance carrier offers a settlement that the policyholder thinks is unsatisfactory? When this happens, the policyholder begins by filing an appeal with the insurer. The policy should spell out the appeals process. After the appeal, if the policyholder still does not agree with the settlement offer, the policy likely spells out the next options. These options typically involve arbitration. **Arbitration** is the process of bringing the dispute in front of a professional mediator. A **mediator** looks at both sides of the case, favoring neither side, and then makes a judgment. The result of this process is binding to both parties, whether they agree with the outcome or not.

It is important for the policyholder to use the insurance when it is needed. But, before filing a claim, policyholders need to consider the possible impact to their insurance coverage. Someone who has several claims against an automobile policy in one year, for example, may find the insurance carrier will not renew the policy for the next year. Or, the carrier may renew the policy, but raise the premium. If the damage is something the policyholder can afford to handle without insurance, that option should be considered.

Real World Case

The insurance carrier that sold a homeowner's policy to Jacob's older brother, Silas, recently canceled it. Silas filed several claims for damages throughout his first year of coverage. For example, he filed for storm damage when he had to replace shingles on his roof. Then he filed to replace his gutters when another storm ripped them from his house.

How could Silas have done things differently to maintain his coverage? He could have replaced the shingles himself after the first storm. The cost of fixing the roof was $750, and Silas' deductible was $500. It was not worth filing the claim to only receive $250 for the repair.

If Silas had contacted the agent who sold him the policy, he could have been advised on the impact his claims might have on his coverage status.

Checkpoint 10.3

1. What is the process of documenting a loss against a policy?
2. What insurance professional is responsible for arriving at a final settlement with the policyholder after a claim has been made?
3. The result of what dispute-resolution process is binding on both sides?
4. When are the services of a mediator needed?
5. What should a policyholder carefully consider before filing a claim?

Build Your Vocabulary

As you progress through this course, develop a personal glossary of insurance terms. This will help you build your vocabulary and prepare you for a career in insurance. Write out a definition for each of the following terms, and add it to your personal insurance glossary.

claim
loss adjuster
arbitration
mediator

Section 10.4
Consumer Resources

Objectives
After completing this section, you will be able to:
- Describe the role of ratings agencies in the insurance market.
- Identify how states offer information to the consumer on insurance companies.

Terms
ratings agencies
financial analyst
statisticians
state insurance departments

Ratings Agencies

You know that insurance companies put a lot of resources into figuring out what risk a consumer represents to them. But, how do consumers know what risk an insurance company represents to them? Two information sources can give consumers information on insurance companies—ratings agencies and state insurance departments.

Ratings agencies provide an expert opinion on the health of companies and investment products. These agencies employ hundreds of financial analysts and statisticians who work together to come up with the ratings. **Financial analysts** research companies to determine their ability to pay their debts. **Statisticians** collect and analyze numerical data.

Consumers and investors can use ratings information when making financial decisions. However, the ratings are opinions, *not* facts or guarantees. Ratings agencies took some of the blame for the economic recession that began in 2007. This economic crisis reminded investors not to rely solely on ratings agencies to make investment decisions.

Among the most well-known US ratings agencies are Moody's, Standard & Poor's, and A.M. Best. All ratings agencies use a letter grading system to identify the financial health of a company. Each uses its own set of criteria to analyze companies and its own set of ratings. Figure 10-1 shows how three ratings agencies grade insurers.

State Consumer Resources

Ratings assigned by ratings agencies are educated *opinions* about an insurer's financial health. Consumers should consider the ratings, but also use other information to make a decision. Another good resource is state insurance departments.

Agency	Ratings Scale	
Moody's	Aaa =	Exceptional
	Aa =	Excellent
	A =	Good
	Baa =	Adequate
	Ba =	Questionable
	B =	Poor
	Caa =	Very poor
	Ca =	Extremely poor
	C =	Lowest
Standard & Poor's	AAA =	Superior
	AA =	Excellent
	A =	Good
	BBB =	Adequate
	BB =	Adequate but vulnerable
	B =	Vulnerable
	CCC =	Extremely vulnerable
A.M. Best	A++, A+ =	Superior
	A, A- =	Excellent
	B++, B+ =	Good
	B, B- =	Fair
	C++, C+ =	Marginal
	C, C- =	Weak
	D =	Poor

Figure 10-1. Rating Scales

Each state makes and enforces insurance laws. **State insurance departments** supervise and regulate insurers in their respective states. For example, states collect consumer complaints about insurers. Information about insurers can typically be found on a state's insurance agency website. You will read more about state insurance departments in Chapter 12.

Checkpoint 10.4

1. What service do ratings agencies perform?
2. What role does the financial analyst play in a ratings agency?
3. How do ratings agencies give their opinion of a company's financial health?
4. What professional collects and analyzes numerical data for ratings agencies and other companies?
5. What entities supervise and regulate insurers?

Build Your Vocabulary

As you progress through this course, develop a personal glossary of insurance terms. This will help you build your vocabulary and prepare you for a career in insurance. Write out a definition for each of the following terms, and add it to your personal insurance glossary.

ratings agencies
financial analyst
statisticians
state insurance departments

Chapter Summary

Section 10.1 Insurance Contracts

- An insurance contract, or policy, is legally binding to you and the insurance company.
- Most insurance contracts are based on forms from ISO and include sections for declarations, insuring agreement, definitions, exclusions, conditions, and endorsements.

Section 10.2 How Insurers Manage Risk

- An important way insurance companies manage risk is through the law of larger numbers, which says the accuracy of a statistic increases with the sample size.
- The process of determining whether to accept the risk of an applicant and what premium to charge is underwriting, and the main goal is to guard against adverse selection.

Section 10.3 Insurance Claims

- Most insurance claims are straightforward and settled quickly, but a more-complex claim may involve an independent loss adjuster.
- If a policyholder does not agree with the settlement offer, it can be appealed, and it may end up in arbitration.

Section 10.4 Consumer Resources

- Ratings agencies employ financial analysts and statisticians who provide an expert opinion on the health of companies and investment products.
- State insurance departments supervise and regulate insurers in their respective states.

Check Your Insurance IQ

Now that you have finished this chapter, see what you know about insurance by taking the chapter post test.
www.m.g-wlearning.com
www.g-wlearning.com

Review Your Knowledge

Match the following terms with the definition that fits best.

A. claim
B. conditions
C. credit score
D. declarations
E. endorsements
F. exclusions
G. inspection report
H. insurance contract
I. insurance score
J. reinsurance

1. A legally binding document also called a policy.
2. Describes the responsibilities the policyholder has when a loss occurs.
3. Losses the insurance carrier will not cover.
4. Lists a policy number, the name of the policyholder, and the insurance company.
5. A more-detailed look at the applicant's finances, health habits, occupation, and character.
6. A numerical value that reflects a person's credit history.
7. Numerical value that reflects the risk the applicant represents to the insurance company.
8. An insurance company transfers some of its risk to another insurance company.
9. The process of documenting the loss against the policy.
10. Details agreements that are not otherwise part of the policy.

On a separate sheet of paper or in a word processing document, answer each of the following questions.

11. Describe the role of the ISO.
12. Explain how the law of large numbers affects an insurance company's profitability.
13. What roles do smart systems play in the insurance application process?
14. What does a loss adjuster do?
15. What function does the insuring agreement portion of an insurance policy serve?

Apply Your Knowledge

16. Do you think an insurer should be permitted to use an applicant's insurance score to determine what kind of risk they may present? Why or why not? Explain your answer.
17. Think of an example not mentioned in the text of how a policyholder or an insurance agent can break utmost good faith. What processes are in place to make sure that the insurance agent and the policyholder are behaving honestly?
18. Think of an instance in which it may be better for the insured not to file an insurance claim even if the damage may be covered. Why would someone decide not to file a claim?
19. Conduct an Internet search for the term "insurance fraud". What types of fraud are at the top of your search? Why do you think this is the case? From the reports you read, how do you think that fraud could have been prevented?
20. Create a one-act play that shows the interaction between an agent and an applicant or an investigator and a claimant. Be sure the dialogue shows the nature of the relationships.

Working in Teams

Working in a team, conduct an Internet search to find applications for insurance policies. Beyond a person's name, what other information is included in the application? Why would having this information help an insurance carrier determine the potential risk an applicant represents? Create a chart that shows what questions are used most frequently and what they tell the company about the applicant.

G-W Learning Mobile Site

Visit the G-W Learning mobile site to complete the chapter pretest and post test, to review the History of Insurance articles, and to practice vocabulary using e-flash cards. If you do not have a smartphone, visit the G-W Learning companion website to access these features.

G-W Learning mobile site: www.m.g-wlearning.com
G-W Learning companion website: www.g-wlearning.com

Common Core

College and Career Readiness

Reading. Research information about one of the three major ratings agencies. Analyze the structure the author uses to organize the facts about the agency you choose. Provide an accurate summary of your reading, making sure to incorporate key information about the agency.

Writing. Conduct a short research project to answer the question: How do ratings agencies help the consumer make informed decisions regarding which insurance carrier to choose? Write an informative report consisting of several paragraphs that synthesize the information you collected.

Careers

Many competitive events for career and technical student organizations (CTSOs) offer events that include various finance careers. This competitive event may include an objective test that covers multiple topics. Participants are usually allowed one hour to complete the event. One of the topics that may be included on the test is careers in insurance. To prepare for the careers portion of the insurance test:

1. Read the Careers in Insurance features in each chapter of the text. As you read each career, note an important fact or two that you would like to remember.

2. Do an Internet search for "careers in insurance". Review any careers that you have not already read about. Make notes on important facts about each.

Chapter 11
How Insurance Companies Make Money

Section 11.1
Premiums

Section 11.2
Investments

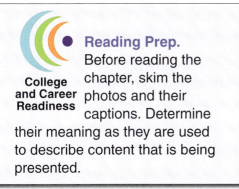

Reading Prep. Before reading the chapter, skim the photos and their captions. Determine their meaning as they are used to describe content that is being presented.

College and Career Readiness

Insurance companies have two ways of making money. The first is the premiums they charge to insurance policyholders. Premiums must be set carefully so the insurance company avoids paying out more in claims than it receives in payments. The second source of income is investments. Investments typically produce more income to insurers than the premiums they collect. This chapter covers how insurance companies use premiums and investments to make money.

Increasingly, insurance companies are developing environmental policies that apply to all aspects of their business, including their vendors. To this end, many insurance companies are working with preferred vendors to make sure that when repairs are made as the result of a claim, they are done so in an environmentally responsible manner.

Check Your Insurance IQ

Before you begin this chapter, see what you already know about insurance by taking the chapter pretest.

www.m.g-wlearning.com
www.g-wlearning.com

Section 11.1
Premiums

Terms
premium
underwriter
risk class
preferred risk class
substandard risk class
underwriting policy
group health plan
demographics
individual market
mortality table
ratemaking
pure premium
load
gross premium
catastrophe
catastrophe modeling

Objectives
After completing this section, you will be able to:
- Discuss how premiums contribute to an insurance company's profit.
- Identify how underwriting relates to premiums.
- Define the role of ratemaking in setting premiums.
- Explain how insurance companies account for unknown future catastrophes.

Overview of Premiums

One source of income for insurance companies is premiums. A **premium** is the fees a policyholder pays in return for insurance coverage. Insurance companies have to manage their businesses so that income from premiums at least equals claims paid to policyholders and their operational expenses. Otherwise, the companies might lose money. Ideally, premiums bring in more money than the insurer has to pay out in claims and expenses. For example, the US property and casualty insurance industry wrote policies totaling more than $420 billion in premiums in 2010. It incurred over $300 billion in losses the same year.

Calculating competitive insurance premiums is an important function of an insurance company.

Source: Shutterstock (Stocklite)

While premiums can be high for some people, they are generally affordably priced. The market is competitive, and insurance companies will lose money if they are unable to set affordable premiums. Health insurance on the individual market is a common exception. You will read about it later in this chapter.

Underwriting

The **underwriter** in an insurance company deals with the selection of risk. It is the underwriter who determines whether or not to issue a policy to an applicant and at what premium. For example, a health insurance underwriter in the individual health insurance market will consider an applicant's age, lifestyle, current health, and family health history. A property and casualty underwriter will look at what risks a given property is exposed to and steps an applicant has taken to reduce those risks.

Risk Classes

The underwriter also determines an applicant's risk class. A **risk class** is a category based on the risk an applicant represents to the company.

A fit 25-year-old runner may be put in a **preferred risk class** for life insurance, for example, because he or she is a low risk to the company. The premium would be lower than that of a 50-year-old smoker. This older applicant might be put in a **substandard risk class** because he or she is a high risk to the company. The premium would be higher to help the company cover future claims. Figure 11-1 outlines the risk classes underwriters commonly use in the life insurance industry.

History of Insurance

A fire raged for five days in 1666, nearly destroying London, England. The Great Fire of London led to the formation of fire insurance. A physician who entered the construction business to rebuild the city also started insuring the homes he built against fire. His successful insurance business led others to get into the industry.

www.m.g-wlearning.com
www.g-wlearning.com

Class	Description
Standard	Insured receives standard policy without restrictions or surcharge.
Preferred	Insured is in a class with above-average mortality risk (less likelihood of premature death) and receives a lower premium rate.
Substandard	Insured is in a group that is not expected to live as long as others who are not subject to the same hazards, such as physical condition or occupational risk. Insured pays a higher premium and may receive a restricted policy.
Uninsurable	Applicant is denied coverage because of a high physical or moral hazard.*

*Moral hazard is the potential for an individual to engage in risky behavior because he or she has insurance coverage that protects from the financial consequences.

Figure 11-1. Life Insurance Underwriting Risk Classes

Underwriting Policy

An underwriter bases decisions on the company's underwriting policy. The **underwriting policy** establishes the:
- kinds of insurance the company will offer;
- geographic locations in which insurance will be sold; and
- maximum amount of coverage the insurer can offer.

Sound underwriting policies are critical for the financial health of an insurance company.

Underwriting in the Health Insurance Market

In the health insurance market, underwriting is a little bit different. More than half of Americans receive health insurance through their employers. A health insurance plan that employers offer to employees is known as a **group health plan.** If an insurance company is establishing a group health plan, it will not underwrite each individual employee. Instead, the underwriter sets a premium based on certain characteristics of the group as a whole. The claims history, demographics, and geographic location of the group may be considered. **Demographics** are statistics, such as age and income, about a group of people.

In health insurance, the **individual market** is where a single person or family purchases health insurance. Applicants in this market go through an extensive underwriting process. While most people are healthy most of the time, everyone is likely at some point to have an illness or suffer an injury that will be expensive. The risk to the insurance company is not spread over a large group. As a result, underwriting in the individual market is much more selective. Those with health conditions, such as diabetes or depression, may pay a high premium, receive limited benefits, or be rejected for coverage.

Because of the recession that began in 2007, millions of people lost their jobs and their employer-provided health insurance. Many were unable to afford health insurance policies in the individual market. Many people found themselves unemployed for longer periods than was the case in the recent past, leaving them without health insurance over a longer time. When people found work, it may not have been full time or offer group health-care benefits. The inability to afford health insurance is one reason more than 50 million people are uninsured.

Source: Shutterstock (stefanolunardi)

The loss of a job can include loss of insurance as well.

The Role of Actuaries in Underwriting

In the health insurance market, actuaries predict the likelihood of injuries and diseases, like heart disease, stroke, and cancer. In the life insurance market, actuaries predict how long someone may live. Their predictions are based on mortality tables. **Mortality tables** show the rate of deaths by age group. The premiums are set based on the risk the individual or group represents to the insurer. Figure 11-2 shows projections of how long men and women may live from birth, if they reach age 65, and if they reach age 75.

Ratemaking

To arrive at a premium, insurance companies begin with a process called ratemaking. **Ratemaking** is when actuaries determine a premium rate per unit of insurance. For example, a standard unit of fire insurance is $100. So, in ratemaking, the actuary assigns a premium rate per every $100 of fire insurance coverage. The rate the actuary applies to each unit is expected to cover losses and expenses. An actuary's data sources and assumptions are critical in setting a rate that allows the insurance company to remain financially sound. A poorly estimated rate or inappropriately set premium can spell financial disaster for an insurer.

The **pure premium** is the amount of the premium that should cover expected losses. Take a look at fire insurance, for example. As noted, one unit of fire insurance is $100 of coverage. Assume the actuary comes up with a rate of $10 per unit. The insurer multiplies this rate by the number of units a person is purchasing to find the pure premium. How much would the pure premium be for a $1,000 fire insurance policy?

rate × (policy amount ÷ unit size) = pure premium
$10 per unit × ($1,000 ÷ $100 per unit) = $10 per unit × 10 units = $100

Ethical Insurance Practices

Underwriting fraud can carry severe penalties. Take the example of a man who ran a school bus operation in New York City, but registered his buses in Pennsylvania for lower rates. He used an address in Pennsylvania to obtain driver's licenses and to secure registration and insurance for the buses. He stated on his insurance application that the buses would be used for non-commercial purposes and would be used primarily in one county in Pennsylvania. This man was charged with criminal conspiracy, insurance fraud, and other violations. He could serve up to seven years in jail and pay $15,000 in fines.

	Men	Women
At birth	75.4	80.4
At Age 65	82.2	84.9
Age 75	85.6	87.5

Figure 11-2. Life Expectancy in the US by Gender

The pure premium is not what the customer pays. The customer's premium also takes into account the load. The **load** is the expenses the insurer has for creating, selling, and maintaining the policy. Adding the pure premium and the load produces the gross premium. The **gross premium** is the amount of the policyholder's premium.

State regulations require insurance companies to document how they arrived at the rate they use. Further, regulations require insurance companies to set their rates based loosely on four criteria. The rates are required to be:
- reasonable;
- not excessive;
- not inadequate; and
- not unfairly discriminatory.

You will read more about insurance regulations in Chapters 12 and 13.

Accounting for Disasters

The biggest unknown for a property and casualty actuary, and the variable with the largest potential impact, is unexpected catastrophes. In insurance terms, a **catastrophe** is any event that results in $25 million or more in losses involving many policyholders and insurers. For example, Hurricane Katrina was a catastrophe. It tops the list of most insured losses for a hurricane in the US. The 2005 hurricane totaled $47.4 billion in insured losses. Hurricane Irene, in 2011, was also a catastrophe, with estimates of losses topping $20 billion. From 1990–2009, hurricanes in the US caused insurance losses of $152.4 billion. Over the same period, tornadoes in the US caused $97.8 billion in insured losses.

To estimate the cost of future catastrophes, actuaries rely in part on catastrophe modeling. **Catastrophe modeling** seeks to identify the likelihood of a major disaster in a given region and estimate how much loss could occur. Modeling takes a hazard and identifies an insurance company's

Catastrophe modeling helps insurance companies plan losses a natural disaster can cause.

Source: FEMA (Eliud Echevarria)

covered properties in a potentially affected area. This is designed to help the insurer set a premium that is sufficient to cover catastrophic losses.

For example, a model may look at a hurricane in southern Florida. It projects losses to the properties the insurer covers in this area based on vulnerabilities, like what the properties are made of, their age, and height. The model takes into account the coverage the insurance policies provide. It then produces an estimate of the financial impact of a hurricane in that region.

Real World Case

A fierce tornado swept through Joplin, Missouri in May 2011. Jacob's cousins had a home there. The family survived unharmed, but unfortunately more than 100 people died as a result of the storm. His cousins' home was flattened in 200-mile-per-hour winds. Even their trees disappeared. Fortunately, they were able to rebuild because their homeowner's insurance policy covered the damages.

Checkpoint 11.1

1. What is the fee a policyholder pays in return for insurance coverage?
2. What is meant by gross premium?
3. What strategy does the insurance industry use to help project costs that may be associated with huge disasters?
4. When an actuary formulates a rate for a unit of insurance, what is it expected to cover?
5. What actuarial tool helps set life insurance premiums?

Build Your Vocabulary

As you progress through this course, develop a personal glossary of insurance terms. This will help you build your vocabulary and prepare you for a career in insurance. Write out a definition for each of the following terms, and add it to your personal insurance glossary.

premium
underwriter
risk class
preferred risk class
substandard risk class
underwriting policy
group health plan
demographics
individual market
mortality table
ratemaking
pure premium
load
gross premium
catastrophe
catastrophe modeling

Section 11.2
Investments

Terms
investing
float
tail
short-tail insurance
long-tail insurance

Objectives
After completing this section, you will be able to:
- Discuss insurance companies using investments as a source of income.
- Identify how insurance companies use float to generate income.
- Explain the difference between a short-tail and long-tail insurance policy.

Income from Investments

Investing is committing money to something with the expectation of earning money. Insurance companies invest in the stock market, bonds, real estate, cash markets, and other areas. Investments from property and casualty insurers totaled $1.32 trillion in 2010. Life and health insurance companies had $3.2 trillion invested in the same year.

Investing can produce high returns, and it can also produce losses. Bonds are less risky than real estate and stock investments. Because they need to pay future claims, the majority of insurance industry investments are in the bond market. However, insurers lost billions during the global financial crisis that started in 2007. The property and casualty insurance industry, for example, experienced $19.8 billion in investment losses in 2008.

Losses are realized when an investment is sold for less than the purchase price. A loss is unrealized if the investment is worth less than what was originally paid for it, but was not sold. If an insurance company has a bond with an unrealized loss, for instance, it can still realize income from that bond as the bond issuer pays dividends. Those dividends help it pay the claims and expenses it needs to pay claims.

Float

With most types of insurance policies, there is a lag between when premium money comes in and when expenses and claims money goes out. During the lag, insurers can invest a portion of the incoming premiums. Any resulting returns are the insurance company's to keep.

Float is the amount of collected premiums that have not yet been paid out in claims. The more float an insurance company has, the more money it has to invest. Returns on these investments represent a large portion of an insurer's profits.

Careers in Finance
Insurance Services

What Does an Insurance Policy Processing Clerk Do?

Insurance policy processing clerks handle applications and changes to insurance policies. They work directly with policyholders and insurance agents. A **policy processing clerk**:
- reviews new insurance applications and processes them;
- collects initial premium payments;
- verifies policy data, such as age, name, address, and the value of insured property;
- handles client requests to make changes to policies;
- maintains files for policyholders; and
- enters data into computer software programs.

What Is It Like to Be an Insurance Policy Processing Clerk?

Policy processing clerks take in new applications and review them for completeness. They work in offices, communicating with policyholders to answer questions and handle requests. Processing clerks must be personable and highly organized. **Policy processing clerks** need to be comfortable working with computers as well as dealing with customers. In any kind of communication, they must follow accepted guidelines for use of e-mail, social networking, blogs, and texting. Business attire is usually required, but depends on individual office policy. Most **policy processing clerks** receive on-the-job training in the use of computerized databases and word processing software.

What Education and Skills Are Needed to Be an Insurance Policy Processing Clerk?
- a high school diploma, with a two-year degree preferred
- strong communications skills
- solid computer skills
- good time-management skills

Short-Tail and Long-Tail Policies

Tail is the length of time an insurance company has between receiving a premium payment and making a claims payment. For **short-tail insurance,** there is little time between receiving the premium and paying a claim. Automobile insurance generally is short tail. When an insured driver has an accident, the insurance company

Careful investing helps keep insurance companies profitable.

pays out the claim once damages are reported and assessed. This may take only a few weeks. Medical, dental, and short-term disability insurance are also short-tail insurance.

For **long-tail insurance,** there can be a long time between receiving the premium and paying a claim. Take a product like long-term disability insurance, for example. The premium received in a particular year is intended to cover any claims that begin in that year. But some of those claims could last for decades, and the insurer's claim payments would be spread out over that period. During this period, the insurance company invests the money received as premium payments. The money received as returns on the investments is income and is used to help pay the continuing costs of the claim.

Checkpoint 11.2

1. Committing money to something with the expectation of getting more money back in return is called what?
2. In addition to money collected from premiums, how else do insurance companies make money?
3. What is the time between when the premium is received and when a claim is paid?
4. What is the money that insurers may invest that has been collected, but has not yet been paid out in claims?
5. What advantage does a long-tail policy have over a short-tail policy for the insurance company?

Build Your Vocabulary

As you progress through this course, develop a personal glossary of insurance terms. This will help you build your vocabulary and prepare you for a career in insurance. Write out a definition for each of the following terms, and add it to your personal insurance glossary.

investing
float
tail
short-tail insurance
long-tail insurance

Chapter Summary

Section 11.1 Premiums
- Income from premiums must at least equal claims paid to policyholders, but should be greater.
- The underwriter determines whether or not to issue a policy to an applicant and what premium to charge.
- Through ratemaking, actuaries determine a rate per unit of insurance that is applied to how many units of insurance is purchased, and the result is added to the load to determine the policyholder's premium.
- Actuaries use catastrophe modeling to identify the likelihood of a major disaster in a given region and estimate the cost of losses.

Section 11.2 Investments
- Insurance companies use investments in the stock market, bonds, real estate, and cash markets as a source of income.
- The amount of premiums that insurance companies collect that have not been paid out in claims is the float, which is invested to produce income.
- Short-tail insurance has little time between receiving a premium and paying a claim, while long-tail insurance has a long time.

Check Your Insurance IQ
Now that you have finished this chapter, see what you know about insurance by taking the chapter post test.
www.m.g-wlearning.com
www.g-wlearning.com

Review Your Knowledge

On a separate sheet of paper or in a word processing document, match the following terms with the definition that fits best.

A. catastrophe
B. catastrophe modeling
C. float
D. gross premium
E. load
F. long tail
G. mortality table
H. short tail
I. smart systems
J. substandard risk class

1. Insured losses are $25 million or more.
2. Computer applications that underwriters use to analyze risk.
3. Workers' compensation is this type of insurance.
4. The premium amount the policyholder pays.
5. Individuals in this group will pay higher premiums.
6. The time between premium collection and claims payments.
7. The amount added into a premium that accounts for operational expenses.
8. Estimate of how long people will live.
9. An actuary uses this to estimate potential losses from future disasters.
10. An automobile policy is an example of this kind of insurance.

On a separate sheet of paper or in a word processing document, answer each of the following questions.

11. Describe how actuaries use catastrophe modeling.
12. Explain the function investing plays in an insurance company's profitability.
13. What role does the load and the pure premium play in the premium a policyholder pays?
14. Explain the difference between the float and the tail.
15. What effect would being in a preferred risk class have on the premium an individual would pay?

Apply Your Knowledge

16. Do you think premiums or investments produce more income for an insurance company? Explain your answer.
17. What impact do you think the recent economic downturn had on insurance company investments?
18. Do you think it is fair that people with chronic diseases have to pay higher premiums or may be denied health-care coverage altogether? Explain your answer.
19. Do you think the use of smart systems to determine an insurance applicant's premium and rate benefits the insurance carrier or the consumer more? Explain your position.
20. Why do you think the insurance industry sets criteria for an event being designated a catastrophe?

Working in Teams

Working with a classmate, study Figure 11-1 in this chapter. Create a character for each of the four underwriting risk classes described there. One of you can draw the character and the other one can write a paragraph that explains how it matches the class designation. Share the characters you created with the rest of the class.

G-W Learning Mobile Site

Visit the G-W Learning mobile site to complete the chapter pretest and post test, to review the History of Insurance articles, and to practice vocabulary using e-flash cards. If you do not have a smartphone, visit the G-W Learning companion website to access these features.

G-W Learning mobile site: www.m.g-wlearning.com
G-W Learning companion website: www.g-wlearning.com

College and Career Readiness

Common Core

Reading. Read a magazine, newspaper, or online article about a natural disaster that has taken place over the past three years that could be considered a catastrophe. Determine the central ideas and conclusions of the article. Provide a summary of the material that contains all of the most important details.

Writing. Research current trends in the stock market in the US and worldwide. How does stock market performance affect insurance company profits? Write a report that answers this question and describes the trends as well as the outlook for future stock market performance.

Job Interview

Job interviewing is an event you might enter with your organization. By participating in the job interview, you will be able to showcase your presentation skills, communication talents, and ability to actively listen to the questions asked by the interviewers. For this event, you will be expected to write a letter of application, create a résumé, and complete an application. You will also be interviewed by an individual or panel. To prepare for the job interview, do the following.

1. Read the guidelines provided by your organization.
2. Review the interviewing techniques presented in this chapter.
3. Write your letter of application, résumé, and complete the application (if provided for this event).
4. Solicit feedback from your peers, teacher, and parents.
5. Make certain that each piece of communication is complete and free of errors.

In 1945, the McCarran-Ferguson Act was signed into law, giving states the authority to regulate the business of insurance within their respective states.

Source: Shutterstock (mattesimages)

Chapter 12
State Regulation of Insurance

Reading Prep. As you read this chapter, think about what you are learning. Determine the central idea of the chapter. After you finish the chapter, summarize your findings without using prior knowledge of the subject matter.

Insurance plays an important role in the financial security of policyholders. It is important that individuals have faith in the insurance system so they can purchase coverage with confidence. This is primarily why states regulate the insurance industry. Regulations are intended to protect policyholders and to ensure fair pricing. This chapter discusses state regulation of the insurance industry.

Section 12.1
Purpose of State Regulation

Section 12.2
What States Regulate

Section 12.3
State Risk Pools

There is an international trend toward requiring that all businesses carry environmental damage insurance in addition to general liability insurance. Many insurance companies that provide this coverage are actively pursuing standards within various industries, from construction to nuclear power, that would reduce the chance of environmental damage and thus the likelihood of damage claims.

Check Your Insurance IQ

Before you begin this chapter, see what you already know about insurance by taking the chapter pretest.

www.m.g-wlearning.com
www.g-wlearning.com

Section 12.1
Purpose of State Regulation

Terms
McCarran-Ferguson Act
solvency
insolvent
liquidation
National Association of Insurance Commissioners
guaranty funds

Objectives
After completing this section, you will be able to:
- Identify the purpose of state insurance regulation.
- Describe the roles of state governmental bodies in insurance regulation.
- Identify what consumer protections are offered by states.

Why States Regulate the Insurance Industry

States, rather than the federal government, have the authority to regulate insurance. The federal government granted this authority through the McCarran-Ferguson Act. The act, however, includes a condition that the federal government will not regulate insurance as long as the states are doing a good job regulating it.

Many debate the effectiveness of regulations and if they are even needed. Others argue for more regulation or that the federal government should regulate the industry. These debates were especially intense following the Great Recession of 2007–2009. Regardless of the debates, states continue to regulate the industry. These regulations focus on making sure companies are financially strong and protecting consumers from unfair practices.

The decisions of politicians directly influence regulation of insurance and related industries.

Source: FEMA

Roles of State Government Branches

All three branches of state government are involved in the regulation of insurance within a state's borders. States have legislative, judicial, and executive branches. Figure 12-1 identifies the main roles of each branch with respect to the insurance industry.

Legislative Branch

State legislators make the laws by which insurance companies must abide when conducting business in the state. These include rules on establishing an insurance company based within the state. State laws also govern selling insurance by companies not based in the state. The licensing of companies and sales agents also fall under state laws.

State laws establish rules aimed at insuring the solvency of each insurance company in the state. **Solvency** is the ability of the company to pay claims and other debts. These laws attempt to protect customers in the state from situations where a company cannot afford to pay a legitimate claim.

Judicial Branch

The judicial branch is involved in insurance regulation through court cases. These decisions often involve the legal meaning of insurance policy terms. Court cases often result in modifying regulations to make them clearer. Cases also come before the court to determine if insurance laws and the actions of regulators are appropriate under the state's constitution.

Additionally, if a company is found to be insolvent by the state, the state court will order liquidation. **Insolvent** means the company does not have enough cash and assets to pay its claims and debts. **Liquidation** is the process of dividing up the company's assets among parties with a financial interest.

History of Insurance

The US Congress enacted the McCarran-Ferguson Act in 1945. It made the insurance industry largely immune from federal regulation. It is the only law through which Congress explicitly assigns to the states the role of regulating an industry. It is also the only law where Congress explicitly denies regulation of an industry by the federal government.

www.m.g-wlearning.com
www.g-wlearning.com

Branch	Role
Legislative	Creates laws under which insurance companies must operate. Oversees state insurance departments.
Judicial	Regulates the industry through court cases. Clarifies legal meaning of policy terms, determines if laws and regulators' actions are appropriate under the state's constitution.
Executive	Supervises the industry through an insurance commissioner. Seeks to ensure the financial health of the industry for the benefit of policyholders, assists policyholders with complaints, and steps in to help financially troubled insurers to stabilize.

Figure 12-1. Role of State Government in Insurance Industry Regulation

Careers in Finance
Insurance Services

What Does an Insurance Claims Processing Clerk Do?

Insurance claims processing clerks manage incoming claims. They collect information from insured parties and review filed claims for accuracy and completeness. Much of their work involves using a computer and speaking with policyholders and others involved in a claim. A claims processing clerk:
- reviews incoming claims;
- reviews insurance policies to determine coverage;
- contacts policyholders or other parties to track down missing information;
- enters data into computer software programs; and
- sends questionable claims to be investigated.

What Is It Like to Be an Insurance Claims Processing Clerk?

Claims processing clerks need to be comfortable working with computers. With advances in technology, an **insurance claims processing clerk** may work in a traditional office setting, in a call center, or from home. No matter the working environment, **insurance claims processing clerks** will have virtual or actual contact with customers and agents and should at all times conduct themselves in a professional manner. In any kind of communication, the **insurance claims processing clerk** must follow accepted guidelines for use of e-mail, social networking, blogs, and texting. The attire required is dependent on the work setting. Business-casual or professional attire is usually required for those who work in an office or call center.

What Education and Skills Are Needed to Be an Insurance Claims Processing Clerk?

- a high school diploma, with a two-year degree preferred
- strong communications skills
- solid computer skills
- good time management skills

Executive Branch

Each state has a commissioner of insurance in its executive branch. The commissioner supervises the industry and administers insurance laws. The commissioner also deals with consumer complaints.

If an insurance company becomes financially troubled, the state commissioner steps in to help the company stabilize. If it is not possible to fix the company's financial problems, then the commissioner goes to the state courts to request liquidation.

State insurance commissioners coordinate their efforts through the National Association of Insurance Commissioners (NAIC). The purpose of the **National Association of Insurance Commissioners** is to assist state governments with the regulation of the insurance industry. Commissioners meet four times a year and make recommendations for legislation and policy. Acceptance of the recommendations is voluntary, but states commonly agree to them.

State's Role in Consumer Protection

To help compensate policyholders if an insurer goes out of business, states maintain guaranty funds. State insurance departments also work with consumers when they encounter a problem related to their insurance contracts.

State Guaranty Funds

A main focus of state insurance regulation is the financial health of insurers. If a company is no longer able to pay claims, the state steps in. Each state runs a **guaranty fund** to cover a policyholder's losses if the insurance company cannot. Funding comes from insurance companies that do business in the state. Typically, when a company becomes insolvent, the state insurance department assesses each insurer a share of the losses. This means that solvent companies pay into a fund that covers policyholder losses of the insolvent company.

Typically, the fund pays claims after a deductible, but only up to a limit. For example, most states cover life insurance benefits up to $300,000. The maximum amount for property and casualty insurance products varies from state to state. Texas, for example, pays up to $300,000. On the other hand, Tennessee pays up to $150,000.

Consumer Complaints

A major area of focus of state insurance departments is handling consumer complaints. Combined, state insurance departments employ more than 1,600 consumer services personnel. They handle on average 2.3 million inquiries and 370,000 formal complaints each year. While complaints vary across insurance lines of business, the most common are claims-processing delays, claims denials, and unsatisfactory settlements. Most states allow residents to file complaints online or by e-mail.

Source: Shutterstock (Norman Pogson)

State consumer services personnel handle various complaints and inquiries from policyholders.

States use data on complaints to offer company comparisons. For example, the Texas Department of Insurance posts a complaint index by line of insurance for each calendar year. Here, consumers can compare companies by how often the state receives legitimate complaints. The average complaint ratio is 1.0 on the scale used by Texas. Companies with averages below 1.0 have fewer complaints. Companies with averages above 1.0 have more complaints.

In addition, the NAIC collects complaint information from the states. It produces a comparison index using the information states file. The NAIC also runs an online consumer information source portal. Through it, policyholders can file complaints, download financial information about insurance companies, and report suspicions of fraudulent activity.

Most states and the NAIC offer consumer information materials about insurance as well. The NAIC's consumer information portal is Insure U. It maintains a library of consumer guides, posts consumer alerts, and provides tips about insurance needs and decisions.

Checkpoint 12.1

1. What effect does the McCarran-Ferguson Act have on the insurance industry?
2. What is the main purpose of state insurance regulation?
3. What happens if a company is found to be insolvent by the state?
4. How are policyholders protected in the event an insurance carrier cannot pay claims?
5. What is the purpose of the National Association of Insurance Commissioners?

Build Your Vocabulary

As you progress through this course, develop a personal glossary of insurance terms. This will help you build your vocabulary and prepare you for a career in insurance. Write out a definition for each of the following terms, and add it to your personal insurance glossary.

McCarran-Ferguson Act
solvency
insolvent
liquidation
National Association of Insurance Commissioners
guaranty funds

Section 12.2
What States Regulate

Objectives
After completing this section, you will be able to:
- Name two tracking systems states use to monitor insurance company solvency.
- Discuss the focus of state market regulation of insurance companies.
- Identify five ways rate setting may be regulated.

Terms
licensing
capital
surplus
risk-based capital requirements
Insurance Regulatory Information System
Financial Analysis and Solvency Tracking System
financial statement
audit
reserves

Solvency

State regulation of the insurance industry centers primarily on solvency, market regulation, and rate regulation. For state insurance departments, the financial health of insurance companies is a critical area of focus. The goal of solvency regulations is to detect and prevent insolvencies before they happen.

Licensing

Each state has specific financial requirements an insurance company must meet before it can be licensed to do business in the state. In an insurance context, **licensing** is when a state gives permission to engage in a regulated activity. In addition, the state insurance commissioner will judge the competence of a company before issuing a license. If a company fails to comply with state insurance regulations, the state can suspend or revoke its license.

Individual insurance sales agents must also be licensed to sell insurance in each state. Insurance contracts are highly technical and often complex. States require an insurance sales agent to prove an understanding of the products that will be sold. States also want to know the agent understands the laws that govern the sale of insurance. To receive state licensing, an insurance sales agent must study and complete exams for each line of insurance he or she will sell.

Capital Requirements

Most states require insurance companies to have a minimum amount of capital and surplus. **Capital** is cash and assets that are easily sold to produce cash. **Surplus** is excess capital beyond what the company needs to meet its liabilities. In the 1990s, the NAIC developed

Ethical Insurance Practices
The Illinois Department of Insurance partnered with Illinois State University and others to create the Institute for Insurance Ethics in 1997. The expressed mission of the Institute is to "develop programs that will educate members of the insurance and financial services industry, as well as the consuming public about the nature of ethics, social responsibility, and the application of high ethical standards." Most states require insurance agents to take continuing education courses every two years, focusing in part on industry ethics.

risk-based capital requirements (RBC), which most states adopted. **Risk-based capital requirements** represent the minimum amount of capital an insurer should hold, not what it needs to pay all of its obligations. The states monitor these minimum requirements. The insurer or the regulators must take action when a company's capital falls below its RBC minimum.

Financial Reports

States require insurers to submit financial reports four times a year (quarterly) and annually. Insurers also must file these reports with the NAIC. The reports include information on assets, liabilities, income, claims payments, expenses, and investments.

Data from financial reports go into the NAIC's Insurance Regulatory Information System (IRIS). The **Insurance Regulatory Information System** runs financial tests on the data to flag potential problems.

An additional NAIC tool is the Financial Analysis and Solvency Tracking System (FAST). The **Financial Analysis and Solvency Tracking System** helps detect financial distress. The system looks at certain information in a company's financial statement to determine if it needs further review. A **financial statement** is an annual report of a company's financial condition. Companies are identified as routine, priority, or immediate. A second FAST analysis looks at a company's financial statement over five years. Altogether, these data help regulators determine the need and priority of regulatory review.

State Audits

Typically, states conduct audits of insurance companies every three years. An **audit** is an examination of the company's bookkeeping, financial assets, and other aspects of the operation. The state can choose to audit an insurance company anytime the state deems necessary, however. These audits are rigorous. They involve on-site examination of all aspects of the insurer's operations.

Reserves

An insurance company's **reserves** are the money set aside for future claims. States regulate how insurance companies calculate their reserves.

Setting the appropriate amount of reserves is critical. If reserves are set too high, an insurance company may need to raise premiums to bring in enough money to fill the reserves. If the reserves are set too low, the company may not be able to pay all claims.

Investments

Investments are a significant income source for insurance companies. States regulate these investments to limit the risk of financial loss that could cause financial problems. So, each state spells out investment rules for each type of insurance company. The rules differ between states, but generally provide common sense guidance. For example, a state may strictly limit how much an insurer can invest in real estate or rule that insurers cannot invest in insolvent companies. Figure 12-2 identifies the investment holdings of the property and casualty insurance industry as a whole in 2008. Total investments amounted to $1.25 trillion.

Market Regulation

In addition to solvency concerns, states also engage in market regulation of the insurance industry. Market regulation focuses on the fair treatment of policyholders by insurance companies.

Policy Forms

Because insurance contracts are complex, states try to protect consumers from unfair provisions. State regulators also want to be sure insurers do not over-promise coverage because of competitive pressure. So, states regulate what goes into insurance contracts. Typically contracts must include certain provisions. Also, the policy forms need to be filed with the state.

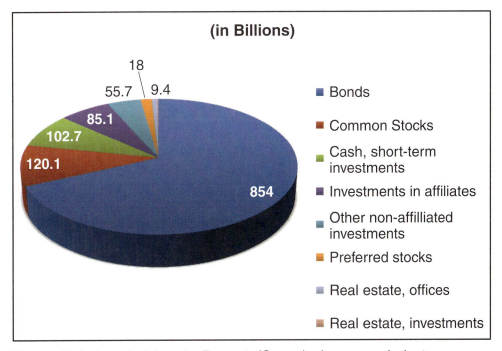

Figure 12-2. Invested Assets, Property/Casualty Insurance Industry

Unfair Practices

Each state has laws that prohibit unfair trade practices. These laws prohibit insurance companies from making false claims in advertisements and from conducting business in any other unfair manner. The laws also prohibit companies from unfairly discriminating in the underwriting process. Unfair-practice laws also seek to encourage insurers to pay legitimate claims in a timely basis.

Rate Regulation

The reason states regulate ratemaking is that the ability of an insurer to pay promised claims directly relates to the rates it charges for its policies. Therefore, the process of setting rates is subject to government regulation. Currently, every state except Illinois regulates ratemaking.

Ratemaking

Recall from Chapter 11 that ratemaking is the process of determining the pricing of insurance products. As Figure 12-3 shows, states require that rates must be adequate, not excessive, and not unfairly discriminatory. Legislation in all regulating states requires ratemaking to follow these principles. Enforcement varies from state to state and from one insurance product to another, however.

Types of Rate Regulation

State regulation of life insurance rates primarily focuses on the ability of insurers to pay claims. Rate regulation for property and casualty insurance tends to go much further. As outlined in Figure 12-4, states take different approaches to regulating changes in property and casualty rates.

Rates must be...

Adequate	Combined with investment returns, rates must be sufficient to cover all losses and expenses.
Not excessive	Rates should result in profits that are not excessive, given the essential nature of insurance to consumers.
Not unfairly discriminatory	An insurer is unable to charge wildly different rates to two policyholders that represent similar risk.

Figure 12-3. Ratemaking Principles

Law	Requirements
Prior Approval	The insurer files the data it used to arrive at a given rate, and the commissioner approves or denies the use.
No Filing	The insurer documents how it arrived at a given rate, but it does not have to file its rationale with the state. The commissioner can request the information.
File-and-Use	Insurers have to file documentation to support their rate changes, but they do not have to wait for approval to use them. The commissioner can subsequently disallow the rate change, however.
Informational Filing	The commissioner does not approve rate changes, but does require filing the changes for informational purposes.
Flex Rating	The state sets a range for insurance rates. As long as rate changes stay within the range, insurance companies do not have to file for state approval. Changes outside of the range require approval.

Figure 12-4. Rate Regulation Approaches

Checkpoint 12.2

1. Cash together with assets that can be readily sold are known as what?
2. What is it called when there is more capital than is needed to pay obligations?
3. What essential company document is examined by insolvency-tracking systems to determine a company's financial health?
4. What is the approach to rate regulation that does not require state approval of rate changes within certain predetermined boundaries?
5. What characterizes an adequate rate?

Build Your Vocabulary

As you progress through this course, develop a personal glossary of insurance terms. This will help you build your vocabulary and prepare you for a career in insurance. Write out a definition for each of the following terms, and add it to your personal insurance glossary.

licensing
capital
surplus
risk-based capital requirements
Insurance Regulatory Information System
Financial Analysis and Solvency Tracking System
audit
reserves

Section 12.3
State Risk Pools

Terms
state risk pool
Preexisting Condition Insurance Plan
preexisting condition
health insurance exchanges

Objectives
After completing this section, you will be able to:
- Identify the reason why states began creating insurance pools.
- Identify what will take the place of state risk pools beginning in 2014.

Purpose of Risk Pools

Millions of Americans lack health-care coverage. Many people are uninsured because they do not have access to group health coverage, and they either cannot afford or do not qualify for individual coverage. State Medicaid programs limit coverage to people with low incomes. Medicare is generally available only to seniors. This leaves many Americans with no access to affordable health insurance coverage.

In response to the crisis of the uninsured, many states run health insurance risk pools. A **state risk pool** is intended to be a way for Americans to access affordable health insurance when it is otherwise unavailable to them. These risk pools typically provide hospital services, nursing home care, and prescription drug coverage. Between 1976 and 2009, 35 states created high-risk pools.

Premiums pay for some of the cost of running state risk pools. The rest of the money comes from various sources, depending on the state. Some states charge health insurers an assessment to help cover costs. Others use income taxes. The federal government provides some money for state risk pools, as well.

Replacing Risk Pools

In 2010, Congress passed the Patient Protection and Affordable Care Act (PPACA). This was a major effort intended to reform the US health system. One provision established the Preexisting Condition Insurance Plan (PCIP). The **Preexisting Condition Insurance Plan** is a health insurance risk pool for people who have been denied coverage because of preexisting medical conditions. A **preexisting condition** is a disease or health condition that exists at the time a person applies for health coverage. The PCIP can be administered either by the individual states or by the federal government.

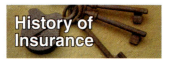

History of Insurance

The first state risk pool was started by Minnesota in 1976. Since then, 34 other states have established their own high-risk pools. While state risk pools represent an important means of obtaining insurance for people who otherwise cannot access it, enrollment is quite low. Minnesota's pool remains the largest, but covers just 1% of its population.

www.m.g-wlearning.com
www.g-wlearning.com

By 2014, PPACA will prohibit health insurance plans from denying coverage to individuals with preexisting conditions. At that time, the PCIP will be replaced by state-run health insurance exchanges. **Health insurance exchanges** will offer private health insurance plan options. States will run the exchanges, which the federal government will fund in part. Alternatively, states can partner with the federal government to establish and run exchanges. The goal is that uninsured individuals will be able to shop for affordable insurance coverage through these exchanges. About half of all states have begun developing these exchanges.

Checkpoint 12.3

1. What purpose do state insurance risk pools serve?
2. Why do millions of Americans lack health insurance?
3. What is a Preexisting Condition Insurance Plan as established by the Patient Protection and Affordable Care Act?
4. What is a health insurance exchange?
5. How can a preexisting condition affect a person's ability to get health insurance?

Build Your Vocabulary

As you progress through this course, develop a personal glossary of insurance terms. This will help you build your vocabulary and prepare you for a career in insurance. Write out a definition for each of the following terms, and add it to your personal insurance glossary.

state risk pool
Preexisting Condition Insurance Plan
preexisting condition
health insurance exchanges

Chapter Summary

Section 12.1: Purpose of State Regulation

- The purpose of state insurance regulation is to ensure companies are financially strong and consumers are protected from unfair practices.
- State legislatures, the judiciary, and executive branch are all involved with insurance regulation.
- The state insurance commissioner supervises and administers state insurance regulation and handles consumer complaints.

Section 12.2: What States Regulate

- Solvency regulation includes establishing capital requirements, licensing companies and agents, overseeing financial reporting, conducting state audits, and regulating reserves and investments.
- Market regulation focuses on the approval of policy forms and the prevention of unfair trade practices.
- Rate regulation seeks to ensure that companies follow ratemaking principles, which require rates to be adequate, not excessive, and not unfairly discriminatory.

Section 12.3: State Risk Pools

- Thirty-five states run health insurance risk pools as a way to make insurance coverage available to people who are otherwise uninsurable.
- Beginning in 2014, states will sponsor health insurance exchanges, intended to provide competitive health insurance options for uninsured Americans.

Check Your Insurance IQ

Now that you have finished this chapter, see what you know about insurance by taking the chapter post test.
www.m.g-wlearning.com
www.g-wlearning.com

Chapter 12 State Regulation of Insurance

Review Your Knowledge

On a separate sheet of paper or in a word processing document, match the following terms with the definition that fits best.

A. audit
B. capital
C. financial statement
D. guaranty funds
E. insolvent
F. liquidation
G. reserves
H. risk-based capital requirements
I. solvency
J. surplus

1. The ability of a company to pay claims and other obligations.
2. Covers losses if the insurance company cannot.
3. Cash and assets easily sold to produce cash.
4. Excess capital.
5. An examination of a company's bookkeeping, financial assets, and other aspects of the operation.
6. The money set aside for future claims.
7. The process of dividing up the company's assets among parties with a financial interest.
8. An annual report of a company's financial condition.
9. Inability of a company to pay claims and other obligations.
10. The minimum amount of capital an insurer should hold.

On a separate sheet of paper or in a word processing document, answer each of the following questions.

11. What are the three principles that guide state regulation?
12. What two tracking systems are used to check for insurance solvency?
13. What effect does the McCarran-Ferguson Act have on the way the insurance industry is regulated?
14. What does the National Association of Insurance Commissioners do?
15. What is the difference between risk-based capital requirements and reserves?

Apply Your Knowledge

16. Do you think it is fair that strong insurance companies have to pay into state guaranty funds when insolvent companies cannot pay their obligations? Why or why not? Explain your answer.
17. What are the pros and cons of leaving insurance regulation in the hands of the individual states? Do you think this is a good system?
18. Why do you think that rate regulation is more stringent for property and casualty insurance than it is for life insurance?
19. A central principle of appropriate ratemaking is that rates should not be unfairly discriminatory. What do you think that means? Give an example of fair discrimination as far as insurance ratemaking is concerned and an example that may be considered unfairly discriminatory.
20. Why do you think that some states have established risk pools and Preexisting Insurance Plans and others have not?

Working in Teams

Together with a partner, create a map that shows which states have high-risk insurance pools. Conduct research to determine the common characteristics of those with risk pools and those without. Present your map and your conclusions to the class.

G-W Learning Mobile Site

Visit the G-W Learning mobile site to complete the chapter pretest and post test, to review the History of Insurance articles, and to practice vocabulary using e-flash cards. If you do not have a smartphone, visit the G-W Learning companion website to access these features.

G-W Learning mobile site: www.m.g-wlearning.com
G-W Learning companion website: www.g-wlearning.com

College and Career Readiness

Common Core

Reading. Read a magazine, newspaper, or online article about the State Children's Health Insurance Program (known as SCHIP or CHIP). As you read, jot down answers to the *who, what, when, why,* and *how* of the article. Determine the central ideas and conclusions. Provide an accurate summary of your reading that is brief, yet complete.

Writing. Research which states have the highest percentage of residents without health insurance coverage. Do these states have state-sponsored high-risk pools? Write a report that spells out your findings and draws well-supported conclusions about the reasons why so many people remain uninsured.

Business Calculations

The business calculations event is an objective test that covers multiple problems related to various business applications. Participants are usually allowed one hour to complete the event. One of the topics that may be included on the test is insurance. To prepare for the business calculations test, complete the following activities.

1. Well in advance of the date of the event, visit the organization's website.
2. Download any posted practice tests.
3. Time yourself taking the tests with the aid of a non-graphing calculator. Check the answers and correct any mistakes you may have made.
4. Review the Math features throughout this book.
5. Visit the organization's website often to make sure information regarding the event has not changed.

Chapter 13
Federal Insurance Industry Regulations

Reading Prep. Before reading this chapter, read the end-of-chapter summary. The summary highlights important information that was presented in the chapter. Compare and contrast what you learned from the summary with what you learned in the chapter.

College and Career Readiness

States are largely responsible for insurance regulation, but the federal government has some authority, particularly in the health insurance arena. Congress has enacted three federal laws that have had a significant impact on the health insurance industry. They are COBRA, HIPAA, and PPACA.

Section 13.1
COBRA

Section 13.2
HIPAA

Section 13.3
PPACA

Go Green

Simple things when widely applied can make a big difference. This is true with the practice in many insurance companies of providing desk-side recycling bins to all those who work at a desk. In some cases, this simple step can reduce by half the quantity of discarded material that is sent to the landfill.

Check Your Insurance IQ

Before you begin this chapter, see what you already know about insurance by taking the chapter pretest.

www.m.g-wlearning.com
www.g-wlearning.com

Section 13.1
COBRA

Terms
COBRA
continuation coverage
private-sector group health plans
public-sector group health plans

Objectives
After completing this section, you will be able to:
- Describe the intent of COBRA with respect to its health insurance provisions.
- List the circumstances under which COBRA applies.
- Name the federal agencies that regulate COBRA coverage.

Overview of COBRA

COBRA stands for the Consolidated Omnibus Budget Reconciliation Act of 1986. A provision of COBRA enables individuals to continue group health benefits in certain circumstances.

You have read about group and individual health plans in earlier chapters. Premiums for group plans are typically lower than for individual plans. Also, people with medical conditions may not be able to get insurance in the individual market. So, when a worker changes jobs, for example, COBRA allows him or her to keep the group coverage from the previous employer for a period of time.

Continued access to health care is especially important for those with chronic diseases who need ongoing treatment.

Source: Shutterstock (Monkey Business Images)

Eligibility

COBRA applies to employers that sponsor a health plan and have 20 or more workers. **Continuation coverage** is an extension of an employee's group coverage after the employee leaves the employer. Covered employers must offer COBRA continuation coverage to participants in these circumstances:
- job loss
- reduction in hours worked, if the reduction means the worker loses health coverage
- transition between jobs, death, divorce, and other life events

COBRA continuation coverage typically lasts for 18 months. In the event of divorce, COBRA coverage can last up to three years.

Most employers pay part of their workers' health insurance premiums. This benefit, however, does not extend to COBRA coverage. A person who opts for COBRA pays the full premium, with administrative expenses added in. The premium may be high, but it is often cheaper than buying individual coverage. Plus, preexisting conditions are not an issue under COBRA, where they might be when purchasing individual coverage.

Ethical Insurance Practices

The vast majority of those working in the insurance industry behave ethically and professionally. Those who breach ethical codes can make the whole industry look bad. Industry professionals who are not susceptible to ethical lapses are those who look beyond their own self-interest and focus on the ethical guidelines established by the industry.

Real World Case

Maria, her mom, and her siblings had health benefits through her dad's job. When Maria's mom and dad divorced, Maria and her siblings remained on her dad's health plan. Her mom was self-employed at the time and qualified for COBRA continuation coverage. Even though Maria's mom had to pay a higher premium, it was worth it, because she was being treated for high blood pressure. She may not have qualified for coverage by an individual plan because of her condition.

COBRA helps those who have lost their jobs continue insurance coverage for a set period of time.

Source: Shutterstock (Denizo71)

Consumer Laws

The newest federal health law, the Patient Protection and Affordable Care Act, eliminates the right of insurers to deny coverage due to preexisting conditions, beginning in 2014. You will read more about this law later in the chapter.

Regulation and Enforcement

Three federal agencies regulate COBRA. The US Treasury Department and the Department of Labor enforce rules related to eligibility, coverage, and premiums for private-sector group health plans. **Private-sector group health plans** are employment-based plans offered by companies in the private sector. The US Department of Health and Human Services is generally responsible for administering COBRA for public-sector group health plans. **Public-sector group health plans** are plans sponsored by federal, state, or local governments.

Checkpoint 13.1

1. How long does COBRA continuation coverage typically last?
2. Under what circumstance can COBRA coverage last up to three years?
3. Who pays the COBRA premium?
4. What advantage does COBRA have for a person with a preexisting condition?
5. In addition to change in employment, what other circumstances make an individual eligible for COBRA?

Build Your Vocabulary

As you progress through this course, develop a personal glossary of insurance terms. This will help you build your vocabulary and prepare you for a career in insurance. Write out a definition for each of the following terms, and add it to your personal insurance glossary.

COBRA
continuation coverage
private-sector group health plans
public-sector group health plans

Section 13.2
HIPAA

Objectives
After completing this section, you will be able to:
- Describe the intent of HIPAA with respect to its health insurance provisions.
- Explain HIPAA's preexisting conditions rule.
- Define reasons for special enrollment under HIPAA.
- Explain the circumstances under which HIPAA guarantees health-insurance coverage.

Terms
HIPAA
significant break in coverage
special enrollment rule
individual health plan rule

Overview

HIPAA stands for the Health Insurance Portability and Accountability Act of 1996. Like COBRA, HIPAA helps people keep their insurance in certain circumstances. HIPAA also contains provisions dealing with electronic medical records and privacy. This section focuses only on Title I, the health insurance portion of the law. HIPAA's major provisions are listed in Figure 13-1.

Source: Shutterstock (iofoto)

Before HIPAA, a preexisting medical condition could mean that a new employee was excluded from the health insurance plan offered by the new employer.

Preexisting conditions	Limits the ability of employer health plans to exclude coverage for preexisting medical conditions.
Special enrollment	Gives individuals more options for enrolling in group health plans when they lose coverage.
Individual access	Guarantees access to individual health insurance for certain individuals.

Figure 13-1. HIPAA Health Insurance Provisions

Preexisting Conditions Rule

Prior to HIPAA, a new employee with a preexisting medical condition could be excluded from employer-offered health insurance. HIPAA limits a plan's ability to deny this coverage. If the health plan covers a particular medical condition, it has to cover a new enrollee with that condition. However, if the new employee had been treated for the condition in the six months before enrolling, the plan can exclude coverage for the condition for up to a year.

Individuals can shorten this period if they had prior health-care coverage. If, for example, a new employee with kidney disease had insurance under the old employer, that coverage counts against the one-year exclusion. So, if coverage under the old plan was for 12 months or longer, the condition is immediately covered under the new plan. However, if the coverage lasted four months under the old plan, for example, then the exclusion period under the new plan would last eight months.

The only catch with the exclusion period for a preexisting condition is if the individual had a significant break in coverage. Under the law, a **significant break in coverage** is 63 days. If a new employee had a significant break in coverage, any prior health coverage will not count toward reducing the exclusion period.

For example, suppose somebody with asthma has worked as a waiter for three years and had health insurance coverage through the restaurant. Then, the restaurant goes out of business, and the person loses health insurance. It takes the person four months to find another job with health insurance, but the plan excluded coverage for the asthma. How long was the exclusion period, given the prior coverage?

History of Insurance

The Employee Retirement Income Security Act (ERISA) is the main federal law that governs the regulation of health insurance plans. It also covers pension plans. ERISA covers health plans that purchase coverage from insurance companies and outlines some state regulatory responsibilities. The federal government has sole responsibility for regulating self-insured plans. These are plans in which the employer assumes the financial risk of offering health-care insurance without involving a health insurer.

www.m.g-wlearning.com
www.g-wlearning.com

Years with health insurance: 3 years
Break in coverage: 123 days
Exclusion period: **12 months**
12 months – 0 months eligible previous coverage = 12 months exclusion period

Since there was a significant break in coverage, the three years of coverage does not count against the exclusion period in the new plan. What if the break in coverage was only one month?

Years with health insurance: 3 years
Break in coverage: 31 days
Exclusion period: **0 months**
12 months − 36 months eligible previous coverage = 0 months exclusion period

The prior coverage fully offsets the 12-month exclusion, because the break in coverage was less than 63 days.

Special Enrollment Rule

Group health insurance plans typically have a specific annual enrollment period. During this time window, employees can sign up for a health plan or change plans if others are available. Typically, employees cannot enroll in the plan outside of this time window.

HIPAA has a **special enrollment rule** that requires a health insurance plan to offer enrollment outside of the annual window in some cases. For one, an employee can enroll if coverage is lost from another source. Say, for example, a family has coverage through the wife's job. If the wife loses the coverage for any reason, the husband can request enrollment in his employer's plan, even if the timing is outside of the annual enrollment period. The request for enrollment must be made within 30 days of losing the other coverage. Other cases where the special enrollment rule applies are marriage, birth, and adoption.

Individual Health Plan Rule

HIPAA has an **individual health plan rule** that guarantees access to health insurance for people who are unable to obtain group coverage. This rule only applies if the individual:
- had coverage for at least 18 months, most recently in a group health plan, without a significant break;
- lost group coverage for reasons other than fraud or unpaid premiums ;
- is not eligible for COBRA coverage, or had COBRA coverage and it ended; or
- is not eligible for coverage under another group health plan, Medicare, or Medicaid and has no other coverage.

Each state has rules concerning whether people can get coverage through a state-run risk pool or if private insurers must offer policies. In Texas, for example, HIPAA-eligible individuals can get coverage through the state's risk pool. On the other hand, in New York, all health insurance companies that sell individual policies must make coverage available to HIPAA-eligible people.

Checkpoint 13.2

1. In addition to helping people maintain insurance coverage, what else does HIPAA seek to do?
2. Under HIPAA, what period of time constitutes a significant break in coverage?
3. What does the special enrollment rule provision of HIPAA do?
4. What HIPAA provision guarantees coverage for an individual who had been covered during the preceding 18 months in a group health plan, but whose circumstances make them no longer eligible for that plan?
5. Who provides the guaranteed health insurance HIPAA promises?

Build Your Vocabulary

As you progress through this course, develop a personal glossary of insurance terms. This will help you build your vocabulary and prepare you for a career in insurance. Write out a definition for each of the following terms, and add it to your personal insurance glossary.

HIPAA
significant break in coverage
special enrollment rule
individual health plan rule

Chapter 13 Federal Insurance Industry Regulations

Section 13.3
PPACA

Objectives

After completing this section, you will be able to:
- Describe the intent of PPACA with respect to health-insurance coverage.
- Identify how PPACA expands health-insurance coverage.
- List changes to health-insurance plans required by PPACA.
- Explain what changes will occur in Medicare under PPACA.

Terms

PPACA
PCIP
uncompensated care
federal poverty level

PPACA Overview

In 2010, Congress passed PPACA. **PPACA** stands for Patient Protection and Affordable Care Act. The law intends to address several problems in our health-care insurance system. While some parts of the law have been put into place, several others will become effective in 2014.

PPACA is a complex law that politicians intensely debated. There are lawmakers who hope to repeal some or all of its provisions. If the law remains intact, it will make significant changes in the availability of health-insurance coverage.

PPACA allows many people in their 20s continuous coverage under their family's health-insurance plans.

Source: Shutterstock (Andresr)

Many of PPACA's provisions will go into effect in 2014 and are discussed later in this chapter. Here are provisions of PPACA that are currently in place.

- Young adults can stay on their parents' health plan until they turn 26. This provision intends to address the high rate of the uninsured among people in their 20s. Federal data show that 30% of this age group was uninsured prior to PPACA.
- PPACA established the Preexisting Condition Insurance Plan (PCIP). **PCIP** is a risk pool that covers people who have been denied insurance due to medical conditions. PCIP is a temporary measure. By 2014, federal law will prohibit insurance plans from excluding coverage for preexisting conditions.
- PPACA prohibits preexisting condition exclusions for children under age 19.
- PPACA provides a special tax credit to small businesses for buying group health insurance.

Expanding Coverage

PPACA will require most of us to buy health insurance. Some exceptions apply, but for the most part, people who do not carry insurance will pay a penalty. One reason for this provision is to cut down on uncompensated-care costs. **Uncompensated care** is health-care services provided to the uninsured. The cost to the federal and state governments for uncompensated-care was $62.1 billion in 2009.

Another way PPACA seeks to expand coverage is by expanding Medicaid. Currently, states have different eligibility rules. PPACA makes the income limit the same across the states, at 138% of the federal poverty level. The **federal poverty level** is a guideline that low-income-assistance programs use to determine benefits based on a family's size and income.

Also, states will set up health insurance exchanges. Individuals and small businesses will be able to shop for coverage through them. Federal subsidies will help low-income individuals pay their premiums.

Finally, employers with more than 50 workers will pay a penalty for not offering a health-insurance plan. The penalty intends to encourage employers to offer coverage.

Health Plan Changes

Beginning in 2014, provisions in PPACA will place certain requirements on health insurance plans. Plans will:
- not be able to place annual or lifetime dollar limits on care;
- cap how much participants have to pay out-of-pocket each year;
- not be able to exclude coverage for preexisting conditions;
- have to cover a minimum set of services; and
- have to cover the full cost of preventive services.

Careers in Finance
Insurance Services

What Does an Insurance Loss Control Representative Do?

Insurance loss control representatives assess risks insurance companies face. They play an important role in helping insurance companies price policies appropriately. They also help clients understand ways to limit their exposure to risk. A loss control representative:
- inspects business operations;
- analyzes historical data on workplace injuries and automobile accidents;
- assesses potential for natural hazards, business practices, and unsafe work conditions that could cause catastrophic loss;
- makes recommendations on ways to mitigate risks; and
- helps underwriters price accounts.

What Is It Like to Work as an Insurance Loss Control Representative?

Insurance loss control representatives serve as inspectors. Their work helps insurance companies significantly reduce the probability of loss. **Insurance loss control representatives** mostly work outside of the office, travelling to locations where losses have occurred or to conduct interviews. Some representatives work from home-based offices. In any kind of communication, the **insurance loss control representative** must follow accepted guidelines for use of e-mail, social networking, blogging, and texting.

What Education and Skills Are Needed to Be an Insurance Loss Control Representative?

- a college degree preferred
- strong interpersonal skills
- excellent time management skills
- solid computer skills

Medicare Changes

Rising costs are having a significant impact on Medicare. Once the PPACA is fully implemented, it is projected to cut about $400 billion in government payments to Medicare.

PPACA cuts costs by constraining annual payment increases to certain Medicare providers. It also raises taxes on high-income earners. Other revenue provisions seek to improve the efficiency and quality of Medicare services.

For beneficiaries, PPACA closes an existing coverage gap for prescriptions. It also ends copayments for some preventive services.

Provisions of PPACA are intended to improve the efficiency and quality of Medicare services.

Source: Shutterstock (AVAVA)

Checkpoint 13.3

1. How does PPACA address preexisting condition exclusions?
2. How long can a child stay on a parent's health-insurance plan because of PPACA?
3. What effect does uncompensated care have on state and federal government expenditures?
4. What effect will uniform income eligibility have on Medicaid?
5. What must a business with more than 50 employees do under PPACA rules?

Build Your Vocabulary

As you progress through this course, develop a personal glossary of insurance terms. This will help you build your vocabulary and prepare you for a career in insurance. Write out a definition for each of the following terms and add it to your personal insurance glossary.

PPACA
PCIP
uncompensated care
federal poverty level

Chapter Summary

Section 13.1 COBRA

- COBRA allows individuals to continue group health insurance coverage in certain situations.
- COBRA applies when job loss, reduction in hours, or a transition between jobs occurs or death, divorce, or other qualifying life event takes place.
- The Departments of the Treasury and Labor regulate COBRA coverage for private-sector health plans, while the Department of Health and Human Services regulates COBRA coverage for public-sector health plans.

Section 13.2 HIPAA

- HIPAA helps individuals keep health-insurance coverage and deals with electronic medical records and privacy.
- HIPAA allows continuing coverage from previous insurance for preexisting conditions, unless there has been a significant break in coverage.
- There are certain special enrollment conditions covered by HIPAA that allow enrollment in a group health insurance plan outside of the normal enrollment window.
- HIPAA guarantees health-insurance coverage for individuals under four specific circumstances.

Section 13.3 PPACA

- PPACA transforms several aspects of health-insurance coverage, from eliminating exclusions for preexisting conditions to extending the age to which young adults can be covered by parents' insurance.
- PPACA expands health-insurance coverage by requiring most people to purchase coverage.
- PPACA requires several changes to health insurance, from removing lifetime dollar limits, to capping the yearly out-of-pocket expenses for policyholders.
- Medicare under PPACA will see a projected $400 billion in cuts.

Check Your Insurance IQ

Now that you have finished this chapter, see what you know about insurance by taking the chapter post test.
www.m.g-wlearning.com
www.g-wlearning.com

Review Your Knowledge

On a separate sheet of paper or in a word processing document, match the following terms with the definition that fits best.

A. continuation coverage
B. federal poverty level
C. HIPAA
D. individual health care plan rule
E. preexisting condition rule
F. private-sector group health plan
G. public-sector group health plan
H. significant break in coverage
I. special enrollment
J. uncompensated care

1. Prevents employer-provided plans from excluding coverage for preexisting conditions.
2. Gives individuals who lose coverage more options for enrolling in group health plans.
3. Guarantees access to individual health insurance for certain individuals.
4. An extension of employer group coverage after the employee leaves a job.
5. Employment-based plans offered by companies in the private sector.
6. Plans sponsored by federal, state, or local governments.
7. Sixty-three days or more without health-care coverage.
8. Health-care services provided without payment.
9. Guideline used to determine benefits based on a family's size and income.
10. Provides a way for individuals with preexisting conditions to continue health-insurance coverage.

On a separate sheet of paper or in a word processing document, answer each of the following questions.

11. Under what circumstances can an individual continue health benefits through COBRA?
12. What are the three major provisions of HIPAA that relate to access to health insurance?
13. Name three requirements of insurers beginning in 2014 under PPACA.
14. What three federal agencies regulate COBRA?
15. What plan benefits children of insured parents up to age 26?

Chapter 13 Federal Insurance Industry Regulations

Apply Your Knowledge

16. If regulation of insurance companies is left to the individual states, why do you think COBRA and HIPAA are regulated by the federal government?
17. After working for two years at a job where you received health-insurance benefits, the company relocates out of state. As a result, you are out of work for six months before finding another job with health-care benefits. How long must you wait until your preexisting asthma condition is covered under your new employer-provided insurance?
18. Create a Venn diagram that compares and contrasts COBRA and HIPAA.
19. At what age do you think children should no longer be carried on their parents' insurance policies? Explain your answer.
20. Look up the Medicaid eligibility criteria for your state. In addition to the federal poverty level, what other factors are taken into account? Why do you think these factors are included?

Working in Teams

Working with a classmate, research health-insurance costs over the past ten years. Create a chart or other visual that depicts your findings. What conclusions can you draw from the data? Present the results of your research to your class.

G-W Learning Mobile Site

Visit the G-W Learning mobile site to complete the chapter pretest and post test, to review the History of Insurance articles, and to practice vocabulary using e-flash cards. If you do not have a smartphone, visit the G-W Learning companion website to access these features.

G-W Learning mobile site: www.m.g-wlearning.com
G-W Learning companion website: www.g-wlearning.com

Common Core

College and Career Readiness

Reading. Read a magazine, newspaper, or online article about access to or the affordability of health care in the US. Determine the central ideas and conclusions of the article. Provide an accurate summary of your reading, making sure to incorporate the *who, what, when, where, why,* and *how* of the issue.

Writing. Conduct research into the Patient Protection and Affordable Care Act. What provisions of the act are the most controversial? Which groups support it and which groups find it objectionable? Write an informative report, giving both sides of the argument. Include your conclusions as well as any effects the act may have on you and your family.

Business Communication

The insurance competitive event may include an objective test that covers multiple topics. One of the topics that may be included is business communication. This portion of the event will likely touch on all aspects of effective writing, speaking, and listening skills as applied to a business environment. To prepare for the business communication portion of the event, complete the following activities.

1. On your own, review the essential principles of business communication, such as grammar, spelling, proofreading, capitalization, and punctuation.

2. Visit the organization's website and look for business communication tests that were used in previous years. Many organizations post these tests for students to use as practice for future competitions. Up to 30% of the questions from tests previously used in competition will be reused. So, this material is an especially important resource.

3. Study all elements of business communication, taking care not to overlook digital communication such as e-mail correspondence and Netiquette.

4. Use the Internet to find additional resources that will help you prepare. Print the information you find for use as study material.

Chapter 14

Legal Principles

 Reading Prep. Before reading this chapter, go to the Review Your Knowledge section at the end of the chapter. This will prepare you for the content that will be presented. Can you determine the relationship between the content and the questions?

College and Career Readiness

The basic legal principles behind insurance contracts offer important protections for the insured and the insurer. Neither party could rely on an insurance contract without these principles in place. This chapter covers the concepts most often cited as the basic legal principles of insurance contracts.

Section 14.1
Utmost Good Faith

Section 14.2
Insurable Interest

Section 14.3
Indemnity and Subrogation

Go Green

Many insurance companies are recognizing the energy savings that can be achieved by moving from desktop computer workstations to laptops. Laptops use significantly less energy, but have the same processing power. By moving from desktops to laptops and other handheld devices, insurance companies are reducing their impact on the environment.

Check Your Insurance IQ

Before you begin this chapter, see what you already know about insurance by taking the chapter pretest.

www.m.g-wlearning.com
www.g-wlearning.com

Section 14.1
Utmost Good Faith

Terms
utmost good faith
material misrepresentation
concealment
warranty

Objectives
After completing this section, you will be able to:
- Explain the concept of utmost good faith.
- Define the three components of utmost good faith.

Principle of Utmost Good Faith

If you make a deal with a friend to help move to a new apartment, your friend expects you to show up. If you never intended to help your friend, you acted in bad faith. Utmost good faith boils down to honesty.

The principle of **utmost good faith** in the insurance industry is that the insurance company and the policyholder are truthful with one another. If an applicant lies about being a smoker, he or she has acted in bad faith. Likewise, if an insurance agent withholds important information about the coverage when selling a policy, he or she has acted in bad faith.

Think of how long it would take to buy an insurance policy if the company had to investigate every statement on every application. Instead, companies investigate claims when a loss occurs. If an applicant lied to obtain an insurance policy, the insurer can deny claims, cancel the policy, or pursue fraud charges through local authorities.

Source: Shutterstock (OtnaYdur)

The principle of utmost good faith is central to the business relationship between the policyholder and the insurance carrier.

Three Components of Utmost Good Faith

A policyholder can run afoul of utmost good faith in one of three ways: material misrepresentation, concealment, and warranty. Figure 14-1 defines these terms, and the next sections discuss the concepts.

Material misrepresentation	False statements made on an insurance application.
Concealment	A failure to disclose certain information.
Warranty	Promise by an applicant to satisfy certain requirements.

Figure 14-1. Components of Utmost Good Faith

Material Misrepresentation

An insurance company can void a policy if any representation on an application is material and the applicant knows it is untrue. This is known as **material misrepresentation**. *Material* means it is relied on by the insurer.

For example, say an applicant for car insurance says the car is parked in a garage at night. The insurer relies on this information to issue the policy, therefore it is material. A lower premium is assigned to the policy to reflect the reported practice of parking off the street overnight. If the insurer later finds out the car is not parked in a garage, it can void the policy. Even worse, it can deny a claim if the car is hit on the street or vandalized.

Concealment

With **concealment,** the applicant withholds certain information from the insurer. For an insurer to deny a claim or void a policy due to concealment, it has to prove two things. First, it must prove that the policyholder knew the fact was important with respect to the policy. Second, it needs to prove that the policyholder intended to deceive the insurance company.

For example, a young person gets hit hard playing soccer and thinks a few ribs are broken. The person does not have health insurance and cannot afford to pay for treatment, so he or she applies for health insurance. If he or she does not disclose the injury, the company can deny the claim for treatment. The act of withholding the health status is concealment.

Ethical Insurance Practices

It is unethical to ignore a situation or condition you should be aware of. A mother, unaware her son received a speeding ticket, who states on an insurance form that her family has been ticket free for more than a year is making a negligent representation. Making a negligent misrepresentation is unethical and can negatively affect your insurance coverage.

Real World Case

When Jacob's Uncle Phil took out a life insurance policy, the agent asked if he was a smoker. His uncle said he was not. Unfortunately, Uncle Phil was in a serious traffic accident not long after taking out the policy and did not survive. When his insurer investigated the claim, it found that Phil was in fact a smoker. Uncle Phil was not honest on his application, so he did not uphold the principal of utmost good faith. The insurer denied the claim based on material misrepresentation. So, Uncle Phil's wife received no life insurance benefit.

Warranty

A **warranty** is a statement or promise a policyholder makes that becomes part of the insurance contract. For example, a policyholder gets a good rate for a homeowner's policy because of an alarm system. Then the homeowner suffers a break-in and the thief takes off with thousands of dollars in electronic equipment. Because the homeownder failed to set the alarm, the insurance company can deny the claim. However, state laws limit the degree to which an insurance company can rely on warranty to deny a claim.

Source: Shutterstock (Greg Epperson)

Someone without insurance who sustains an injury then applies for insurance without disclosing the injury is engaging in concealment.

Checkpoint 14.1

1. What is the principle of mutual trust between the insurer and the policyholder called?
2. List three reasons for an insurer to void a policy.
3. When an insurance sales agent withholds important coverage information from a client, it is an example of what?
4. When a potential policyholder provides information during the insurance application process he or she knows to be untrue, it is an example of what?
5. If you get into an accident while street racing your motorcycle, your insurance company can refuse to pay your claim or even void your policy under what principle?

Build Your Vocabulary

As you progress through this course, develop a personal glossary of insurance terms and add it to your portfolio. This will help you build your vocabulary and prepare you for a career in insurance. Write out a definition for each of the following terms, and add it to your personal insurance glossary.

utmost good faith
material misrepresentation
concealment
warranty

Section 14.2
Insurable Interest

Objectives
After completing this section, you will be able to:
- Explain how insurable interest applies in property insurance.
- Describe how insurable interest applies in life insurance.

Terms
insurable interest
liable

Insurable Interest in Property and Casualty Insurance

Insurable interest is an important principle behind all insurance contracts. **Insurable interest** basically means the policyholder must have a financial interest in what is being insured.

For example, a policyholder can take out a homeowner's policy on his or her own house because damage or loss of the home would have a financial impact on him or her. That same person cannot own a valid homeowner's policy on the neighbor's house. This is because he or she lacks insurable interest. He or she suffers no financial hardship if the neighbor's house burns to the ground.

Ownership shows an obvious insurable interest. For example, a car owner has an auto policy to protect against the financial loss that may come from an accident. The parking garage the car is stored in may also take out a policy on the car. This is because the parking garage owner may be liable for damage to the car while it is in the parking garage. **Liable** means responsible according to law. In both cases, the policyholders show an insurable interest.

These business partners have insurable interest in one another.

Source: Shutterstock (Yuri Arcurs)

It is important to recognize that insurable interest must exist at the time of a loss. Take the example of a parking garage owner. There is no insurable interest if a customer's car is damaged somewhere other than on the property.

Insurable Interest in Life Insurance

With life insurance policies, insurable interest is a bit different. First of all, insurable interest exists if the relationship between the policyholder and the life being insured is one of love and affection. In other words, a financial interest is not necessary. Also, this interest needs to be in place only when the policy is purchased, not at the time of loss. For example, a wife purchases a life insurance policy on her husband, and they later divorce. Years later, the ex-husband dies. The ex-wife collects the policy benefit because she had an insurable interest at the time of the contract's purchase.

Another example of insurable interest in a life insurance policy could be co-owners of a business. Each owner has an insurable interest in the other, which is a financial interest. Therefore, each partner can take out a life insurance policy on the other. Even if the business closes, the policies will still be in effect. This is because they both had an insurable interest when they bought the policies.

The intent of insurance is to compensate an individual for his or her loss, not someone else's loss. Laws to require insurable interest first appeared in the 18th century.

History of Insurance

Before the Life Insurance Act of 1774 in England, people could take out life insurance policies on anyone. After its passage, other governments picked up on it. Now, most states in the US require insurable interest for a policy to be valid.

www.m.g-wlearning.com
www.g-wlearning.com

Checkpoint 14.2

1. What is the concept that a policyholder must have a financial interest in the property being insured known as?
2. In an insurance context, what does *liable* mean?
3. What is the purpose of insurance?
4. Insurable interest in a life insurance context does not require what factor that is required with other kinds of insurance?
5. If an insurable interest exists between a policyholder and a beneficiary at the beginning of the insurance contract, it does what?

Build Your Vocabulary

As you progress through this course, develop a personal glossary of insurance terms and add it to your portfolio. This will help you build your vocabulary and prepare you for a career in insurance. Write out a definition for each of the following terms, and add it to your personal insurance glossary.

insurable interest
liable

Section 14.3
Indemnity and Subrogation

Objectives
After completing this section, you will be able to:
- Explain the purpose behind indemnity.
- Identify three benefits of subrogation.

Terms
indemnity
actual cash value
depreciation
valued policies
valued policy laws
replacement cost insurance
subrogation

Indemnity

The principle of **indemnity** is that a policyholder cannot end up in a better financial position than he or she was before an insured loss occurs. In other words, the existence of an insurance contract should not provide an incentive for the policyholder to destroy property to collect more than what it was worth. Think of it as replacing a piece of a missing puzzle. The insurance company restores the missing piece—it does not pay for a new puzzle.

An insurance company determines what it will pay for a loss based on actual cash value. **Actual cash value** is an item's replacement cost minus its depreciation. **Depreciation** is the loss in value of an item because of age or wear and tear.

Indemnity does not apply to life insurance policies, where the "actual cash value" of a life is not measurable. The payout on a life insurance policy is simply its face value. Three other exceptions to the principle of indemnity are listed in Figure 14-2.

Valued policies came out of ocean marine insurance in the early days of insurance contracts. When a ship was lost at sea, it could be

Exception	Explanation
Valued policies	Insured collects full face value regardless of the actual cash value. Commonly applies to works of art.
Valued policy laws	State requires that face value of the policy must be paid if a total loss is caused by a specified peril, such as a tornado.
Replacement cost insurance	Payment for a loss without allowing for depreciation. The policyholder pays more for this type of coverage.

Figure 14-2. Exceptions to the Principle of Indemnity

months before the amount of loss became known. So underwriters and ship owners came up with an agreed value of the ship and its contents to write the policy. In the event the ship was lost at sea, the insurer would pay the full face value of the policy. Today, valued policies pay out the full face value of the policy, regardless of the actual amount of financial loss.

Valued policy laws exist in about half of the states. Interestingly, they fly in the face of the principle of indemnity. Valued policy laws state that, in the event of a specific occurrence (tornado, lightning, fire, etc.), the insurance company must pay the actual face value of the policy to the insured. For example, a person could insure a house for $200,000, even though it is only worth $100,000. If the property is destroyed in ways specified by the state law, the insurance company has to pay out $200,000. Where the principle of indemnity is to prevent policyholders from profiting through insurance contracts, valued policy laws allow just that.

With **replacement cost insurance,** an insurance company pays the market cost of replacing a given item without accounting for depreciation. The cost to replace a couch that was bought for $1,500 in 2005 might be $1,700 in 2011. If the couch is destroyed in 2011, the insurance company will pay $1,700 to replace it. Replacement cost insurance is common in homeowner's insurance policies.

Subrogation

Suppose a woman is in a traffic accident caused by another driver. The woman suffers damage to her car and ends up in the emergency room for a concussion. The injured woman eventually files a claim with her insurance company, and the company pays it. For the injured woman, this is the end of the story. For the insurance company, the tale continues.

Replacement cost insurance can help homeowners recover some losses in a case of fire and property destruction.

Source: Shutterstock (Candace Schwardron)

Careers in Finance
Insurance Services

What Does a Financial Planner Do?

Financial planners help clients see the big picture when it comes to their personal finances. They can help clients focus on a single financial goal or multiple goals. If they work for a financial services company, they receive a salary. If they are independent, they can either charge a flat fee for their services, work only for commissions, or some combination of the two. A financial planner:
- works with clients to set financial goals;
- examines assets, income, liabilities, taxes, insurance, as well as savings and investments;
- develops a plan and puts it into action; and
- uses networking skills to identify prospective clients.

What Is It Like to Work as a Financial Planner?

A **financial planner** helps clients manage their finances so clients can meet their goals. These may include buying a home, sending kids to college, retirement planning, or other matters. **Financial planners** may work for large financial services companies or they may have their own business.

What Education and Skills Are Needed to Be a Financial Planner?

- minimum of a bachelor's degree in a finance-related area
- excellent interpersonal skills
- solid verbal and written communication skills
- licenses to sell certain products, preferably the Certified Financial Planner (CFP) designation

---

Insurance contracts all work under the principle of **subrogation,** which allows the insurance company, in place of the insured, to claim damages from the person at fault. In the case of the injured woman, subrogation allows her insurance company to go after the negligent driver for reimbursement. The woman gives up her right to recover losses from the other driver. This gets back to the principle of indemnity. The woman cannot profit because of her insurance policy. If she could collect from her insurance company *and* from the driver that caused the accident, she would receive compensation for twice the amount of her loss.

In addition to preventing the insured from collecting twice for the same accident, subrogation makes the person who caused the damage financially responsible for his or her actions. Subrogation also keeps insurance premiums down by allowing insurers to recover claims payments.

Checkpoint 14.3

1. What insurance principle is meant to prevent policyholders from profiting through insurance contracts?
2. Replacement value minus depreciation is known as what?
3. What kind of policy pays out the full face value of the policy?
4. If you purchased a lamp four years ago for $50 and it was destroyed by fire this year, what type of insurance would pay the cost of purchasing a new lamp just like it?
5. What insurance principle allows an insurance company to go after the responsible third party for damages and prohibits the policyholder from getting paid by the insurance company?

Build Your Vocabulary

As you progress through this course, develop a personal glossary of insurance terms and add it to your portfolio. This will help you build your vocabulary and prepare you for a career in insurance. Write out a definition for each of the following terms, and add it to your personal insurance glossary.

indemnity
actual cash value
depreciation
valued policies
valued policy laws
replacement cost insurance
subrogation

Chapter Summary

Section 14.1 Utmost Good Faith

- In the insurance industry, utmost good faith refers to the understanding between the policyholder and the insurer that they will be truthful with each other.
- The three components of utmost good faith are material representation, concealment, and warranty.

Section 14.2 Insurable Interest

- With property insurance, the policyholder must have a financial interest in what is being insured.
- The principle of insurable interest relates to the principle of indemnity in that they are both safeguards against someone benefitting from an insured loss.
- With life insurance, the policyholder need not have a financial interest in the person being insured.
- Spouses, former spouses, and business partners can have an insurable interest in an individual.

Section 14.3 Indemnity and Subrogation

- Indemnity is the idea behind all insurance: that you should be made "whole" after a loss, but should not be in a better position.
- Three benefits of subrogation are that it prevents the insured from collecting twice for the same accident, makes the person who caused the damage financially responsible for his or her actions, and allows insurers to recover claims payments, which keep premiums down.

Check Your Insurance IQ

Now that you have finished this chapter, see what you know about insurance by taking the chapter post test.
www.m.g-wlearning.com
www.g-wlearning.com

Review Your Knowledge

On a separate sheet of paper or in a word processing document, match the following terms with the definition that fits best.

A. material misrepresentation
B. concealment
C. warranty
D. insurable interest
E. liable
F. indemnity
G. actual cash value
H. valued policies
I. replacement cost insurance
J. subrogation

1. Allows the insurance company to claim damages from the person at fault.
2. An item's replacement cost less depreciation.
3. Compensation for a loss.
4. Failure to disclose certain important information.
5. False statement made on an insurance application.
6. Full stated value is paid regardless of the actual cash value.
7. Lawfully accountable.
8. Promise by an applicant to fulfill certain requirements.
9. Pays the market value of replacing a given item.
10. The policyholder must have a financial interest in the item being insured.

On a separate sheet of paper or in a word processing document, answer each of the following questions.

11. Explain the principle of utmost good faith.
12. Explain the idea of insurable interest.
13. Describe what it means for someone to be *liable* for an accident.
14. What insurance principle is meant to prevent policyholders from profiting through insurance contracts?
15. Explain the purpose and advantages of subrogation.

Chapter 14 Legal Principles

Apply Your Knowledge

16. Do you think that a policy should be voided if someone applying for automobile insurance doesn't tell the truth about how many miles he or she drives the car per year? Explain what led you to your opinion.

17. Imagine how things would be different if the principle of insurable risk did not exist. Write a short story or essay that describes what you think it would be like.

18. Give several examples of material misrepresentations that would cause a life insurance policy to be voided.

19. Do you think it is fair that a former spouse or former business partner is considered to have an insurable interest in a policyholder even after the personal or business relationship has ended? Explain why or why not.

20. Search the term "insurance disclaimer" on the Internet. Choose a site and read the material provided. Describe how the information provided in the disclaimer relates to the principle of utmost good faith.

Working in Teams

With a partner, work together to create a four-panel comic strip or storyboard that depicts one of the three components of utmost good faith. Be prepared to share your work with the class.

G-W Learning Mobile Site

Visit the G-W Learning mobile site to complete the chapter pretest and post test, to review the History of Insurance articles, and to practice vocabulary using e-flash cards. If you do not have a smartphone, visit the G-W Learning companion website to access these features.

G-W Learning mobile site: www.m.g-wlearning.com
G-W Learning companion website: www.g-wlearning.com

Common Core

College and Career Readiness

- **Reading.** Read a magazine, newspaper, or online article about a current issue pertaining to insurance. The issue could be availability, cost, coverage, or something similar. Determine the central ideas and conclusions of the article. Provide an accurate summary of your reading, making sure to incorporate the *who, what, when,* and *how* of this situation.

Writing. Conduct research on the McCarran-Ferguson Act of 1945. Write an informative report, consisting of several paragraphs to describe your findings on this legislation and its implications for the insurance industry.

Business Law

Business law is an individual event in which participants take an objective test that covers multiple legal topics. Participants are usually allowed one hour to complete the event. One of the topics that may be included on the test is insurance as a means of risk management. To prepare for the business law event:

1. Well in advance of the date of the event, visit the organization's website.
2. Download any posted practice tests.
3. Time yourself taking the tests. Check the answers and correct any mistakes you may have made.
4. Conduct some research on the Internet regarding the legal topics that will be covered on the test. Print out the information you find to use as study material.
5. Visit the organization's website often to make sure information regarding the event has not changed.

Chapter 15
Ethics and Social Responsibility

 **Reading Prep.** As you read this chapter, make a list of three things you think are important in the content.

College and Career Readiness

The insurance industry plays an important role in society. It distributes risk to shield individuals and businesses from devastating financial losses. The transaction of insurance relies on trust. The industry has several codes of ethics that all share common themes. Their intent is to help insurance professionals make ethical decisions when faced with a dilemma. Insurance fraud costs the industry billions of dollars a year.

Section 15.1
Insurance Industry Ethics

Section 15.2
Insurance Fraud

Section 15.3
Industry's Role in Society

 Insurance companies are establishing green committees in their offices whether at the local or corporate level. Members of different departments meet (online or in person) to brainstorm ways the company can be more environmentally responsible in its daily operations.

Check Your Insurance IQ

Before you begin this chapter, see what you already know about insurance by taking the chapter pretest.

www.m.g-wlearning.com
www.g-wlearning.com

Section 15.1
Insurance Industry Ethics

Terms
ethics
kickback
The Institutes
seven canons of ethics
civil penalty
Interstate Insurance Product Regulation Commission (IIPRC)

Objectives
After completing this section, you will be able to:
- Describe the importance of ethical behavior in the insurance industry.
- Identify market regulation activities that states undertake to ensure ethical treatment of consumers.

Ethical Codes in the Insurance Industry

What stops the auto technician from overcharging a customer to service a car's brakes? What makes the teenager who gets an extra $20 at the checkout return it to the cashier? The answer to both questions is ethics.

Ethics are principles that define behavior as right, good, and proper. Your own ethics are behind the voice in your head that tells you to do the right thing. Ethics involves the ability to gather and question facts, make a value judgment based on those facts, and behave in a fair and just manner. Ethics requires a willingness to overlook our own personal benefit.

Companies and industries commonly develop their own codes of ethics. The insurance industry is a good example. The transaction of insurance relies on the insurer behaving in an ethical manner. It is not hard to see how an unethical insurance sales agent could sell a product a client does not need. The agent might be driven by a desire to earn a higher commission or to meet a sales goal. Likewise, a claims

Honestly and truthfully evaluating an insurance claim is part of the job for claims adjusters.

Source: Shutterstock (Gina Sanders)

adjuster might have a financial incentive to send wrecked cars to a certain repair shop in return for cash. This is known as a **kickback.** Ethics come into play in these situations.

The insurance industry has several membership and educational organizations, many of which have a stated code of ethics. For example, **The Institutes** (www.aicpcu.org) is an educational, nonprofit organization with a focus on property and casualty underwriters. However, it offers courses on ethics that apply to all insurance professionals. Its publication "Ethical Guidelines for Insurance Professionals" defines ethics and its importance to the industry. The guidelines contain ethical-dilemma scenarios. Figure 15-1 shows the Institute's **seven canons of ethics.**

Another example of ethics comes from The American College (www.theamericancollege.edu). It is a nonprofit educational institution for financial-services professionals. Its Center for Ethics in Financial Services seeks to raise awareness of ethics in the industry and raise the level of ethical behavior. The American College has also put forth a professional pledge:

> "In all my professional relationships, I pledge myself to the following rule of ethical conduct: I shall, in light of all conditions surrounding those I serve, which I shall make every conscientious effort to ascertain and understand, render that service which, in the same circumstances, I would apply to myself."

Basically, the pledge is a version of the Golden Rule, "do unto others what you would have them do unto you."

State Regulation of Ethics

Each state regulates the behavior of insurance professionals to some degree. States try to provide guidance in areas where doing the right thing may not be clear-cut. Ethical codes work together with state regulations. What if an insurance agent wants to sell an unnecessary

Ethical Insurance Practices

Would it be okay for an insurance agent to backdate a policy by one day to cover a policyholder's loss? Although you may think it is in the client's best interests, backdating the policy is insurance fraud. The agent could lose his or her license and possibly serve jail time.

Canon	Insurance professionals should …
1.	Endeavor to place the public interest above their own.
2.	Continually seek to maintain and improve their professional knowledge, skills, and confidence.
3.	Obey all laws and regulations and avoid any conduct or activity that would cause unjust harm to others.
4.	Be diligent in the performance of their occupational duties and should continually strive to improve the functioning of the insurance mechanism.
5.	Aspire to raise the professional and ethical standards in the insurance business.
6.	Strive to establish and maintain dignified and honorable relationships with those whom they serve, fellow insurance practitioners, and members of other professions.
7.	Assist in improving the public understanding of insurance and risk management.

Figure 15-1. The Institutes Ethical Guidelines for Insurance Professionals

State regulation encourages insurance agents to be fair and honest.

Source: Shutterstock (Jami Garrison)

policy to a client? It may be technically legal to sell the policy, but is it ethical to do so? Respect for a code of ethics is important to navigate situations like this.

The primary responsibility of state insurance regulators is to protect the interest of insurance consumers. As you read in Chapter 12, state regulations focus on licensing, financial regulation, consumer services, market regulation, and product regulation. The latter two focus on the ethical conduct of insurance professionals.

State Market Regulation

State insurance regulators seek to ensure fair and reasonable prices, products, and trade practices to protect insurance consumers. They periodically conduct examinations. Consumer complaints can also lead to an examination. Examinations may look for unfair practices like:
- overpricing;
- excessive sales pressure;
- inappropriate risk classification;
- failure to pay claims; and
- sale of unsuitable products.

If regulators find violations, the state insurance department recommends actions that will bring the company into compliance with state law. Some violations can result in civil penalties, license suspension, or license revocation. A **civil penalty** is a fine the government imposes to enforce regulations.

State Product Regulation

State regulators protect consumers by reviewing insurance policies to see that they comply with state law, are reasonable and fair, and do not contain major gaps in coverage that might be misunderstood by consumers. As you might imagine, the process of reviewing products

Ethical Insurance Practices

Insurance professionals need a working knowledge of their states' laws and regulations. Failure to understand the laws and regulations is no excuse for not following them.

Chapter 15 Ethics and Social Responsibility

before they are permitted into the market can be cumbersome and lengthy. In 2002, The National Association of Insurance Commissioners (NAIC) formed a commission to streamline product regulation efforts. The Interstate Insurance Product Regulation Commission (IIPRC) was established in 2006 to serve this need.

The **Interstate Insurance Product Regulation Commission (IIPRC)** provides 41 member states with a vehicle to develop uniform national product standards to protect consumers of life insurance, annuities, disability income, and long-term care insurance products. The IIPRC is also a central point for filing and reviewing new products. Many insurers sell the same policy in several states. The commission gives these companies the opportunity to file a new product one time, versus filing with dozens of states.

States can opt out of IIPRC standards. For example, Indiana opted out of the commission's long-term care insurance standards. It is one of four states to join a long-term care insurance partnership pilot program that allows easier access to Medicaid benefits for long-term care policyholders. Since Indiana requires non-partnership policies to be similar to partnership policies, state regulators believed consumers' best interests would be served by retaining review of the policies.

Products in other insurance lines, like automobile, health, and homeowners' policies, are reviewed at the individual state level. These policies are more sensitive to local costs and conditions, so uniform standards would be more challenging.

Checkpoint 15.1

1. What defines ethical behavior?
2. What consequences can result if state insurance regulators find violations?
3. What three features of the insurance business are monitored by each state's market-regulation authority?
4. Professional practice standards that require insurance professionals to behave in a certain way, but do not have the force of law are called what?
5. What part does the Interstate Insurance Product Regulation Commission (IIPRC) play in insurance regulation?

Build Your Vocabulary

As you progress through this course, develop a personal glossary of insurance terms and add it to your portfolio. This will help you build your vocabulary and prepare you for a career in insurance. Write out a definition for each of the following terms, and add it to your personal insurance glossary.

ethics
kickback
The Institutes
seven canons of ethics
civil penalty
Interstate Insurance Product Regulation Commission (IIPRC)

Section 15.2
Insurance Fraud

Terms
fraud
hard fraud
soft fraud
opportunity fraud
external fraud
internal fraud

Objectives
After completing this section, you will be able to:
- Describe the main types of fraud in insurance.
- Provide examples of external fraud.
- Provide examples of internal fraud.

Overview of Insurance Fraud

Unethical behavior can possibly lead to fraud. **Fraud** is when someone uses deception for personal or financial gain. In insurance, an unethical policyholder may lie about the value of household belongings that were destroyed in a fire, for example. Fraud can happen within the industry, too. For example, the insurance adjuster who receives kickbacks for sending policyholders to a certain contractor is committing fraud.

Insurance fraud can be hard or soft. **Hard fraud** is when someone stages an incident to cause a loss the insurance policy covers. Faking a car accident or an in-home burglary to obtain an insurance payment

An example of opportunity fraud is representing that an injury is more serious than it truly is.

Source: Shutterstock (Lisa F. Young)

are examples. **Soft fraud,** also called **opportunity fraud,** is when someone exaggerates a legitimate claim or makes untrue statements on an application for insurance.

It is difficult to put a dollar amount on fraud, primarily because it continually evolves. States have laws to penalize those who commit fraud, whether inside the industry or outside. Every state treats fraud as a crime. Often, insurance crime crosses the line into federal crime, carrying with it long prison sentences.

External Fraud

External fraud occurs when somebody not involved in the insurance industry engages in insurance fraud. Sometimes, unethical people bring attention to themselves in the actions they take. For example, an applicant that provides a post office box as an address or appears overly anxious to get coverage started could be a warning sign to the agent. And, there is the policyholder who files for losses that occur soon after the coverage goes into effect. Or, the one who submits a claim for losses that seem beyond the policyholder's buying capacity.

Fraud occurs more frequently with automobile insurance, workers' compensation, and health insurance. In the automobile insurance industry, applicants may lie about miles driven to get lower rates. Dishonest policyholders have been known to stage car accidents to get the insurance payment. Workers' compensation fraud may involve employers misrepresenting employees' occupations for a lower premium. It may also involve an employee whose compensation claim is false or inflated. With health insurance, fraudulent companies will sell coverage that does not exist.

Real World Case
Police caught a Florida woman selling bogus automobile policies. She made the mistake of selling one of the fake policies to a detective. She went to jail, convicted on 16 felony charges.

History of Insurance
One of the biggest cases of health insurance fraud occurred in 1991. Two brothers set up mobile medical labs in several states to conduct unnecessary tests on unsuspecting patients. In addition, they submitted claims for tests that were not performed. The brothers were arrested and convicted. They admitted to taking more than $1 billion in the fraud.

www.m.g-wlearning.com
www.g-wlearning.com

Internal Fraud

Fraud also occurs from within the industry. This is **internal fraud.** Much of the opportunity to commit internal fraud lies with agents and adjusters.

Internal fraud can include agents not disclosing information related to a false claim by a policyholder. Adjusters have committed fraud by scheming with policyholders to inflate claims for compensation.

Real World Case

A New Jersey insurance company owner and agent sold commercial insurance to nightclubs and bars. His initial scheme was to overcharge for premiums (by as much as 800%). Then, he and a collaborator began selling fake policies. He was eventually caught and sentenced to 40 months in prison and ordered to pay back $618,480.

Checkpoint 15.2

1. What three insurance products are most susceptible to fraud?
2. An agent failing to disclose information related to a policyholder's fraudulent claim is an example of what?
3. When a policyholder tells a "little lie" about how much a neck injury hurts after an accident, it is called what?
4. An employee who hurts his or her back over the weekend helping a friend move, but files a workers' compensation claim that says the injury occurred on the job, has committed what kind of fraud?
5. What two insurance industry professionals have the greatest opportunity to perpetrate a fraud?

Build Your Vocabulary

As you progress through this course, develop a personal glossary of insurance terms and add it to your portfolio. This will help you build your vocabulary and prepare you for a career in insurance. Write out a definition for each of the following terms, and add it to your personal insurance glossary.

fraud
hard fraud
soft fraud
opportunity fraud
external fraud
internal fraud

Section 15.3
Insurance Industry's Role in Society

Objectives
After completing this section, you will be able to:
- Identify benefits of the insurance industry to society.
- Describe the insurance industry's responsibility to society.

Terms
fidelity
impaired insurer

Social and Economic Contributions

The insurance industry provides important benefits to society. Through insurance, a society spreads the cost of losses by paying a known premium. This process reduces uncertainty, allowing people and businesses to spend money on other economic activities. Insurance helps families, communities, and businesses rebuild following disasters.

Think of a society without insurance, where everyone had to save enough to manage every type of loss. Jobs would be hard to come by because the few employers that would exist could not afford more workers. Economic activity would be negligible, with workers unwilling to spend their money. And, to be sure, many people would not have enough savings to cover certain losses. Then imagine the impact on this society's government, trying to provide a safety net against financial ruin for millions of people. The society would grind to a halt. Thank insurance for not having to worry about that scenario.

Capital investment by the insurance industry helps provide money to build schools and other projects that benefit society.

Source: Shutterstock (Monkey Business Images)

The insurance industry is an important source of capital for economies. Investors fuel society by providing money to build companies, roads, and schools, for example. By investing funds that they collect for their products, insurance companies support the health of financial markets. In 2009, the industry held $5 trillion in stocks, bonds, and government securities.

Responsibility to Society

As a society, we hold the insurance industry responsible for acting with integrity, honesty, and fidelity. **Fidelity** is the principle that promises should be kept. We rely on insurers to sell solid protection from potential losses. We look to the industry to responsibly pay claims and treat policyholders respectfully. Importantly, the industry has a responsibility to remain unimpaired. An **impaired insurer** is one that is having significant financial problems, and its ability to pay claims is in question. Society expects each insurer to:
- invest its money wisely;
- be an economic engine for society; and
- be financially capable of paying claims into the future.

Careers in Finance
Insurance Services

What Does an Insurance Marketing Manager Do?

An **insurance marketing manager** uses several tools to promote the company's insurance products to independent agents and consumers. A marketing manager:
- reviews data on industry trends and consumer interests to identify opportunities for new products;
- conducts market research through surveys and focus groups to understand what potential customers are interested in, or on how they may react to a new product;
- is responsible for advertising and promotional efforts, including media outreach; and
- may engage in sales and customer service.

What Is It Like to Be an Insurance Marketing Manager?

Insurance marketing managers spend their time coming up with strategies to sell new and existing products to consumers. In any kind of communication, the insurance marketing manager must follow accepted guidelines for use of e-mail, social networking, blogs, and texting.

What Education and Skills Are Needed to Be an Insurance Marketing Manager?
- an advanced degree in marketing preferred
- strong organizational skills
- good leadership skills
- solid verbal and written communication skills

Checkpoint 15.3

1. What effect does the ability to manage risk through purchasing insurance have on a society?
2. What effect does the capital investment made by insurance companies have on the economy?
3. What principle is required of insurers that addresses their commitment to providing protection against financial loss?
4. What term is used for an insurance carrier that is financially incapable of paying claims in the future?
5. How does society expect insurance companies to invest their money?

Build Your Vocabulary

As you progress through this course, develop a personal glossary of insurance terms and add it to your portfolio. This will help you build your vocabulary and prepare you for a career in insurance. Write out a definition for each of the following terms, and add it to your personal insurance glossary.

fidelity
impaired insurer

Chapter Summary

Section 15.1 Insurance Industry Ethics

- The highest ethical conduct of those working within the insurance industry is essential to safeguard policyholders as well as the industry itself.
- Insurance industry regulators in each state scrutinize the suitability, price, and function of insurance products as well as market practices within the given state.

Section 15.2 Insurance Fraud

- Insurance fraud can be categorized either as hard fraud (such as staging an accident) or soft fraud (when a policyholder suffers an actual loss but exaggerates the extent of the damage).
- External fraud is perpetrated by someone not working within the insurance industry, such as a policyholder, doctor, or auto body shop operator.
- Internal fraud is committed by someone working within the insurance industry, such as an insurance agent who backdates the start of coverage for a customer.

Section 15.3 Industry's Role in Society

- The insurance industry provides many benefits to society, such as spreading the cost of losses, providing the funds to rebuild after disasters, saving people from financial ruin because of an accident, injury, or illness, and investing funds that they collect for their products back into the economy.
- The insurance industry has a responsibility to invest its money wisely, be an economic engine for society, and be financially capable of paying claims into the future.

Check Your Insurance IQ

Now that you have finished this chapter, see what you know about insurance by taking the chapter post test.
www.m.g-wlearning.com
www.g-wlearning.com

Review Your Knowledge

On a separate sheet of paper or in a word processing document, match the following terms with the definition that fits best.

A. civil penalty
B. ethics
C. fidelity
D. fraud
E. hard fraud
F. impaired insurer
G. internal fraud
H. kickback
I. seven canons of ethics
J. soft fraud

1. Principles that define behavior as right, good, and proper.
2. An improper payment to someone in authority to direct business toward the person making the payment.
3. Code of ethics developed by The Institutes.
4. A fine the government imposes to enforce regulations.
5. Use of deception for personal or financial gain.
6. An event manufactured for the purpose of receiving money from an insurance claim.
7. Also known as opportunity fraud.
8. A scheme to defraud an insurer carried out by someone within the industry.
9. The commitment to keep a promise.
10. An insurance carrier in a poor financial condition.

On a separate sheet of paper or in a word processing document, answer each of the following questions.

11. List at least four unfair insurance practices.
12. For what four insurance product lines does the Interstate Insurance Product Regulation Commission (IIPRC) provide national product standards?
13. What four benefits does the insurance industry provide to society?
14. Staging a car accident to get an insurance payment is an example of what?
15. What four characteristics of an insurance product do state regulators typically look for to deem it acceptable for sale?

Apply Your Knowledge

16. What type of fraud do you feel is more serious: external fraud or internal fraud? Explain your answer.
17. If you were your state's insurance commissioner, what kind of measures would you put in place to help prevent insurance fraud?
18. Write a short story that illustrates a day in the life of a person living in a fictional society where there is no insurance.
19. Research on the Internet other professions that have established a code of ethics for their industry. Compare the ones you find with the ones for the insurance industry. What similarities and differences do you find?
20. What do you think the saying, "Just because it's legal doesn't make it right" means? Consider the difference between a law and an ethical standard.

Working in Teams

In a small group or with a partner, share a time when you were confronted with an ethical dilemma—a situation that had the voice in your head nagging at you. Discuss how you each handled the situation and if you did so in an ethical manner. Have a representative of the group report to the whole class the key points of your group's discussion.

G-W Learning Mobile Site

Visit the G-W Learning mobile site to complete the chapter pretest and post test, to review the History of Insurance articles, and to practice vocabulary using e-flash cards. If you do not have a smartphone, visit the G-W Learning companion website to access these features.

G-W Learning mobile site: www.m.g-wlearning.com
G-W Learning companion website: www.g-wlearning.com

Common Core

College and Career Readiness

Reading. Go to the insurance commission website for your state. Review the process for registering a complaint. Create a flowchart that shows the steps in the complaint process.

Writing. Research how much insurance fraud costs the insurance industry and consumers through higher premiums. Write a one-page paper describing your findings and giving suggestions regarding how the incidence or extent of fraud can be reduced.

Proper Attire

Some competitive events for career and technical student organizations (CTSOs) require appropriate business attire from all entrants and those attending the competition. This requirement is in keeping with the mission of CTSOs: to prepare students for professional careers in business. To make certain that the attire you have chosen to wear at the competition is in accordance with event requirements:

1. Visit the organization's website and look up the most current dress code.
2. The dress code requirements are very detailed and gender specific. Some CTSOs may require a chapter blazer be worn when competing.
3. Do a dress rehearsal when practicing for your event. Are you comfortable in the clothes you have chosen? Do you present a professional appearance?
4. In addition to the kinds of clothes you can wear, be sure the clothes are clean and pressed. You do not want to undermine your appearance or event performance with wrinkled clothes that may distract judges.
5. Make sure your hair is neat and worn in a conservative style. If you are a male, you should be clean shaven. Again, you do not want anything about your appearance detracting from your performance.
6. As far in advance of the event as is feasible, share your clothing choice with your organization's sponsor to make sure you are dressed appropriately.

Unit 3 Summative Assessment

On a separate sheet of paper or in a word processing document, use what you have learned in this unit to answer the questions that follow.

True/False Questions

1. *True or False?* The central purpose of state insurance regulation is to make sure companies are financially strong and to protect consumers from unfair practices.
2. *True or False?* The former employer pays the COBRA premium.
3. *True or False?* Insurance companies transfer their risk by purchasing reinsurance.
4. *True or False?* Capital in excess of that needed to pay obligations is called a windfall.
5. *True or False?* Providing information during the insurance application process that an applicant knows to be untrue is an example of breach of warranty.

Multiple Choice Questions

6. What consequences can result if state insurance regulators find violations?
    A. Civil penalties.
    B. License suspension.
    C. License revocation.
    D. All of the above.
7. What principle is based on the idea that the greater the pool of policyholders, the lower the risk is to the insurance company?
    A. Adverse selection.
    B. The law of large numbers.
    C. Speculative risk.
    D. Risk ratio.
8. Which of the following is an example of insurable interest?
    A. An insurance company that issues homeowner's policies.
    B. An insurance company that issues life insurance policies.
    C. A person who would lose out financially if an item was lost or damaged.
    D. A person who previously owned a home or automobile that was insured.
9. What entity supervises and regulates insurers?
    A. The Insurance Services Office.
    B. State insurance departments.
    C. The Medical Information Bureau.
    D. The Department of Health and Human Services.
10. What effect does the McCarran-Ferguson Act have on the insurance industry?
    A. It granted the federal government the right to regulate the insurance industry.
    B. It prohibited the sale of term-life insurance policies.
    C. It was the model for the Patient Protection and Affordable Care Act.
    D. It granted states the authority to regulate the insurance industry.

Unit 4 Careers

Insurance carriers and agencies are the main industry employers. Carriers usually employ 250 or more workers. Agencies tend to be small. They typically employ fewer than 20 workers. Other industry employers provide insurance-related services, such as medical-claims processing. The insurance industry currently employs about 2.2 million workers.

Chapter 16
Roles and Responsibilities

Chapter 17
Benefits of a Career in the Insurance Industry

Chapter 16
Roles and Responsibilities

 **Reading Prep.** As you read this chapter, think about what you are learning. How does this compare and contrast with similar information you have learned in other classes?

The insurance industry offers a wide variety of career opportunities. Administrative roles make up about 42% of insurance industry jobs. The remaining opportunities range from selling insurance to managing the operations of an insurance company, with many points between. About two-thirds of industry jobs are with insurance companies. Analysts expect the industry will continue to create jobs, given the population growth and the insurance needs of the 78-million strong Baby Boom generation.

Section 16.1
Licensing and Professional Designations

Section 16.2
Administrative-Support Occupations

Section 16.3
Management Occupations

Section 16.4
Financial Occupations

Section 16.5
Sales Occupations

Go Green
Those who work in the insurance industry, especially claims adjusters, sales agents, and investigators, often travel by car to different locations as part of their jobs. Many insurance companies have begun to use hybrid and electric vehicles to reduce their carbon footprint and improve overall energy efficiency.

Check Your Insurance IQ

Before you begin this chapter, see what you already know about insurance by taking the chapter pretest.

www.m.g-wlearning.com
www.g-wlearning.com

Section 16.1
Licensing and Professional Designations

Terms
state licensing
continuing education
reciprocity
certification
professional designations
Chartered Property Casualty Underwriter (CPCU)

Objectives
After completing this section, you will be able to:
- Explain why states require licensing for insurance professionals.
- Identify career advantages to pursuing designations or certifications.

Licensing

Some roles in the insurance industry require state licensing. **State licensing** ensures that the professional understands the laws that govern the industry and the expectations of ethical behavior. Individuals who pursue a state license also undergo a criminal background check. Licensing is a way to protect consumers.

Obtaining a license requires coursework and testing. States require separate licensing for life and health and property and casualty insurance. Once an individual receives a license, he or she has to take continuing education classes to maintain it. **Continuing education** classes keep professionals current on the knowledge they need to perform their jobs.

While states have their own licensing rules and procedures, most offer **reciprocity**. This means that one state will honor licensing from other states. For example, say a licensed insurance agent in Texas wants to sell policies in Georgia. Rather than having to take the state exam and undergo continuing education requirements in Georgia, he or she submits a request for a license and the application used in Texas. There may be a fee, but the process relieves the agent from taking continuing education for two different states.

Source: Shutterstock (Yuri Arcurs)

The principle of reciprocity can allow an insurance agent to sell policies in more than one state.

Certification and Professional Designation

For industry professionals to distinguish themselves, they can pursue **certifications** or **professional designations.** These are ways to prove expertise in a given area. To receive a certification or professional designation, the professional must complete coursework and testing. These are offered through industry associations, community colleges, and other schools. It may take several years to complete the coursework and pass the exams.

Extra certification can increase the earning power of insurance professionals. The **Chartered Property Casualty Underwriter (CPCU)** certification is a great example. To receive the CPCU certification, a professional must pass exams for three courses in personal or commercial insurance and one elective course. Insurance professionals with the CPCU designation earn 29% more on average than their colleagues in the same area with the same amount of time in the industry. The designation is not just for underwriters. Property and casualty industry professionals also seek it. The industry estimates that more than 1,100 insurance industry chief executive officers and presidents hold the CPCU designation.

Figure 16-1 lists some other certifications and designations insurance professionals can pursue. There are well over 100 professional designations available.

Ethical Insurance Practices

To obtain a state insurance license, professionals are required to take coursework in ethics. Most certifications and professional designations require ethics coursework, too.

Certification or Designation	Meaning	What It Specifies
AIC	Associate in Claims	Coursework improves technical claims-handling abilities, communication and negotiation skills
ARM	Associate in Risk Management	Coursework provides comprehensive understanding of the risk-management process
ACLA	Automobile Claim Law Associate	Addresses the interaction between the principles of law and the principles of coverage in auto claims
CII	Certification in Insurance	Coursework provides core qualification for insurance staff
CFE	Certified Fraud Examiner	Accrediting process for investigators. Identifies the investigator as having expertise in resolving fraud allegations, gathering evidence, testifying to findings, and more.
MSFS	Master of Science in Financial Services	A degree program focused on advanced financial planning topics emphasizing case studies and client/practitioner issues

Figure 16-1. Select Insurance Industry Professional Certifications and Designations

Professional designations and certifications can increase a person's career potential and earning power.

Source: Shutterstock (Yuri Arcurs)

Checkpoint 16.1

1. Why do states require licensing for some insurance professionals?
2. How might a professional designation or certification help an insurance professional's career?
3. What certification is pursued by property and casualty professionals as well as underwriters?
4. What is the purpose of continuing education classes for a licensed insurance professional?
5. If an insurance adjuster who lives in Florida wants to move to South Carolina to work, what practice allows him or her to continue working without having to start the education and licensing procedure over?

Build Your Vocabulary

As you progress through this course, develop a personal glossary of insurance terms and add it to your portfolio. This will help you build your vocabulary and prepare you for a career in insurance. Write out a definition for each of the following terms, and add it to your personal insurance glossary.

state licensing
continuing education
reciprocity
certification
professional designations
Chartered Property Casualty Underwriter (CPCU)

Section 16.2
Administrative-Support Occupations

Objectives
After completing this section, you will be able to:
- Describe the work involved in a secretarial/administrative assistant career.
- Explain what accounting and auditing clerks do.
- Describe the role of policy- and claims-processing clerks.
- Identify why customer service representatives are often required to be certified.

Terms
secretary
administrative assistant
accounting clerk
auditing clerk
policy-processing clerk
claims-processing clerk
customer service representative

Secretaries and Administrative Assistants

Administrative-support jobs are largely the same across all industries. **Secretaries** and **administrative assistants** perform routine functions like drafting letters, organizing files, and scheduling appointments. The positions require strong computer and communication skills. Most employers require at least a high school diploma, though a two-year degree is typically preferred. Some employers look for candidates with skills in specific types of software, like project management and desktop publishing applications.

Source: Shutterstock (Stephen Coburn)

The duties of an administrative assistant are essential to the operation of many insurance companies.

Accounting and Auditing Clerks

Accounting clerks and **auditing clerks** deal with an insurance company's financial transactions and recordkeeping. They record and calculate data to keep financial records complete and accurate. While an accounting clerk deals with payments and billings, an auditing clerk verifies records posted by other workers.

Accounting and auditing clerks use specialized software, spreadsheets, and databases, so computer skills are a must. At minimum, employers look for a high school diploma. Some may seek candidates with a two-year degree in business or accounting.

Policy- and Claims-Processing Clerks

Processing clerks handle policies or claims, depending on the role. **Policy-processing clerks** take in new applications and review them for completeness. They take calls from policyholders, answering questions or handling requests for policy changes.

Claims-processing clerks, as the name implies, handle claims. They collect information from insured parties and review filed claims for accuracy and completeness.

Policy- and claims-processing clerks need analytical skills to be able to interpret provisions in insurance policies. Their jobs require solid computer skills. Processing clerks need to be detail-oriented and feel comfortable working with numbers. They also need strong communication skills. Candidates need a high school diploma and preferably a two-year degree in business or accounting.

Customer Service Representatives

Customer service representatives do a lot of what processing clerks do, but also provide direct customer contact. They often handle ongoing communication with existing clients. Customer service representatives may even sell new policies to current clients. Figure 16-2 represents an actual advertisement of an insurer seeking a customer service representative.

Many insurance customer service representatives work in call centers that are open around the clock. They need to understand the insurance products the company offers to be able to advise clients. For this reason, many states require customer service representatives to obtain a license.

Help Wanted: Customer Service Representative

Insurance-licensed individual needed for a full-time commercial lines customer service role in a busy property and casualty agency. One year of agency experience preferred. Will train a newly-licensed, entry-level candidate or a qualified candidate with less than one year of agency experience. Must have good computer/data entry skills overall. Ability to quote new business with multiple carriers is a necessity. Familiarity with a broad array of class codes/markets is a plus. Will need to work independently, both with the agency's producers and its carriers. Local resident with territorial familiarity preferred. High school degree minimum.

Figure 16-2. Job Advertisement for a Customer Service Representative

Checkpoint 16.2

1. What two administrative-support roles use their strong computer and communication skills to draft letters, organize files, and schedule appointments as a central part of their jobs?
2. What is the difference between the duties of an accounting clerk and an auditing clerk?
3. What part does a policy-processing clerk typically play in the insurance industry?
4. What can most customer service representatives do that other administrative support personnel cannot?
5. What aspect of many customer service representatives' work environments lead to the need for them to obtain state licenses?

Build Your Vocabulary

As you progress through this course, develop a personal glossary of insurance terms and add it to your portfolio. This will help you build your vocabulary and prepare you for a career in insurance. Write out a definition for each of the following terms, and add it to your personal insurance glossary.

secretary
administrative assistant
accounting clerk
auditing clerk
policy-processing clerk
claims-processing clerk
customer service representative

Section 16.3
Management Occupations

Terms
top executive
succession planning
marketing manager
focus groups
sales manager
leads

Objectives
After completing this section, you will be able to:
- Identify common management careers at the top executive level in the insurance industry.
- Describe the work involved in a marketing manager career.
- Explain the qualifications for a sales manager career.

Top Executives

Management jobs account for about one-third of insurance industry careers. As in other industries, managers may be responsible for supervising employees, overseeing projects, setting budgets, and handling issues as they arise. Managers typically require the same educational background across industries. Employers typically look for at least a four-year degree. A master's degree helps managers move up in the company.

Top executives in insurance, as with any other industry, direct the operations of the organization. The positions have various titles, such as president, executive director, and chief executive officer. Top executives set the direction for the company and oversee its operations.

Top executives often come from internal promotions. They know the business inside and out, are skilled strategic planners, and should have the ability to motivate and lead their employees. They also have to be constantly mindful of filling positions when needed across the organization. The focus is on ensuring that the company is attracting and retaining professionals who have the potential to fill key leadership roles. This is a concept known as **succession planning**.

Marketing Managers

Marketing managers run a company's efforts at promoting existing and new types of insurance products. They develop strategies for selling products to customers. To understand customer interests and needs, marketing managers use market research, like surveys and focus groups. A **focus group** is a gathering of potential customers who participate in a guided discussion about a given product.

Marketing managers analyze trends in the market and keep an eye on the competition. They also engage in advertising and promotion, sales, outreach to the media, and customer service. Most employers look for candidates with an advanced degree in marketing, strong organizational and communication skills, as well as leadership skills.

Sales Managers

Sales managers are responsible for training and overseeing sales agents. They are also charged with identifying and managing sales opportunities, called **leads.** Leads can come through existing clients or prospective customers. Sales managers typically work in the local sales offices of insurance companies or independent agencies.

Employers look for candidates with prior sales experience and licensing. Sales managers need strong communication skills, the ability to manage their time well, and good computer skills.

History of Insurance

Benjamin Franklin founded the first property insurance company in the US in 1752. He and his fellow firefighters opened The Philadelphia Contributionship to help protect property owners from losses due to fires. The full name of this new business was The Philadelphia Contributionship for the Insuring of Houses from Loss by Fire.

www.m.g-wlearning.com
www.g-wlearning.com

Checkpoint 16.3

1. What role do top executives such as presidents, executive directors, and chief executive officers, play in a corporation?
2. How could a company benefit from elevating its existing employees into top executive roles?
3. Attracting and retaining professionals who have the potential to fill key leadership roles is a concept known as what?
4. What is the role of a marketing manager in the insurance industry?
5. Through what means are sales opportunities typically developed?

Build Your Vocabulary

As you progress through this course, develop a personal glossary of insurance terms and add it to your portfolio. This will help you build your vocabulary and prepare you for a career in insurance. Write out a definition for each of the following terms, and add it to your personal insurance glossary.

top executive
succession planning
marketing manager
focus groups
sales manager
leads

Section 16.4
Financial Occupations

Terms
appraiser
claims adjuster
health-claims examiner
life insurance-claims examiner
insurance investigator
loss-control representatives
underwriter
actuary

Objectives
After completing this section, you will be able to:
- List the types of claims-examiner careers.
- Describe the role an investigator performs.
- Explain how a loss-control representative functions in the insurance industry.
- Discuss the requirements for a career as an underwriter.
- Explain the role of actuaries in the insurance industry.

Claims Examiners

The insurance industry has several different roles that involve the examination of claims. While the type of work is similar among them, the focus varies. An appraiser works for automobile insurers. An adjuster works in the property and liability insurance field. Health-claims examiners work in the health insurance industry. Life-claims examiners work strictly in the life insurance industry.

Most states require professionals in these positions to obtain a license. However, some positions can be covered by the insurance company's license, so individual licensing is not needed. This varies by state.

Employers typically prefer candidates who possess a college degree in business, accounting, or engineering. Examiners and adjusters can also pursue special designations and certifications that help further their careers.

Appraisers

Most insurance **appraisers** specialize in estimating the cost to repair damage to automobiles. They work with auto repair shops to negotiate the cost of fixing the vehicle and to schedule the work. An appraiser also works directly with policyholders.

An appraiser can work for one insurance company or with an independent appraisal firm. Either way, they often work from home offices.

Appraisers need a high school diploma, though some college education is preferred. They need good negotiating skills, the ability to use math to solve problems, and good communication skills. Figure 16-3 shows a job advertisement for an appraiser.

> ## Help Wanted: Appraiser
>
> This position is designed to take initial claims electronically, via fax, mail, or phone from our agent, insured, or claimant. The adjuster sets up the claim, investigates the accident or loss, and makes a liability and deductible decision and decision to pay along with applying an appropriate surcharge or subrogation demand.
>
> **Responsibilities:**
> - sets up claims on WMS from information received electronically via fax, mail, or phone call from our agent, insured, or claimant
> - identifies and applies coverages and limits
> - gathers information from witnesses, claimants, and insured in order to establish liability and damages
> - uses various software and databases to adjust claim
> - applies Massachusetts At-Fault Standard to establish liability
> - applies the appropriate surcharge according to the Massachusetts General Law
> - identifies all subrogation opportunities
> - makes liability and deductible decision and decision to pay
> - fosters and maintains relationship with agents through communication and customer service skills
>
> **Qualifications:**
> - college degree preferred
> - superior organization skills and detail orientation required
> - customer service experience required
> - excellent communications skills required
> - bilingual a plus
> - ability to work cooperatively within a team environment

Figure 16-3. Job Advertisement for an Auto Property Claims Appraiser

Claims Adjusters

Claims adjusters work in the property and liability insurance industry. They decide whether customers' policies cover their claims. Some work outside the office inspecting damage claims, while others work in a centralized claims center. A claims adjuster inspects property damage, estimates repair costs, and determines the insurer's financial responsibility. An adjuster typically interviews witnesses, physically inspects damage, undertakes computer research, develops a report, and negotiates a settlement with the claimant. An adjuster should possess strong communication skills, the ability to interview well, and strong computer skills.

Health-Claims Examiner

Health-claims examiners review claims applications for accuracy and completeness and make decisions to approve or deny claims. Their review also includes making sure costs are reasonable based on a given diagnosis. Health-claims examiners use an industry-specific guide that outlines average periods of disability, hospital stays, and treatments based on illness or injury.

A health insurance-claims examiner's job includes interviewing medical specialists, verifying information on claims, referring claims for further research, and authorizing or denying payments for claims. This role requires good communication and computer skills as well as solid analytical skills. Employers prefer college-educated candidates with a medical background.

Life-Claims Examiner

Life insurance-claims examiners review the cause of death in life-insurance claims. They also review life-insurance applications to make sure applicants have no serious illnesses that would put them at high risk to insure.

Life-claims examiners interview medical specialists, consult policy files to verify information reported on a claim, refer claims for further investigation, and authorize or deny payments for claims. The job requires good communication and computer skills and solid analytical skills. Employers prefer college-educated candidates.

Investigators

Insurance investigators are called in when a claim is questionable. They look into possible fraud by researching, interviewing claimants and witnesses, and conducting surveillance. Investigators do a lot of work with lawyers and are often called to testify in court. Insurers tend to hire former law enforcement detectives or private investigators for this role. Sometimes, claims adjusters and examiners can become investigators.

Investigators must have strong interviewing and interpersonal skills and not be afraid of confrontation. A minimum of a two-year degree is typically preferred. Investigators are licensed by the state, but requirements vary.

Loss-Control Representatives

Loss-control representatives are the eyes and ears of the insurance industry. They inspect property and business operations of insurance applicants and assess the likelihood of hazards, accidents, and financial loss. Loss-control representatives analyze historical information on their area of specialty, whether automobiles, workplaces, or construction sites. They often recommend actions to ensure safety and mitigate loss.

Loss-control representatives typically work from a home-based office, but travel from one site to another to inspect and consult. They prepare reports of findings and recommend actions for applicants or policyholders to take. They need technical background in their field, good communication skills, and exceptional writing skills, solid organizational skills, and computer proficiency. Employers typically look for candidates with a bachelor's degree, but some prefer or require a master's degree.

Loss-control representatives can pursue the designation of Certified Safety Professional (CSP). To obtain the CSP, professionals first need a bachelor's degree in any field or an associate's degree in health, safety, or the environment. They also need at least three years of professional safety experience. Then they must pass two rigorous exams. The extra effort is worth it. According to the Board of Certified Safety Professionals, CSPs earn $300,000 more on average over a lifetime than their non-certified colleagues.

Underwriters

Underwriters make decisions on whether or not to issue policies to applicants. They also set insurance premiums. Underwriters are an important link between insurance agents and the insurance company.

To start as an entry-level underwriter, applicants generally need a bachelor's degree, preferably in business or finance. However, since much of an underwriter's work is learned on the job, the area of study is often a lesser consideration. Most underwriters start as trainees, helping collect information on applicants and evaluating applications. Underwriters can earn professional certifications and designations to further their careers. Figure 16-4 lists some of these designations.

Underwriters spend a lot of time on computers, using research tools and special underwriting software programs. So, computer skills are a must. Underwriters also must possess good judgment and be detail-oriented. They work directly with agents and other professionals. They need good communication and interpersonal skills.

Actuaries

An **actuary** analyzes a lot of different information to come up with models that help predict the likelihood of accidents or other causes of loss. Actuaries use a deep understanding of math and statistics to produce their models. Insurers use these data to set insurance premiums. Models also help determine how much income an insurer needs in order to pay expected future claims while earning a profit.

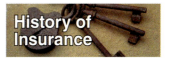

Back in 1688, a man by the name of Edward Lloyd kept a coffeehouse in London where individuals could insure ships and their cargo. These individuals were among the first underwriters in the new insurance industry. This was the start of what later became Lloyd's of London, an insurance marketing association that is well-known today.

www.m.g-wlearning.com
www.g-wlearning.com

Certification or Designation	Meaning	What It Specifies
AU	Associate in Commercial Underwriting	Solid foundation in good underwriting practices.
CLU	Chartered Life Underwriter	In-depth knowledge of insurance needs of individuals, business owners, and professional clients.
CPCU	Chartered Property Casualty Underwriter	Broad understanding of property/casualty industry focusing on legal, financial, and operational aspects of risk management, insurance, and financial services.
RHU	Registered Health Underwriter	Comprehensive understanding of group insurance benefits and health insurance for individuals and families. Helps keep professional current on major benefit laws.

Figure 16-4. Underwriter Certifications and Designations

Employers look for actuaries with degrees in actuarial science, math, or statistics. Alternatively, candidates may have a business-related degree, like finance, business, or economics. For an actuary to achieve full professional status, he or she has to pass a series of national exams. It can take up to 10 years to complete these exams.

About 60% of actuaries work in the insurance industry. Others may work for pension funds or financial-services companies.

Checkpoint 16.4

1. What field(s) does a claims adjuster work in?
2. What type of property do insurance appraisers deal with?
3. What background do employers prefer when hiring investigators?
4. What does a CPCU designation mean for an underwriter?
5. What percentage of actuaries work in the insurance industry?

Build Your Vocabulary

As you progress through this course, develop a personal glossary of insurance terms and add it to your portfolio. This will help you build your vocabulary and prepare you for a career in insurance. Write out a definition for each of the following terms, and add it to your personal insurance glossary.

appraiser
claims adjuster
health-claims examiner
life insurance-claims examiner
insurance investigator
loss-control representatives
underwriter
actuary

Section 16.5
Sales Occupation

Objectives
After completing this section, you will be able to:
- Identify two types of agents.
- Explain how agents earn income.

Terms
independent agent
commission
captive agent
sales agent
producer
multiline agent
sales and revenue goals

Overview

People in the business of selling insurance are called agents and must be licensed by the state. An agent may be an **independent agent** and sell products of one or more insurance carriers. In this case, they work on **commission,** which is a percentage of sales. Agents may also work for a single insurance company and sell only those products. These agents, known as **captive agents,** typically earn a salary and receive a commission.

Agents must take exams to get licensed by the state to sell insurance. States require separate licenses for life and health and property and casualty products.

Sales Agents/Producers

Insurance **sales agents,** also known as **producers,** sell insurance products to consumers and businesses. They may be captive or independent agents selling one line of products, like life insurance, or several types of insurance, like life, health, home, and disability. Agents that sell several product types are called **multiline agents.**

Agents identify their own sales leads and then work with applicants to determine what products may fit their needs. Often, agents will help clients when they have a claim.

Many agents work in small offices with just a few people. Independent agents often spend much of their time traveling to meet with clients and close sales. They make their own work schedule, which often includes evenings and weekends to accommodate a client's availability.

Sales agents have **sales and revenue goals.** These are targets for how many policies the agent wants to sell and how much revenue they seek to generate on those sales. To meet these goals, sales agents maintain relationships with clients they have previously sold to and constantly look for potential new customers.

Because agents work directly with the public, they should possess excellent communication and people skills. Employers prefer to hire candidates with a college degree, usually in business, economics, or finance. Figure 16-5 represents an actual advertisement seeking a sales agent.

Help Wanted: Sales Agent

Established insurance agency is seeking an experienced personal lines agent. The agent's principle responsibilities include processing new and renewal business, quotes, and servicing of clients. Qualified candidate will have property and casualty experience. Ability to multitask, pay close attention to detail, and work with minimal supervision. Professional appearance and demeanor with the ability to interact with clients in a friendly and professional manner. Some college preferred.

Figure 16-5. Advertisement for Sales Agent Position

Checkpoint 16.5

1. What is another way to refer to a sales agent?
2. When sales people are paid a percentage of the sales they close, what is this called?
3. An agent that sells homeowner's insurance and life insurance is what kind of agent?
4. What are sales and revenue goals?
5. What strategies do sales agents employ to help meet sales and revenue goals?

Build Your Vocabulary

As you progress through this course, develop a personal glossary of insurance terms and add it to your portfolio. This will help you build your vocabulary and prepare you for a career in insurance. Write out a definition for each of the following terms, and add it to your personal insurance glossary.

independent agent
commission
captive agent
sales agent
producer
multiline agent
sales and revenue goals

Chapter Summary

Section 16.1 Licensing and Professional Designations
- States require licensing for some insurance industry professionals to assure that they uphold high standards of ethical behavior and expertise within the industry.
- Insurance industry professionals attain professional designations and certifications to distinguish themselves as experts in their respective fields.

Section 16.2 Administrative-Support Occupations
- Secretaries and administrative assistants have strong organizational, computing, and communications skills.
- Accounting and auditing clerks deal with transactions and recordkeeping that affect a company's finances.
- Processing new insurance applications and reviewing them for accuracy and completeness is the role of a policy-processing clerk.
- Customer service representatives in the insurance industry are often called upon to answer specific questions regarding coverage and other features of a product and may sell new policies to existing clients. Consequently, they are often required to hold a state insurance license.

Section 16.3 Management Occupations
- Corporate executives (such as presidents, executive directors, and chief executive officers) set the company's direction and lead overall operations.
- A marketing manager uses market research to create strategies that promote the sale of new and existing products.
- Strong skills in communication, time management, and computers as well as prior sales experience and appropriate licensing are among the qualifications for a sales manager position in an insurance company.

Section 16.4 Financial Occupations
- Adjusters, appraisers, health-claims examiners, and life insurance-claims examiners are types of claims examiner careers.
- Investigators look into questionable claims that may involve fraud.
- A loss-control specialist evaluates the chance of hazards, accidents, and financial loss to property and business operations.
- Individuals with careers in underwriting generally have a bachelor's degree, typically in business or finance.
- Actuaries use data to calculate the appropriate price of an insurance premium that will allow the company to remain profitable.

Section 16.5 Sales Occupations
- Sales agents can specialize in only one product (such as life insurance) or several product types or lines (such as homeowner's, automobile, and life insurance).
- Agents earn money through commissions, a percentage of the sales they make.

Check Your Insurance IQ

Now that you have finished this chapter, see what you know about insurance by taking the chapter post test.
www.m.g-wlearning.com
www.g-wlearning.com

Review Your Knowledge

On a separate sheet of paper or in a word processing document, match the following terms with the definition that fits best.

A. administrative assistant
B. captive agent
C. certification
D. commission
E. focus group
F. independent agent
G. investigator
H. leads
I. reciprocity
J. state licensing

1. Proof that a professional knows industry standards and appropriate ethical conduct.
2. One state honors the license earned in another state.
3. Way to prove expertise in a given area.
4. Drafts letters, organizes files, and schedules appointments.
5. A gathering of potential customers who participate in a guided discussion about a given product.
6. Sales opportunities.
7. Investigates potential fraud.
8. Can sell products from many different companies.
9. Percentage of sales.
10. Sells products from only one company.

On a separate sheet of paper or in a word processing document, answer each of the following questions.

11. What is the difference between a captive agent and an independent agent?
12. What is the difference between licensing and certification?
13. Why are sales agents also called "producers"?
14. Why do marketing professionals conduct focus groups?
15. What does a loss-control specialist do?

Apply Your Knowledge

16. Why do you think that insurance sales agents routinely work nights and weekends?
17. Why do you think that insurance sales agents sometimes help their clients with claims even when a claims processing clerk may be available?
18. Log onto the Bureau of Labor Statistics website (www.bls.gov) and find information regarding the earnings and expected job prospects for one of the careers described in this chapter. After reviewing the information, are you more or less interested in the career? Why or why not?
19. Write a help-wanted ad for one of the careers discussed in this chapter that might be posted on an Internet job-search site. In addition to the job title, be sure to list the skills and qualifications the job requires. Research likely salary ranges to include as well.
20. Create a fictional résumé for someone who wants to get a job in the insurance industry. Develop the résumé to show how the applicant's prior experience, skills, and education match the qualifications for one of the careers discussed in this chapter. Be creative, but use appropriate business-communication conventions in your writing.

G-W Learning Mobile Site

Visit the G-W Learning mobile site to complete the chapter pretest and post test, to review the History of Insurance articles, and to practice vocabulary using e-flash cards. If you do not have a smartphone, visit the G-W Learning companion website to access these features.

G-W Learning mobile site: www.m.g-wlearning.com
G-W Learning companion website: www.g-wlearning.com

Working in Teams

In a small group, devise a survey that contains five questions about a particular product. Administer the survey to your class as though they are a focus group. Summarize the findings.

College and Career Readiness

Common Core

Reading. Go to the US Bureau of Labor Statistics website (www.bls.gov). Type the name of one of the insurance occupations (such as "insurance underwriter") that were discussed in this chapter into the search box. Read about the job outlook for that career. Determine whether this career is predicted to experience growth.

Writing. Use the Bureau of Labor Statistics website to determine what insurance careers will be in the greatest demand by the time you graduate. Write a one-page paper that lists the three careers with the best outlook and the reasons behind this demand.

Leave Nothing to Chance

No matter what competitive events you will participate in for a career and technical student organization (CTSO), you will have to be well-organized and prepared. Of course, you will have studied the content exhaustively before the event, but you also have to prepare by making sure all the tools you need for the event, or for travel to the event, are taken care of. Buttoning down all the details well in advance of an event will decrease stress and leave you free to concentrate on the event itself. To prepare for a competition, create a checklist of things you need to bring to the event.

- Appropriate clothing, which includes shoes and appropriate undergarments. See the Event Prep feature in Chapter 15 for an in-depth discussion of appropriate attire.
- All technological resources, including anything that you might need to prepare or compete. Double-check to make sure that any presentation material that is saved electronically is done so on media that is compatible with the machines that will be available to you at the event.
- Identification and registration materials, including a valid form of identification.
- Study materials, including the flash cards and other materials you have used to study for the event.

Chapter 17

Benefits of a Career in the Insurance Industry

Section 17.1
Industry Outlook

Section 17.2
Insights from the Inside

Reading Prep. After you read this chapter, draw a conclusion and explain the author's purpose in providing the content for this chapter.

You will find solid opportunity in the insurance industry. It continues to create jobs, although at a slower pace since the Great Recession. Especially with large insurance companies, the industry offers good pay and benefits. Most insurers offer training on the job, and many offer internships for college juniors and seniors. Through an internship, you get hands-on experience in the industry and build contacts that will be useful when you enter the job market.

Like most other industries, insurance companies post jobs on their corporate websites and other electronic job boards. The company uses less paper in its recruiting efforts, and job seekers use virtually no paper. In most cases, candidates apply online and upload their résumés or credentials. This also leaves out the postal service, further reducing the environmental impact of transporting the application by truck or plane.

Check Your Insurance IQ

Before you begin this chapter, see what you already know about insurance by taking the chapter pretest.

www.m.g-wlearning.com
www.g-wlearning.com

Section 17.1
Industry Outlook

Terms
median income
independent contractor
financial markets
American Insurance Group (AIG)
Dodd-Frank Wall Street Reform and Consumer Protection Act
Federal Insurance Office
total-account approach
mutual fund
annuity

Objectives
After completing this section, you will be able to:
- Describe typical compensation and benefits offered in the insurance industry.
- Identify ways the insurance industry will grow.

Compensation and Benefits

Careers with large insurance companies generally come with good pay and good employee benefits. Figure 17-1 shows data on the median income for the largest insurance occupations. **Median income** means that one-half of workers earn above the amount, and one-half earns below the amount.

Employees in the insurance industry typically receive the following benefits. However, the specific benefits vary from company to company.
- health-care insurance
- dental insurance
- vision insurance
- retirement-savings plans
- paid vacation
- paid holidays

Many employers in the insurance industry will help employees with the cost of pursuing a degree. They also typically offer on-the-job training. Employees may be eligible to receive financial bonuses to earn certain certifications or designations, too. Certifications and designations go a long way in raising an insurance professional's profile and earning power.

Sales agents often work as independent contractors. An **independent contractor** does not receive a regular paycheck or benefits from the company. Rather, the company and agent agree on cash compensation. The agent then conducts sales activities from his or her own office space and sets his or her own schedule. The company supports the agent through things like sales and product training, business planning, and support setting up an office. The company may recognize high performing agents with certain designations and send them to conferences in desirable locations.

Occupation	Median Annual Wages
Underwriter	$59,290
Claims adjusters, examiners, and investigators	$58,620
First line managers of office workers	$47,460
Sales agents	$46,770
Administrative assistants	$30,830
Accounting and auditing clerks	$34,030
Claims and policy processing clerks	$34,760
Customer service representatives	$35,450

SOURCE: BLS Occupational Employment Statistics.

Figure 17-1. Median Annual Wages for Select Insurance Industry Occupations

Captive agents sell products of one company. These agents typically have an employment relationship with the company; so, they receive benefits and a regular paycheck. They also earn commissions or bonuses based on the type of insurance they sell.

Industry Outlook

The global economy suffered a collapse of financial markets beginning in 2007. The **financial markets** include the stock market and other resources that allow businesses and investors to buy and sell stocks, bonds, commodities (like gold and oil), and other financial instruments. The insurance industry lost billions of dollars in investment income as a result. During the recession that followed, income from insurance premiums also significantly dropped.

By the end of 2010, income from investments and premiums had begun to rise. Nevertheless, the collapse and recession have affected the outlook of the insurance industry. At the same time, the industry's growth into new markets and product lines are positive signs for future job seekers.

Is More Regulation on the Horizon?

Debate continues over regulation of the insurance industry. The main reason for this debate involves a blurring of the lines between insurance, banking, and other financial services. Governments are looking for ways to avoid another global economic crisis. So, regulation focused on the financial-services industry may have consequences for the insurance industry.

Ethical Insurance Practices

Some experts see regulation of the financial-services industry as only part of the solution. Professor Ed Conlon, Associate Dean of the Mendoza College of Business at the University of Notre Dame, points to leadership values. He asks, "Can we influence the values of those who decide, ultimately, to participate in the creation of safe financial products? This, at its heart, requires assuring the persons in these positions have the right set of sustainable values."

Another reason for the likelihood of changes in insurance regulation is the collapse of AIG during the crisis. The **American Insurance Group (AIG)** was a complex financial services company. Its demise related to massive risk-taking by its financial-products division.

In July 2010, Congress passed the **Dodd-Frank Wall Street Reform and Consumer Protection Act.** The law made changes to the regulatory structure overseeing the financial-services industry. The impact on the insurance industry may come in the form of a new federal insurance office the act created. The **Federal Insurance Office** is tasked with monitoring the insurance industry. It is required to study the insurance market and recommend improvements to insurance regulation.

Areas of Growth for the Insurance Industry

As a result of the economic crisis and recession, growth in the insurance industry may be somewhat slow, but job openings should be available. Some of the job openings will come from Baby Boomer retirements and employees who move onto other jobs. Other job openings will be newly created positions as companies expand.

Speaking of Baby Boomers, the oldest of them began turning 65 in 2011 at a rate of 10,000 a day. This will continue until 2020. As they retire, Baby Boomers will begin to shift trillions of dollars in retirement assets. Insurers that offer and effectively promote the right solutions to Baby Boomers should come out on top. In fact, in a survey of top insurance executives, more than half see product innovation as a key driver in future growth.

Insurance companies will also seek to grow by entering global markets, such as China. They will continue expanding into the broader field of financial services, as well. At the same time, banks and investment firms' further expansion into the insurance market increases competition.

Today, many insurance agents take a total account approach to improve their earnings prospects. With a **total-account approach,** agents obtain licenses to sell mutual funds, annuities, and other products to provide a comprehensive service to customers. **Mutual funds** are a pool of stocks, bonds, and other investment instruments. By investing in a mutual fund, investors spread the risk of loss over many instruments instead of relying on the performance of a single stock or bond, for example. **Annuities** generally involve paying a lump sum to an insurer in return for steady payments that last until a person's death or for a set period of time, say 20 years. In this way, an agent can take care of most of a client's financial needs.

Baby Boomers represent the largest US generation ever. The generation began in 1946 when the first babies were born to American servicemen and women returning home after World War II. Baby Boomers will have an impact on the insurance industry just as they affected the demand for consumer products, housing, roads and bridges, energy, and other wants and needs.

www.m.g-wlearning.com
www.g-wlearning.com

Chapter 17 Benefits of a Career in the Insurance Industry

Much of the future growth of the insurance industry will likely come from opening markets in other countries.

Source: Shutterstock (Stuart Jenner)

Checkpoint 17.1

1. What is the term for an agent who deals with only one company's products and receives benefits and a regular paycheck from that company?
2. What impact did the financial markets collapse and recession have on the insurance industry?
3. What areas of growth are expected in the insurance industry over the next decade?
4. What is a mutual fund?
5. What is a total account approach?

Build Your Vocabulary

As you progress through this course, develop a personal glossary of insurance terms and add it to your portfolio. This will help you build your vocabulary and prepare you for a career in insurance. Write out a definition for each of the following terms, and add it to your personal insurance glossary.

median income
independent contractor
financial markets
American Insurance Group (AIG)
Dodd-Frank Wall Street Reform and Consumer Protection Act
Federal Insurance Office
total-account approach
mutual fund
annuity

Section 17.2
Insights from the Inside

Terms

work-life balance
recession-proof

Objectives

After completing this section, you will be able to:
- Describe what insurance professionals say they like about their work.
- Identify qualifications employers in the insurance industry will seek.

From the Source

Throughout this text, you learned about insurance products and how they reduce risk for policyholders. You also learned about how companies make money, how they manage risk, and how they are regulated. You have read about the types of careers the industry offers, and you should have a general idea of compensation and benefits. But, what do people with careers in insurance think about their jobs?

Based on informal surveys and discussions, insurance industry professionals report they are very satisfied with their jobs. They appear satisfied with their pay and the benefits they receive. They feel the industry offers effective training. Many also say their job is very meaningful. Helping people and businesses limit the risk they are exposed to is a source of pride. They also take pride in working for their companies.

Many in the industry feel they have a good work-life balance. **Work-life balance** refers to how easy or difficult it is to work and also have time for personal and family interests. In fact, a lot of people will tell you that a good work-life balance is the best thing about a career in insurance. Other positive qualities employees report are feeling challenged and having the opportunity to grow their careers.

Future

The industry was once considered recession-proof. **Recession-proof** refers to industries that can weather tough economic times with little negative impact. But, even the insurance industry lost tens of thousands of jobs in the Great Recession. The careers hardest hit were agents and claims adjusters. By the end of 2010, though, these jobs started returning.

It is always hard to predict the future, of course. But, signs point to a recovery for the insurance industry and opportunity for future careers in the profession. The industry will be especially welcoming to candidates with the right skills and background, a desire to succeed, and a passion for helping protect people and businesses from the biggest financial risks they face.

Checkpoint 17.2

1. What things do people who work in the insurance industry say about their careers?
2. What is work-life balance?
3. What insurance careers were hardest hit by the financial collapse and recession?
4. What is the outlook for the insurance industry?
5. What qualities must a person possess to succeed in the insurance industry in the future?

Build Your Vocabulary

As you progress through this course, develop a personal glossary of insurance terms and add it to your portfolio. This will help you build your vocabulary and prepare you for a career in insurance. Write out a definition for each of the following terms, and add it to your personal insurance glossary.

work-life balance
recession-proof

Chapter Summary

Section 17.1 Industry Outlook

- Median salaries for those in the insurance industry are between $32,000 and $57,000 per year with benefits that typically include medical, dental, and vision insurance as well as paid holidays and vacation time.
- In the future, the insurance industry will likely grow through the development and sale of new products and by entering new markets.

Section 17.2 Insights from the Inside

- Insurance professionals report that they like their work and that a career in insurance allows for a good work-life balance.
- Employers in the insurance industry are looking for candidates with the proper skills, experience, desire, and a passion for helping people.

Check Your Insurance IQ

Now that you have finished this chapter, see what you know about insurance by taking the chapter post test.
www.m.g-wlearning.com
www.g-wlearning.com

Review Your Knowledge

On a separate sheet of paper or in a word processing document, match the following terms with the definition that fits best.

A. annuity
B. Dodd-Frank Wall Street Reform and Consumer Protection Act
C. Federal Insurance Office
D. financial markets
E. independent contractor
F. median income
G. mutual fund
H. recession-proof
I. total-account approach
J. work-life balance

1. Conducts sales activities from his or her own office space.
2. Where stocks, bonds, commodities, and other financial instruments are bought and sold.
3. Changed the regulatory structure of the financial services industry.
4. Established to monitor the insurance industry and recommend changes to the regulatory system.
5. Agents sell mutual funds, annuities, and other products to provide a comprehensive service to customers.
6. A pool of stocks, bonds, and other financial instruments.
7. Payment of a lump sum to an insurer in return for steady payments over time.
8. Having a career while having time for family and other personal interests.
9. The ability to withstand tough economic times with little negative impact.
10. One-half of workers earn above the amount, and one-half earns below the amount.

On a separate sheet of paper or in a word processing document, answer each of the following questions.

11. What is the overall job outlook for the insurance industry?
12. List six benefits employees in the insurance industry typically receive.
13. What is the relative benefit of investing in a mutual fund over investing in an individual stock?
14. What insurance industry occupation listed in Figure 17-1 has the highest median income?
15. What new office was created by the Dodd-Frank Wall Street Reform and Consumer Protection Act?

Chapter 17 Benefits of a Career in the Insurance Industry

Apply Your Knowledge

16. If you were an insurance agent, would you prefer to be a captive agent or an independent contractor? Explain how the characteristics of the position you chose is aligned with your personality and the way you work best.
17. From what you know about the insurance occupations listed in Figure 17-1, what explains the difference in median income among the professions?
18. Log onto the Securities and Exchange Commission (www.sec.gov) website to read more about the Dodd-Frank Wall Street Reform and Consumer Protection Act. What type of protection or regulation does the act provide that has the potential to affect you or someone close to you?
19. Think of any industry or business that is truly recession-proof. If you are unaware of one that actually exists, invent one. What are the characteristics of the business that make it able to withstand economic pressure when others cannot?
20. How important is a work-life balance to you when choosing a career? Explain your answer.

G-W Learning Mobile Site

Visit the G-W Learning mobile site to complete the chapter pretest and post test, to review the History of Insurance articles, and to practice vocabulary using e-flash cards. If you do not have a smartphone, visit the G-W Learning companion website to access these features.

G-W Learning mobile site: www.m.g-wlearning.com
G-W Learning companion website: www.g-wlearning.com

Working in Teams

Working in teams of two, role-play a job interview for a career in the insurance industry. One person plays the role of the hiring associate. The other plays the candidate for the position. The hiring associate should prepare at least ten key questions to ask the candidate. The candidate should prepare for the interview by researching the specific skills and experience the position demands. Consider video-recording the interview so you can each conduct a self-evaluation.

Common Core

College and Career Readiness

Reading. Go to an online job-search site. Search for a job in insurance. Choose two job postings and read each posting carefully. Create a Venn diagram that shows the unique qualifications for each job and the common qualifications.

Writing. Interview someone who has a job in the insurance industry. Ask them what they like best about their job and what they like least as well as several other questions of your own. Write a one-page paper describing what you learned from the interview and whether it affected your desire to have a career in insurance.

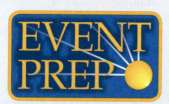

Day of the Event

You have practiced all year for this competition, and now you are ready. Whether it is for an objective test, written test, report, or presentation, you have done your homework and are ready to shine. To prepare for the day of the event, complete the following activities.

1. At least two weeks before you go to the competition, create a checklist of what you need for the event. Include every detail down to a pencil or pen. Then use this checklist before you go into the presentation so that you don't forget anything.

2. If you are making a presentation before a panel of judges, practice what you are going to say when you are called on. State your name, your school, and any other information that has been requested. Be confident, smile, and make eye contact with the judges.

3. When the event is finished, thank the judges for their time.

4. Be sure to get plenty of sleep the night before the event so that you are rested and ready to go.

Unit 4 Summative Assessment

On a separate sheet of paper or in a word processing document, use what you have learned in this unit to answer the questions that follow.

True/False Questions

1. *True or False?* Reciprocity is a strategy for attracting and retaining professionals who have the potential to fill key leadership roles.
2. *True or False?* A claims adjuster works with property and liability claims.
3. *True or False?* A mutual fund provides a place for individuals with preexisting conditions to pool their resources to purchase affordable health insurance.
4. *True or False?* Most of the people who work in the insurance industry report being dissatisfied with their careers.
5. *True or False?* Commissions are paid to sales agents based on the sales they make.

Multiple Choice Questions

6. How might a professional designation or certification help an insurance professional's career?
   A. Increased salary potential relative to others who do not have it.
   B. Decreased likelihood that the professional will commit an ethical violation.
   C. Without it a license cannot be obtained.
   D. Automatically increases the percentage paid in commission.
7. What certification is pursued by property and casualty professionals as well as underwriters?
   A. A Master in Business Administration (MBA).
   B. A Master of Science in Financial Services (MSFS).
   C. The Chartered Property Casualty Underwriter (CPCU) certification.
   D. The Associate of Risk Management (ARM) certification.
8. Why do states require licensing for insurance professionals?
   A. To transfer risk to federal agencies.
   B. To avoid lawsuits.
   C. So that insurance professionals can distinguish themselves as experts within the industry.
   D. To ensure that insurance laws and ethical standards are understood and followed.
9. How is the insurance industry expected to grow over the next decade?
   A. By expanding into global markets and into the broader financial services market.
   B. By reducing payouts of valid claims.
   C. By increasing investment in capital markets and real estate.
   D. All of the above.
10. What can most customer service representatives do that other administrative-support personnel cannot?
    A. Revoke policies.
    B. Authorize claims payments.
    C. Set premium rates.
    D. Sell new policies to current clients.

Glossary

401(k) plan: An employer-sponsored retirement plan in which workers contribute part of their monthly earnings to an investment account. Employers typically contribute, too.

A

accounting clerk: An administrative-support position that deals with payments and billings.

actual cash value: An item's replacement cost minus its depreciation.

actuary: A person who uses statistics, math, computer science, and finance to determine risk for insurance companies.

adjuster: In the property and liability insurance industry, a professional who inspects property damage, estimates repair costs, and determines the insurer's financial responsibility.

administrative assistant: An administrative-support position that involves performing routine functions like drafting letters, organizing files, and scheduling appointments.

adverse selection: A situation in which those purchasing insurance represent a greater risk than the population as a whole.

AIG (American Insurance Group): A complex financial services company that collapsed due to massive risk-taking by its financial products division.

aircraft liability insurance: Protects the insured if an accident causes injury or death to passengers or others.

all-risk policy: A type of insurance contract that list perils it will not cover.

annuity: Payment of a lump sum to an insurer in return for steady payments over time.

appraiser: In the insurance industry, a professional who specializes in estimating the cost to repair damaged automobiles.

arbitration: The process of bringing the dispute in front of a professional mediator.

assets: Things that can be sold to produce income.

audit: An examination of the company's bookkeeping, financial assets, and other aspects of its operation.

auditing clerk: An administrative-support position that deals with verifying records posted by other workers.

automobile insurance: Coverage for passenger vehicles and protects the beneficiary against the financial aspects of a traffic accident.

aviation hull insurance: Covers the aircraft and all parts permanently attached to it.

aviation insurance: Protects against financial loss involving aircraft.

B

bodily injury liability insurance: A type of automobile insurance that protects the person who causes an accident against financial claims.

bond: A loan to a company or government entity that earns interest for the investor.

BOP (business owner's policy insurance): A policy that provides low-cost property and liability coverage to small businesses.

C

California Earthquake Authority: A privately funded, publicly managed organization through which homeowners in the state can purchase earthquake insurance.

capital: Cash and assets that are easily sold to produce cash.

captive agent: An insurance sales agent who works for only one insurance company and typically earns a salary and receives a commission.

cargo war risk policy: Coverage for cargo from the perils of war.

cash value: An item's current value.

cash value component: The savings-account portion of a permanent life policy.

catastrophe: Any event that results in $25 million or more in losses involving many policyholders and insurers.

catastrophe modeling: A process that seeks to identify the likelihood of a major disaster in a given region and estimate how much loss could occur.

Centers for Medicare and Medicaid Services: A federal agency that administers the Medicare and Medicaid programs for the federal government.

certification: A way for a professional to prove expertise in a given area.

Chartered Property Casualty Underwriter (CPCU): Sought by property and casualty professionals and underwriters to distinguish themselves in their professions.

chronic disease: A health condition that lasts for a long time or recurs.

civil penalty: A fine the government imposes to enforce regulations.

claim: The process of documenting the loss against an insurance policy.

claims-processing clerk: An administrative-support position that involves handling claims, including collecting information from insured parties and reviewing filed claims for accuracy and completeness.

COBRA (Consolidated Omnibus Budget Reconciliation Act): A federal law that includes a provision to extend health-plan coverage in certain circumstances.

collision coverage: Pays for the damage to a policyholder's car as the result of the collision.

commercial general liability insurance (CGL): Insurance that covers bodily injury and property damage.

commercial package policy insurance: The combination of two or more insurance products into one policy.

commercial property insurance: Insurance that pays for physical damage or loss of certain kinds of property.

commission: Compensation that is based on a percentage of sales.

complaint ratio: A number that represents the rate of complaints an insurance company receives.

comprehensive coverage: Automotive insurance that pays for damages to a car that result from causes other than collisions.

concealment: Applies to an applicant withholding certain information from an insurer.

conditions: A section of an insurance agreement that describes the responsibilities the policyholder has when a loss occurs.

consumer-driven health plan: Insurance plan with a high annual deductible.

continuation coverage: An extension under certain circumstances of an employee's group coverage after the employee leaves the employer.

continuing education: Classes and workshops that keep professionals current on the knowledge they need to perform their jobs.

copayment: Also called a copay, a small fee to help the insurer defer some of the cost of health services.

cost-of-living adjustments: A change in benefit payments corresponding to the change in the cost of living.

credit report: A collection of data pertaining to an individual's credit and payment history.

credit score: A numerical value that reflects a person's credit history.

custodial care: Nursing home care or in-home care for people who need help with activities like bathing and dressing.

customer service: The manner in which a company engages with its customers.

customer service representative: An administrative support position that provides direct customer contact, ongoing communication with existing clients, and selling new policies to current clients under certain circumstances.

D

damages: Financial compensation awarded to the plaintiff (patient) in a medical malpractice case.

declarations: The section of an insurance agreement that lists a policy number, the name of the policyholder, and the insurance carrier.

deductible: The expense for a claim paid by a policyholder.

defensive medicine: To protect themselves from lawsuits, some doctors order more tests and procedures than patients really need.

definitions: The section of an insurance agreement to clearly define terms used in the contract.

demographics: Statistics, such as age and income, about a particular group of people.

depreciation: The loss of an item's value over time.

depression: A period of more than six months of severe economic decline.

disability insurance: Coverage that pays workers a percentage of their income if they become ill or are injured and unable to work for an extended period of time.

dividend: A voluntary periodic payout from company profits to policyholders.

Dodd-Frank Wall Street Reform and Consumer Protection Act: Made changes to the regulatory structure overseeing the financial-services industry.

E

earthquake insurance: A property insurance policy that covers the damage the shaking ground causes to buildings.

elimination period: Waiting period before a health insurance policy will cover costs related to a preexisting condition.

endorsement: An add-on to a standard insurance policy that details agreements not otherwise part of the policy.

ergonomics: The science of adapting the workstation to fit the needs of the worker and lessen the chance of injury.

ethics: Conduct that is right, good, and proper.

exclusions: Losses the insurance carrier will not cover.

expense-incurred policy: A policy in which a maximum benefit amount is selected when the policy is purchased.

experience rating: A company's history of unemployment claims, which measures the stability of that business' workforce.

external fraud: Fraud that occurs when somebody not involved in the insurance industry engages in insurance fraud.

F

Federal Insurance Office: Tasked with monitoring the insurance industry as well as studying the insurance market and recommending improvements to insurance regulation.

federal poverty level: A guideline based on a family's size and income used by assistance programs to determine benefits.

fee-for-service health plan: A type of health plan in which the plan participant (the insured person) pays a premium, but must also meet a deductible before coverage begins each year.

FICA (Federal Insurance Contribution Act): A legislative act that governs the taxes funding Social Security and Medicare.

fidelity: The principle that promises should be kept.

Financial Analysis and Solvency Tracking System (FAST): A government system that helps detect financial distress.

financial analyst: A professional that researches companies to determine their ability to pay their debts.

financial markets: A combination of stock markets and other outlets that allow businesses and investors to buy and sell stocks, bonds, commodities, and other financial instruments.

financial responsibility laws: Legislation that requires licensed drivers to buy a minimum amount of automobile liability insurance.

financial statement: An annual report of a company's financial condition.

float: The amount of collected premiums that have not yet been paid out in claims.

focus group: A gathering of potential customers who participate in a guided discussion about a given product.

fraud: Unethical or unlawful behavior where deception is used for personal or financial gain.

full-benefit age: The age at which you will receive your projected full retirement benefit from Social Security.

future purchase option: A feature of an insurance policy that gives the policyholder an opportunity periodically to increase his or her policy's benefit amount without having to take a medical exam.

Glossary

G

gap insurance policy: An insurance policy that pays the difference between the cash value of a vehicle and the balance on the loan.

group: A set of people who have an interest in jointly sharing risk.

gross premium: The amount of a policyholder's premium.

group health plans: Plans that cover a group, often employees of a company, as well as their family members.

guaranteed minimum interest rate: Money in an account will earn at least the specified rate of return.

guaranty funds: Money that is provided by the state to cover a policyholder's losses if an insurance company cannot.

H

hacker: Someone who has expertise in manipulating computer technologies.

hacker insurance: A type of insurance that protects the policyholder from losses and liability caused by hackers.

hard fraud: In the case of insurance, fabricating an incident to cause loss an insurance policy covers.

hazard: A condition that increases the likelihood or extent of a loss.

health-claims examiner: A professional who reviews health-insurance claims for accuracy and completeness and makes decisions to approve or deny claims.

health insurance: Insurance policies that protect the policyholder from financial risk associated with the costs of health care.

health-insurance exchanges: As called for in the Patient Protection and Affordable Care Act, a private insurance market from which uninsured individuals can shop for and purchase affordable health-insurance coverage.

health savings account: An account, often a part of a consumer-driven plan, containing untaxed money that can be used to pay for the health-care costs until the deductible is met.

HIPAA (Health Insurance Portability and Accountability Act): Legislation that helps people maintain insurance coverage and requires that electronic medical records and patient privacy be safeguarded.

HMO (health maintenance organization): A managed care plan typically consisting of a network of providers that participants *must* use for their health-care needs. The insurance company does not pay for out-of-network care.

hospice care: Physical care and counseling for terminally ill patients.

hull policy: Marine insurance that covers personal watercrafts.

I

identity fraud: Using a person's personal information to do things like withdraw money from bank accounts and make credit or debit card charges.

identity theft: Stealing someone's personal information and using it to impersonate the victim.

identity theft insurance: Coverage for financial losses that result from identity theft and fraud.

IIPRC (Interstate Insurance Product Regulation Commission): An organization that provides uniform standards for insurance products to its member states.

impaired insurer: An insurance agency or company that is having significant financial problems, and its ability to pay claims is in question.

indemnity: A policyholder cannot profit from an insurance loss.

indemnity policy: A fixed-benefits amount that is paid regardless of actual costs incurred.

independent agent: An insurance sales agent who sells products from several insurance companies.

independent contractor: In the insurance industry, a sales agent who is not employed by an insurance company, but who is paid according to predetermined sales and performance measures.

independent ratings agencies: Agencies that offer expert opinions on the financial strength of the companies they rate.

individual health plan: Health insurance for a single person or family purchased directly from an insurance company by the participant.

individual health plan rule: A provision of HIPAA that guarantees access to health insurance for people who are unable to obtain group coverage.

individual market: The portion of the health insurance market in which a single person or family purchases health insurance.

inflation: The rise in prices that occurs over time.

inland marine insurance: Covers marine property and equipment whether it is on land, in storage, or away from a body of water.

insolvent: When a company does not have enough cash and assets to pay its claims and debts.

inspection report: A report that provides a very detailed look at the applicant's finances, health habits, occupation, and character.

insurable interest: An insurance provision that means the policyholder must have a financial interest in what is being insured.

insurance: A financial product that offers protection against a specific type of loss.

insurance agent: A professional licensed to sell an insurance contract.

insurance contract: Also called a *policy*, a legally binding document that outlines the terms of an insurance agreement between an insurance carrier and policyholder.

insurance investigator: An insurance professional who looks into possible fraud by researching, interviewing claimants and witnesses, and conducting surveillance.

insurance policy: A legally binding document that outlines the terms of an insurance agreement between an insurance carrier and policyholder.

Insurance Regulatory Information System: A government system that runs financial tests on data to identify potential problems.

insurance score: A numerical value that reflects the risk the applicant represents to the insurance carrier.

insuring agreement: The contract between insurance carrier and policyholder that identifies the commitment the insurance carrier has made to the policyholder. It outlines perils the policy does or does not cover.

internal fraud: Fraud that occurs when somebody within the insurance industry engages in insurance fraud.

investing: The process of committing money to something with the expectation of earning additional money.

ISO (Insurance Services Office, Inc): An organization that advises the insurance industry and produces standardized policy forms.

J

jobless recovery: The economy begins to improve from a downturn, but the unemployment rate does not.

joint underwriting association: Group through which insurers join together to offer medical providers affordable malpractice insurance.

K

kickback: An improper payment to someone in authority to direct business toward the person making the payment.

L

law of large numbers: The accuracy of a statistic increases with sample size.

leads: Sales opportunities.

lease: A contract for rental of a car for a specified term, usually three or more years. The car is returned at the end of the term.

legally binding: An agreement, or contract, between parties that can be enforced through legal action if one of the parties fails to abide by the terms of the agreement.

liable: Responsible according to law.

lien: A legal claim of debt against property, such as real estate or a car.

life insurance: Pays a benefit to beneficiaries when the insured dies.

life insurance-claims examiner: A professional in the life insurance industry who interviews medical specialists, consults policy files to verify information reported on a claim, refers claims for further investigation, and authorizes or denies payments for claims.

life stage: A phase of a person's life.

lifetime limit: A maximum amount that a plan will pay out to the insured participant over the course of that person's life.

liquidation: The process of dividing a company's assets among parties with a financial interest in the company.

load: The expenses the insurer has for creating, selling, and maintaining the policy.

loan term: The length of time over which a loan is repaid.

long-tail insurance: A situation in which there is a long time between receiving the premium and paying a claim.

long-term care: Intensive and ongoing care needed because of health challenges.

long-term care insurance: Financial protection that pays the costs of care for long-term, chronic conditions.

long-term disability: The disability coverage that begins after short-term disability expires, typically replacing 40% to 60% of pre-disability income.

loss adjuster: A specialist who visits with the policyholder to determine the cause of a loss and its extent, whether the policy covers the loss, and whether the amount claimed is reasonable.

loss-control representative: An insurance professional who inspects property and business operations of insurance applicants and assesses the likelihood of hazards, accidents, and financial loss.

M

managed-care plans: Plans in which an insurance company enters into contracts with hospitals, doctors, and other providers of care.

mandate: A requirement that carries the force of the law.

marine cargo policy: Covers ocean-shipped cargo from where it is picked up to the buyer's location.

marketing manager: A professional position that involves running a company's efforts to promote existing and new types of insurance products.

material misrepresentation: The willful and knowing misrepresentation of information by an insurance applicant, which can result in a policy being voided.

McCarran-Ferguson Act: Gives authority for regulating the insurance industries to the states in which they do business.

median income: A statistical point at which one-half of workers earn above the amount, and one-half earns below the amount.

mediator: A person who looks at both sides of an arbitration case, favoring neither side, and then makes a judgment.

Medicaid: A federally mandated public health insurance program that helps low-income individuals and some others receive health care.

Medical Information Bureau: An agency that maintains records of applications for life, health, disability, long-term care, and critical-care insurance.

medical malpractice: A situation in which a health-care professional fails to provide appropriate care and as a result causes injury to a patient.

medical malpractice insurance: Protection for physicians and other health-care providers from the financial risk associated with malpractice lawsuits.

Medicare: A public health insurance program run by the federal government that provides health insurance for Americans aged 65 and older.

Medicare Advantage plans: A managed-care plan that delivers health care through provider networks with the aim of controlling costs.

Medicare Part A: A provision of Medicare that provides insurance benefits for hospital stays.

Medicare Part B: A provision of Medicare that generally pays for doctor's visits and medical services.

Medicare Part C: Extra coverage purchased from private companies by Medicare participants to cover health services not provided by Medicare itself.

Medicare Part D: Extra coverage that may be purchased by Medicare participants to help pay for prescription drugs.

Medigap insurance: Also known as Medicare supplemental insurance, an insurance plan available to Medicare Part A and Part B participants that pays otherwise uncovered expenses, such as copays and deductibles.

misdiagnosis: A case in which a physician makes an error in identifying an illness or injury.

mortality table: A statistical table that shows the rate of deaths by age group.

mortgage: A loan borrowed to purchase a property.

motorcycle insurance: Coverage for any two- or three-wheeled motor vehicle that a person rides on roads and highways.

multiline agent: Insurance sales agents that sell several types of products.

mutual fund: A pool of stocks, bonds, and other investment instruments.

N

named-perils policy: A type of insurance contract that only covers losses resulting from the causes listed in the insuring agreement.

National Association of Insurance Commissioners (NAIC): Organization that assists state governments with the regulation of the insurance industry.

net worth: A person's total assets minus the total of his or her liabilities or debt.

O

occupational therapy: A type of therapy that helps individuals live as independently as possible.

ocean marine insurance: Insurance that provides coverage for ocean-going ships and the cargo they carry.

opportunity fraud: See **soft fraud**.

out-of-network: A care provider not part of the provider network contract for a particular insurance plan.

out-of-pocket maximum: The maximum dollar amount the insured person(s) will have to pay in a given year.

outpatient hospital care: Medical care provided in a medical setting that generally does not require an overnight stay.

P

partnership long-term care policy: A way to qualify for Medicaid without first expending all assets. For every dollar a policy pays in benefits, this policy will protect a dollar of assets.

patient compensation funds: State-created funds that serve as a way to address unaffordable malpractice insurance. These funds cover higher-end losses.

Patient Protection and Affordable Care Act (PPACA): A major reform effort intended to reduce costs, make delivery of care more efficient, and provide a means for those who are not otherwise insured to obtain health insurance.

pay-as-you-go system: Money coming in from taxes goes directly out as benefit payments.

payroll tax: A fee an employer pays on the wages of each employee.

pension: An employment-based retirement plan that provides monthly income.

peril: A potential cause of a loss.

permanent life insurance: A policy that lasts for life, also known as whole life insurance, which pays a death benefit to beneficiaries and contains a savings component.

personal watercraft (PWC): A small one- or two-person marine vessel such as a Jet Ski™ or WaveRunner™.

phishing: The use of fraudulent e-mails and copies of legitimate websites to trick people into providing personal, financial, and other data.

physical therapy: Therapy and exercise that helps individuals with illness or injury to recover.

point of service plan (POS): An insurance plan that mixes features of HMOs and PPOs where participants have to choose a primary care provider who coordinates in-network care. Participants can also choose an out-of-network provider and pay more for those services.

policy processing clerk: An administrative-support position that involves taking in new applications and reviewing them for completeness.

policyholder: The person who buys the insurance policy.

pooled-benefit policy: A policy that pays the actual cost of care up to the maximum daily benefit stated in a policy. If the maximum daily benefit is more than what is needed to pay for care, the remaining money goes toward extending your benefit.

portability: Continued access to health insurance regardless of employment.

preexisting condition: A disease or health condition that exists at the time a person applies for health coverage.

preexisting condition exclusions: Clauses in insurance agreements stating that the insurer may not cover costs related to a preexisting condition for a stated period of time.

Preexisting Condition Insurance Plan (PCIP): A health insurance risk pool for people who have been denied coverage because of preexisting medical conditions.

preferred provider organization (PPO): An insurance plan that establishes a network of providers the insurer encourages plan participants to use. Participants may choose to go out of network, but they will pay more out of pocket.

preferred risk class: A risk class that represents a low risk to an insurance carrier.

premium: A fee charged by an insurance company in return for accepting an individual's risk.

preventive services: Medical services that include certain vaccines, wellness visits, and tests that screen for cancer and other diseases.

primary care provider (PCP): A physician who manages all health care for the participant of an HMO.

private-sector group health plans: Employment-based health insurance plans offered by companies in the private sector.

privatize: To put in the hands of individuals as opposed to under governmental control. In terms of Social Security, this could mean having workers to contribute part of their Social Security tax to a stock market account.

producer: See **sales agent.**

professional designation: See **certification.**

progressive: In terms of Social Security benefits, this means that lower-income workers get a higher benefit relative to their income than higher-income workers do.

proof of insurability: A part of acquiring an insurance policy that requires a medical exam as well as information provided on the insurance company's application.

property and casualty insurance: A policy that protects policyholders against financial loss associated with property damage or injury to others.

property damage insurance: Automotive insurance that covers physical damage to a policyholder's car.

property damage liability insurance: Automotive insurance that pays for damages the policyholder's vehicle causes to another person's property in the event of an accident.

provider network: The hospitals, doctors, and other providers of care that are under contract with a particular insurance plan.

public-sector group health plans: Health-insurance plans sponsored by federal, state, or local governments.

purchasing power: The measure of how much money is worth in terms of how many goods and services it can purchase.

pure premium: The amount of the premium that should cover expected losses.

Q

quarter: A three-month segment of a 12-month period, usually within a fiscal or a calendar year.

R

rate of return: The amount of money an investment makes.

ratemaking: The process by which actuaries determine a premium rate per unit of insurance.

ratings agency: An organization that provides an expert opinion on the health of companies and investment products.

ratings bureau: A business collects loss and claims information from across the industry and sells it to insurance companies.

recession: A period of time marked by an overall decline in the economy that lasts for six months or more.

recession-proof: Refers to industries that can weather tough economic times with little negative impact.

reciprocity: In the case of insurance professionals, this means that one state will honor licensing from another.

reinsurance: The transfer of some of an insurance company's risk to another insurance company.

renewability: The requirements to renew a policy if it lapses.

replacement cost: The full cost of replacing a specific item with one just like it.

replacement cost insurance: Property insurance that pays the market cost of replacing a given item without accounting for depreciation.

reserves: Money an insurance company sets aside for future claims.

resources: In terms of eligibility for Supplemental Security Income, assets like cash, bank accounts, life insurance, and personal property.

risk: The probability of an event occurring and the possible consequences of that event.

risk avoidance: Taking steps to eliminate risk.

risk class: A category based on the risk an applicant represents to the company.

risk management: Evaluating risk and choosing how to minimize or manage the loss.

risk reduction: Taking steps to minimize the amount of risk.

risk retention: Planning for losses rather than transferring risk.

risk transfer: Shifting risk of financial loss to an insurance company.

risk-based capital requirements: The minimum amount of capital an insurer should hold rather than just what it needs to pay all of its obligations.

S

sales agent: In the insurance profession, sales agents sell insurance products to consumers and businesses.

sales and revenue goals: Targets for how many policies agents want to sell, and how much revenue they seek to generate on those sales.

sales manager: A professional position that involves training and overseeing sales agents.

schedule: As related to workers' compensation, a list of injuries with a corresponding compensation amount.

scheduling: A specific, rare, or special item and its value are stated on an insurance policy.

secretary: See **administrative assistant.**

self-insure: A business or person assumes risks on its own and pays claims without the help of an insurance plan.

seven canons of ethics: Guidelines from ethical behavior by insurance professionals.

short-tail insurance: A situation in which there is little time between receiving the premium and paying a claim.

short-term disability: Disability coverage that pays a portion of a person's income for up to three months.

significant break in coverage: Sixty-three days or more in which an individual goes without health insurance.

smart systems: Computer software that can quickly analyze applications, recommend whether to deny or accept them, and adjust premiums based on the applicant's risk profile.

Social Security: A federal social insurance that replaces a portion of income in retirement for eligible Americans and pays some disability benefits.

Social Security Disability Insurance (SSDI): A social insurance program that pays benefits to disabled persons who cannot work for a year or more.

Social Security Trust Fund: Takes in money collected from Social Security taxes and pays benefits to qualifying individuals from that revenue.

soft fraud: In the case of insurance, exaggerating a legitimate claim or making untrue statements on an application for insurance.

solvency: The ability of a company to pay claims and other debts.

special enrollment rule: Requires a company to offer health insurance plan enrollment outside of the annual window in certain instances as provided by HIPAA.

spousal benefit: A Social Security benefit paid to retired workers' spouses who have low or no earnings.

state insurance departments: State-level government departments that supervise and regulate insurers in their respective states.

state licensing: Ensures that an insurance professional understands the laws that govern the industry and the expectations of ethical behavior.

state risk pool: State run program for providing access to health insurance for those who would otherwise be denied coverage.

statistician: A professional that collects and analyzes numerical data.

stock: Ownership of a small piece of a company, called a *share*.

subrogation: An insurance principle that allows the insurance company, in place of the insured, to claim damages from the person at fault in a case of a loss.

substandard risk class: A risk class that represents a high risk to the company.

substantial gainful activity: Any physical or mental activity that can be performed for compensation.

succession planning: Ensuring that the company is attracting and retaining professionals who have the potential to fill key leadership roles.

Supplemental Security Income (SSI): A federal program that pays a benefit to low-income people over age 65, the blind, and the disabled to help meet basic needs for food, clothing, and shelter.

surplus: Excess capital beyond what a company needs to meet its liabilities.

surrender value: The cash value, minus certain expenses, a policyholder receives as a payout after cancelling a qualified insurance policy.

survivors benefit: A Social Security benefit that replaces a portion of family income if a spouse or parent dies.

T

tail: The length of time an insurance company has between receiving a premium payment and making a claims payment.

term life insurance: A life insurance policy that covers a person over a set period of years, usually from zero to 30.

The Institutes: An educational, nonprofit organization with a focus on property and casualty underwriters.

title: A public record that lists who owns a given property.

title defect: An issue that disputes the legal ownership of a property, such as deed errors, omissions, or forgery.

title insurance: Provides lenders with coverage for losses and legal fees in the event of a title defect.

top executive: A management position, such as president, executive director, or chief executive officer, who directs the operations of an organization.

total account approach: A situation in which agents obtain licenses to sell mutual funds, annuities, and other products to provide a comprehensive service to customers, thereby expanding their earnings prospects.

totaled: The term is short for "total loss." When an insurer declares that repairs to a car would cost more than the car is worth or that the car simply cannot be repaired.

U

umbrella policy: A safety net that kicks in when the homeowner's insurance reaches the coverage limits.

uncompensated care: Medical care provided to people who have no insurance and are unable to pay for care on their own.

underinsured liability coverage: Automotive insurance coverage that pays for approved damages caused by an underinsured driver to the property or person of the policyholder.

underwriter: Determines whether to accept the risk of an applicant and what premium to charge.

underwriting policy: Establishes the kinds of insurance and the maximum amount of coverage the insurer can offer.

unemployment insurance: A joint federal-state program that provides partial income replacement when people lose their jobs through no fault of their own.

uninsured liability coverage: Automotive insurance coverage that pays the cost of approved losses caused by an uninsured driver to the property or person of the policyholder.

utmost good faith: A central principle of an insurance product that requires the consumer and the insurance agent to be truthful with each other.

V

valued policy: Pays out the full face value of the policy after a covered loss, regardless of the actual cost to replace the damage.

valued policy laws: Mandate that under certain circumstances insurance companies must pay the actual face value of the policy to the insured.

W

war risk insurance: Provides coverage for acts of terrorism and war.

warranty: A statement or promise a policyholder makes that becomes part of the insurance contract.

workers' compensation insurance: A program intended to provide medical and financial support for workers who are injured or made ill on the job.

work-life balance: How easy or difficult it is to work and also have time for personal and family interests.

Y

yacht policy: A marine vehicle coverage plan that covers vessels like yachts, motorboats, and sailboats.

Index

401(k) plan, 161

A

AAA, 56
accounting clerks, 277
actual cash value, 249
actuarial science, 285–286
actuary, 186, 285
administrative assistant, 277
adverse selection, 68, 183
AIG. *See* American Insurance Group
aircraft hull insurance, 61
aircraft liability insurance, 61
all-risk policies, 180
American College, Center for Ethics in Financial Services, 259
American Insurance Group (AIG), 296
annuities, 296
application, 244
appraisers, 57, 282
arbitration, 190
audit, 218
auditing clerk, 277
automobile insurance, 50
aviation insurance, 61

B

Baby Boomers, 149, 164, 296
bodily injury liability insurance, 52
BOP. *See* business owner's policy insurance
business owner's policy insurance (BOP), 43
buying insurance, 178

C

capital, 217
careers in insurance, 293–303
    compensation, 294–295
    future, 298–299
    industry outlook, 295
cargo war risk policy, 58
cash value, 37
cash value component, 98
catastrophe, 202
catastrophe modeling, 202
Centers for Medicare and Medicaid Services, 145
certifications, 275
Certified Safety Professional (CSP), 285
Chartered Property Casualty Underwriter (CPCU), 275
chronic disease, 68
civic penalty, 260
claim, 21, 56–57, 130, 132, 133, 188
    filing, 56
    process, 56–57
    workers' compensation, 130, 132
    unemployment, 133
claimant, 44
claims adjusters, 44, 283
claims approval, 136–137
claims clerk. *See* insurance claims-processing clerk
claims examiner. *See* health insurance-claims examiner
claims philosophy, 189
claims processing clerk, 278
COBRA, 77, 228, 233
collision coverage, 52
commercial general liability insurance, 42
commercial package policy insurance, 42
commercial property insurance, 42
complaint ratio, 28
comprehensive coverage, 53
concealment, 245
conditions, 180
Consolidated Omnibus Budget Reconciliation Act *See* COBRA.
consumer-driven health plans, 75
continuation coverage, 229. *See also* COBRA and HIPAA
continuing education, 274
contract, 179–181
    conditions, 180
    declarations, 179
    definitions, 179
    endorsements, 180
    exclusions, 180
    insuring agreement, 180
    overview, 178
cost-of-living adjustment, 88
CPCU. *See* Chartered Property Casualty Underwriter
credit report, 119
credit score, 55, 186
CSR. *See* customer service representative
custodial care, 146
customer service representative, 27, 153, 278

D

damages, 114
declarations, 179
deductible, 21, 73, 109
defensive medicine, 68
demographics, 200
Department of Labor, 230
depreciation, 37, 110, 249
disability insurance, 86
dividend, 99
driving, 54–55
    and teens, 55
    record, 54
Dodd-Frank Wall Street Reform and Consumer Protection Act, 296

E

earthquake insurance, 36, 39, 111
elimination period, 78
employer-sponsored health plans. *See* group health plans
endorsements, 180
ergonomics, 131
estate planning, 96
ethical insurance policies, 260
ethics, 257–271
    external fraud, 263
    fraud overview, 262–263
    industry codes, 258–259
    internal fraud, 263–264
    society contributions, 265–266
    state regulation, 259–261
exclusions, 180
expense-incurred policy, 93
extended health care, 85–106
    coverage amount, 101
    disability protection, 86–87
    importance of disability insurance, 87
    insuring others, 97
    long-term care policies, 92–94
    long-term insurance benefits, 90–91
    Medicaid, 92
    Medicare, 92
    policy definitions, 87
    Social Security, 88–89
external fraud, 263

F

FAST. *See* Financial Analysis and Solvency Tracking System
Federal Insurance Office, 296
federal poverty level, 236
federal regulations, 227–242
    enforcement, 230
    expanding coverage, 236
    health plan changes, 236
    HIPAA, 231
    individual health plan rule, 233
    Medicare changes, 237–238
    PPACA overview, 235
    preexisting conditions rule, 232–233
    special enrollment rule, 233
    COBRA, 228
    eligibility, 229
fee-for-service health plan, 73
FICA, 145, 169
FICA-HI tax, 146
filing a claim, 56–57
Financial Analysis and Solvency Tracking System (FAST), 218
financial debt analyst, 191
financial health, 27
financial markets, 295
financial planner, 251
financial responsibility laws, 53
financial risk, 19, 24
financial statement, 218
float, 204
flood insurance, 36, 39
focus group, 280
fraud, 262
full-benefit age, 163
future purchase option, 88

G

gap insurance, 109
Great Recession, 212
gross premium, 202
group health plans, 71, 200
group, 71
guaranteed minimum interest rate, 99
guaranty funds, 100, 215

H

hacker, 120
hacker insurance, 120
hard fraud, 262
hazard, 26
health-claims examiner, 284
health insurance-claims examiner, 79
health insurance exchanges, 223
Health Insurance Portability and Accountability Act (HIPAA), 78, 231, 233
    Title I, 231
health insurance, 21, 67–84
    COBRA, 77–78
    consumer-driven plans, 75–76
    costs, 68–69
    fee-for-service plans, 73
    group plans, 71–72
    HIPAA, 78
    individual plans, 73
    managed-care plans, 74–75
    Patient Protection and Affordable Care Act, 69–70
    uninsured, impact, 79–80
health maintenance organization (HMO), 75
health savings account (HSA), 76
HIPAA, 78, 231, 233
    Title I, 231
HMO, 75
homeowner's insurance, 36, 246–247
hospice care, 146
hull policy, 58

I

identity fraud, 117
identity theft, 117
identity theft insurance, 119
IIPRC. *See* Interstate Insurance Products Regulation Commission
indemnity, 250
indemnity policy, 93
independent contractor, 294
independent ratings agencies, 27
individual health plan, 73
individual health plan rule, 233
individual market, 200
inflation, 163
inland marine insurance, 60
insolvent, 213
inspection report, 186
insurable interest, 97, 247
insurance actuary, 162

insurance agent, 178
insurance appraiser, 51
insurance 19–33, 108–109, 112–122
    buying, 27
    earthquake, 111–112
    gap, 109
    hacker, 120
    how companies make money, 197–209
    identity theft, 117–119
    life choices and risk, 25–26
    life stages and risk, 23–24
    managing risk, 21–22
    medical malpractice, 114
    nature of the industry, 177–196
    regulation of, 28, 215, 227–242, 296
    risks of life choices, 25
    service records, 27–29
    title insurance, 112–113
    umbrella liability, 108
insurance claims processing clerk, 214
insurance contract, 178
insurance investigator, 118, 284
insurance loss control representative, 237
insurance marketing manager, 266
insurance policy processing clerk, 205
Insurance Regulatory Information System (IRIS), 218
insurance researcher. *See* insurance investigator
insurance sales agent, 30, 217, 287
insurance sales manager, 185
insurance score, 187
Insurance Services Office, Inc. (ISO), 179
insurance underwriter, 129
insuring agreement, 180
Interstate Insurance Products Regulation Commission (IIPRC), 261
investing, 204
IRIS. *See* Insurance Regulatory Information System
ISO. *See* Insurance Services Office, Inc.

J

jobless recovery, 135
joint underwriting associations (JUAs), 115
JUAs. *See* joint underwriting associations

K

Kelley Blue Book, 53
kickback, 259

L

law of large numbers, 182
leads, 281
lease, 110
legal principles, 243–253
    indemnity, 249
    insurable interest in life policies, 248
    insurable interest in property/casualty, 247
    subrogation, 251–252
    utmost good faith, 178, 244–246
legally binding, 178
liability coverage, 52
liability protection, 36
liable, 247
licensing, 217
lien, 112
life insurance, 96–101
    estate planning, 96
    investment, 101
    permanent life, 98–99
    straight whole life, 99
    term-life, 97–98
    universal life, 99
    variable life, 99
life insurance-claims examiner, 95, 284
life stage, 23
lifetime limits, 73
liquidation, 213
load, 202
loan term, 110
long-tail insurance, 206
long-term care, 91
long-term care insurance, 91
long-term disability, 87
long-term disability insurance, 87
loss adjuster, 188
loss control representatives, 284

M

managed care plan, 74
mandate, 151
marine cargo policy, 58
marine insurance. *See* ocean marine insurance
marketing managers, 280
material misrepresentation, 245
McCarran-Ferguson Act, 212
median income, 294
mediator, 190
Medicaid, 92, 93, 151, 261
Medical Information Bureau, 186
medical malpractice, 11
medical malpractice insurance, 114
Medicare, 92, 145–148
    advantage plans, 148
    Part A, 146
    Part B, 147
    Part C, 148
    Part D, 147
Medigap insurance, 148
misdiagnosis, 114
mortality tables, 201
mortgage, 24, 37
motorcycle insurance, 50
multiline agents, 287
mutual funds, 296

N

NAIC. *See* National Association of Insurance Commissioners
named-peril policy, 180
National Association of Insurance Commissioners (NAIC), 28, 215
natural disaster, 202
net worth, 108
Nixon, Richard, 169

O

occupational therapy, 147
ocean marine insurance, 58–59
operational expenses, 198
opportunity fraud, 263
OSHA, 130
out-of-pocket maximum, 73
outpatient hospital care, 147
overtime, 110

P

package policy. *See* commercial package policy insurance
partnership long-term care policy, 94
patient compensation funds, 115
Patient Protection and Affordable Care Act (PPACA), 22, 69, 149, 153, 235
pay-as-you-go system, 164
payment request. *See* claim
payroll tax, 43, 135
PCFs. *See* patient compensation funds
PCIP. *See* Preexisting Condition Insurance Plan
PCP. *See* primary care provider.
pension, 161
peril, 26

Index

permanent life insurance, 98
personal watercraft (PWC), 58
phishing, 119
physical therapy, 147
point-of-service plans, 75
policy processing clerks, 278
policy types, 36
policyholder, 22, 246
pooled-benefit policy, 94
POS. *See* point-of-service plans
PPACA. *See* Patient Protection and Affordable Care Act
PPO. *See* preferred provider organization
post test, 19, 35, 49, 67, 85, 107, 127, 143, 159, 177, 197, 211, 227, 243, 257, 273, 294
preexisting condition, 222
preexisting condition exclusions, 72
Preexisting Condition Insurance Plan (PCIP), 222, 236
preferred provider organizations (PPO), 74
preferred risk class, 199
premium, 22, 198
pretest, 31, 45, 63, 81, 103, 122, 138, 155, 171, 194, 207, 224, 239, 253, 268, 290, 300
preventive services, 147
primary care provider, 75
private-sector group health plans, 230
privatize, 165
producers, 287
professional designations, 275
progressive, 163
proof of insurability, 97
property and casualty insurance, 36
property damage, 52
property damage insurance, 52
property damage liability insurance, 52
property insurance, 35–65
    automobile insurance, 50–53
    aviation, 61
    business owner's policy insurance, 43
    claims process, 56–57
    commercial insurance, 42–43
    coverage amounts, 40–41
    determining premiums, 54–55
    floods and earthquakes, 39–40
    home protection, 36–37
    homeowner's protection, 40
    inland marine, 60
    marine, 58–59
    policy types, 37–39
    reducing premiums, 55
    renter's insurance, 36
    state requirements, 53–54

public health, 143–158
    public health insurance, 143
    choosing a plan, 149
    health insurance, 144
    Medicaid, role in, 151–152
    Medicare, role in, 145–149
public-sector group health plans, 230
purchasing power, 163
pure premium, 201
PWC. *See* personal watercraft

Q

quarter, 136

R

rate of return, 99
ratemaking, 201
rating scale, 192
ratings agency, 191
ratings bureau, 186
recession, 134, 200
recession-proof, 298
reciprocity, 274
regulation of insurance, 28, 215, 227–242, 296
    federal, 227–242, 296
    state, 192, 212–226
reinsurance, 187
renewability, 88
renter's insurance, 36
replacement cost, 37
replacement cost insurance, 250
reserves, 218
resources, 170
retirement, 23–24, 161–162
retirement age, 163
risk, 19–26
    avoidance, 21
    changes, 23
    financial, 19
    life stages and, 23
    management, 20
    reduction, 21
    retention, 21
    smoking, 26
risk class, 199
risk management, 20
Roosevelt, Franklin D., 159

S

sales agent, 30, 217, 287
sales and revenue goals, 287
sales manager, 281
scheduling, 41, 129
SCHIP. *See* State Children's Health Insurance Program
secretaries, 277
self-insure, 130
selling insurance, 178
seven canons of ethics, 259
SGA. *See* substantial gainful activity
short-tail insurance, 205
short-term disability, 86
significant break in coverage, 232
smart systems, 184
social responsibility, 266
Social Security, 159–175
    disability income, 167–169
    funding, 164–165, 168–169
    how it works, 163
    retirement income source, 160–162
    spousal benefits, 164
    supplemental income, 169
    survivors benefits, 169
Social Security Disability Income, 167
Social Security Disability Insurance, 88
Social Security Trust Fund, 164
soft fraud, 263
solvency, 213
special enrollment rule, 233
spousal benefit, 164
SSDI. *See* Social Security Disability Income (SSDI)
SSI. *See* Supplemental Security Income (SSDI)
Standard and Poors, 27
State Children's Health Insurance Program (SCHIP), 145
state insurance departments, 192
state licensing, 274
state regulation, 212–226
    McCarran-Ferguson Act, 212
    consumer protection, 215–216
    departments of insurance, 192
    governmental branches, 213–215
    markets, 219–220
    rates, 220
    rationale, 212
    risk pools, 222
    solvency, 217–219
state risk pools, 220
statisticians, 191
subrogation, 252
substandard risk class, 199
substantial gainful activity (SGA), 168
succession planning, 280

Supplemental Security Income (SSI), 170
surplus, 217
surrender value, 99
survivors benefits, 169

T

tail, 205
term-life insurance, 97–98
Texas Department of Insurance, 216
The Institutes, 259
title, 112
title insurance, 112
top executives, 280
total account approach, 296
total loss. *See* totaled
totaled, 52

U

umbrella liability insurance, 108
umbrella policy, 40
uncompensated care, 79, 236
underinsured liability coverage, 54
underwriter, 55, 183, 199
unemployment insurance, 133
uninsured liability coverage, 54
utmost good faith, 178, 244–246

V

valued policies, 249
valued policy laws, 250

W

watercraft insurance. *See* ocean marine insurance
war risk insurance, 62
warranty, 246
worker protections, 127–141
    ergonomics, 131
    making a claim, 131
    OSHA, 130
    program administration, 135–136
    safety, 130
    state rules, 130–131
    unemployment insurance, 133–135
    workers' compensation, 87, 128
workers' compensation insurance, 87, 128
work-life balance, 298

Y

yacht policy, 58